TOM SLICK

AND THE

SEARCH FOR THE YETI

TOM SLICK

AND THE

SEARCH FOR THE YETI

LOREN COLEMAN

Faber and Faber

Boston and London

1989

Dedicated to
Bernard Heuvelmans
and the
Tom Slick family

Cover Photo: The 1958 Slick-Johnson Snowman Expedition on the trek to Hongu Khola, Nepal. Photograph by George Holton

Library of Congress Cataloging-in-Publication Data
Coleman, Loren.
Tom Slick and the search for the Yeti / by Loren Coleman.
p.   cm.
ISBN 0-571-12900-5 : $12.95
1. Yeti. 2. Sasquatch. 3. Slick, Tom, d. 1962. 4. Adventure and adventurers—United States—Biography. I. Title.
QL89.2.Y4C65   1989
001.9'44—dc20   89-7943

Design by Nancy Dutting
Printed in the United States of America

CONTENTS

ACKNOWLEDGMENTS

THIS WORK HAS BEEN ALMOST THIRTY YEARS IN the making. In 1960, my mother, Anna, was the first individual to help me with my beginning research on Tom Slick and the yeti. Long before photocopying machines were located at every corner, my mom would, like an ancient Tibetan monk, hand-copy abominable snowmen articles that I had borrowed from the libraries in Decatur, Illinois. I would examine these early handwritten items very carefully and add them to my growing files. Since that time, of course, I have been able to collect originals of most of those selections, and priceless others have been passed my way. Shortly before my father's recent death, for example, he sent me Marlin Perkins's book because I had always been a "Wild Kingdom" follower and was interested in its host's involvement in the pursuit and debunking of the yeti.

In between this family support, friends, colleagues, fellow researchers, and enemies have added pieces of evidence to my large collection of material demonstrating the pivotal role of Tom Slick in the search for the yeti. Indeed, during the last three decades, many people have assisted me in this research. I could never come close to thanking, by name, all of the hundreds of people who have helped me discover various pieces of the Tom Slick puzzle. Therefore, I would like to give my deep appreciation to all of the unnamed librarians, cryptozoologists, yeti searchers, Bigfooters, biologists, folklorists, forteans, reporters, Slick friends, and others who have shared information with me.

Special thanks and credit go to the Tom Slick family for sharing valuable genealogical and archival information; the Federal Bureau of Investigation for selections from its file on Charles Urschel and Machine Gun Kelly; *Fortune* magazine for the use of one of its photographs; Lo Holton for the use of George Holton's photographs; Peter Byrne for original archival material and the use of his photographs; Bernard Heuvelmans for the use of file materials and selections from his book, *On the Track of Unknown Animals*, copyright © 1958, 1989 by Bernard Heuvelmans (Rupert Hart-Davis, London, and Hill & Wang, New York); Teizo Ogawa for a photograph; Dennis Stacy for consultations; Deborah Johnson Head for the Johnson chronicles and the Johnson/Stewart photograph; Desmond Miller, Susan and Bill Coleman for family discernment; Ray Miles for Tom, Sr., data, critiques, and photographic assistance; Mark A. Hall for numerous original materials and critiques; Mark Chorvinsky for the use of his yeti cinema essay as the primary appendix; Jim McClarin for archival material; John Lovett and the University of Oklahoma Western History Collection for a photograph; S. S. Wilson for sharing critical personal data on the Exeter and Yale years; Warren Thompson for old news items; Freda Bernotavicz for translation assistance; Amy Wallace, David Wallechinsky, and Irving Wallace for permission to use my revised *Book of Lists #3* collection as one of my appendices; Karen Mauney for bibliographical organization; David Parnes for photographic consultation; Richard Greenwell and the International Society of Cryptozoology for information on the Lee Brothers; Rene Dahinden, John Green, and Bob Titmus for insights from California and British Columbia; Joseph Zarzynski for some important addresses; Libbet Cone for content consultations; Malcolm Cone-Coleman for his questions about the yeti; and Jerry Coleman for still wanting to search. Many others have assisted along the way, and I have tried to acknowledge those individuals in the text or in the sources credited.

And, lastly, I would like to thank the good folks at Faber and Faber, Inc. who trusted my vision of this work, and encouraged me along the way. Thanks to Tom, Jeanette, Vicki, Anna, Beth, and their army of in-the-field agents for seeing that this book finds many readers. A colorful appreciation to Nancy Dutting for making our vision of the cover come alive, and working out a way to "please get just one more photograph in the book." And finally, Betsy Uhrig, especially, was a challenging editor who helped me see that my next rewrite could say even more about Tom Slick and the search for the yeti.

And thanks to the readers of my previous books who made this book possible by way of your continuing desire to know just a little bit more about these mysterious, yet scientific subjects.

Loren Coleman
Portland, Maine
Summer Solstice, 1989

INTRODUCTION

MYSTERY GRACES THE HIGH PLATEAUS OF THE Himalayas. In this wind-driven land of incredible snows, in a neglected corner of our vast world, hairy subhumanoids long unknown to science are said to roam. For decades throughout the often frog-infested, rain-soaked montane forests of Tibet, Bhutan, Sikkim, and Nepal, elusive lamas and observant shepherds have reported footprints and encounters with strange creatures. A haunting alien cry is heard echoing through the mountain passages, a call that has made people shiver in fear for centuries. The sightings, sound, and sensation are those of yeti.

Meanwhile, half a globe away, during the 1950s, a little remembered adventurer was to make a decision that would change the fate of yeti forever. This man would throw his fortune behind a serious search for the mysterious creatures. Who was this man? He was a handsome, lean, prematurely white-haired man, soft-spoken, with a slight Southern drawl. Tom Slick was his name, more fictional-sounding than real. And in many ways, Tom Slick's life was the life legends are made of.

Two curious beings, yeti and Tom Slick, joined their destinies some three decades ago. The yetis are the forgotten mystery animals of the Himalayas, outshined today by Bigfoot and the Loch Ness Monster. Tom Slick is Texas's forgotten millionaire. He was a very wealthy oil and beef businessman and scientist who became the leader/sponsor of expeditions to Nepal in search of yeti between 1956 and 1959 and to the American Pacific Northwest in pursuit of Bigfoot from 1959 to 1962. Tom Slick was one of the earliest cryptozoologists—those who actively search for hidden animals that have not yet been acknowledged by science. Slick sought other mystery animals besides the yeti and Bigfoot—Scotland's Loch Ness Monster, California's giant salamanders, Alaska's lake monsters, and Sumatra's orang pendeks.

Visionary. Genius. Inventor. Peacemaker. Searcher. Texan. Oilman. Art collector. Engineer. Philanthropist. Father. Tom Slick was given many labels during his short, event-filled life. But today, hardly anyone remembers this amazing individual. And that's a shame.

Thomas Baker Slick, Jr., was raised in a family atmosphere that encouraged him to explore the cutting edge of many subjects. He was willing to take risks, tell people what he really thought, and choose a different path from others. He had the passion and money to pursue things that made him curious, and he did. Yet his uniqueness was sometimes misunderstood. Such was the life of a revolutionary, a pioneer.

Despite his desire for privacy, Tom Slick did attract a little media attention in the late 1950s and early 1960s, when stories about his innovative quests appeared in national newsmagazines. Sadly, the years since Slick's death are strikingly absent of articles about his superb work. Tom Slick's scientifically based and ground-breaking pursuit of yeti, the abominable snowmen of the mountains and valleys near Mount Everest, has been almost totally ignored in recent years. Interestingly, of all of the stories regarding abominable snowmen, the most under-told, under-investigated, and yet intriguing, is the story of Tom Slick, the man and his missions.

Little is known about Tom Slick's yeti expeditions, partly because they ended so abruptly. On the sixth of October, 1962, Slick died at the age of forty-six in a mysterious plane crash. Intrigue surrounded his death. Rumors abounded about the crash, and both researchers and the public craved information on Slick's forward-thinking, scientific cryptozoological efforts. But only silence has existed for decades. Some members of the expeditions fell quiet about their findings, talking instead about conflicts within the group. Research institutes founded by Tom Slick refused to share information, and members of his family stonewalled inquiries.

After Slick's death a new cry was heard across the land: "The abominable snowman does not exist." Since the 1960s, most of the world has believed that statement. But I'm here to say that the yeti, the abominable snowmen of the Himalayas, do exist. The belief in hairy hominids living in the montane valleys of Nepal was lost through a series of events ending in the death of Thomas Baker Slick, Jr.

It's time to rediscover our past so that we may capture the future. Now, after years of research and several months of talking to many people close to the whole affair, I am able to lift the cloak of mystery surrounding Tom Slick and his yeti expeditions for the first time since his death. Ferreting out the story certainly has been enlightening for me. I first became interested in the abominable snowmen of the Himalayas in early 1960. The search for yeti is what drew me into the fledgling science of cryptozoology, and I quickly learned of the importance of Tom Slick. In August 1962, I was finally able to obtain copies of the *New York Journal-American* articles on Slick's yeti research. These newspaper items reflected all that was known of Slick's accomplishments. Still, this small window into Slick's yeti pursuits amazed me. Since that time, I have traveled far afield, talked to scores of yeti and Bigfoot researchers, to Tom Slick's relatives and friends, and searched archives and microfilm files for tidbits of data. I have written letter after letter, received some responses, and reached several dead ends.

The evidence I uncovered, much of it previously unpublished, is revealed here. Much more material may exist out there, but to date, after twenty-seven years of digging, this book reflects what I find to be the highlights of Tom Slick's life and his search for the yeti in particular. I am overjoyed to have this material, despite a few worried moments that some information would not be released, now see the light of day. I am happy to share events heretofore ignored, largely unknown, or only briefly mentioned in a few cryptozoological histories.

The story of the mysterious Tom Slick and his search for the yeti can finally be told.

CHAPTER I

ORIGINS IN ADVENTURE
The Wild Southwest, Oil,
and Machine Gun Kelly

THOMAS BERNARD SLICK WAS BORN IN CLARION, Pennsylvania, on May 6, 1916, to Berenice Frates and Thomas Baker Slick. He was named after his father's onetime oil partner and friend, Bernard B. Jones of Oklahoma. Years later, Tom's name would be changed to Thomas Baker Slick, Jr., after the family had a falling out with his namesake.

It made sense that Tom Slick would search for the yeti someday. He came into a clan built on derring-do and risk-taking, driven by its own history. His was a family deeply loyal to each of its members, who often found themselves touched and pulled together by losses, difficulties, and phenomenal successes.

THE FRATESES

Tom Slick inherited his sense of adventure from both sides of his family. Take, for example, his mother, who could trace her ancestors back to a Portuguese sailor who jumped ship at an American port and decided to stay.

Tom Slick grew up with the stories of the Frateses, especially those about his mother's father. April 23, 1867, saw the birth of Joseph Anthony to Anthony and Mary Enos Frates, then living in Placer County, California, right in the middle of Gold Rush territory. Anthony was in the railroad construction and mining business, traveled widely, and led an exciting life. Mary Enos has been described as "thin as a reed, with fair skin and coal black hair, a lady of great dignity, religious convictions, and tranquillity" (Frates, n.d.).

Young Joseph grew up in Oakland, California, and for a time attended public schools. But not for long. He admired and respected his father and wanted to follow in his footsteps as an engineer and adventurer. Joseph's devout Catholic mother had other ideas. She wanted her son to become a priest. Joseph's restlessness bothered his mother so much that she removed him from public schools and placed him in a special school preparatory for the priesthood. He hated every minute of it. He would run away; his mother would bring him back. Finally, when he was fourteen, he climbed the fence and never again returned. Instead, he joined the legacy of his father, and went into railroading.

Early in his career, Joseph Frates learned telegraphy as a railroad man. Because of the scarcity of good telegraph operators in those days, the youthful Frates was able to write his own ticket and moved from one place to another as he pleased. Mostly, in the beginning, he would relocate from one California town to another.

From Daggart, California, famous for its beautiful women, dance halls, saloons, restaurants, and gambling houses, Frates, still in his late teens, went on to other exciting Wild West locales—a town of 2000 named Los Angeles and the up-and-coming Tuscon, Arizona, and El Paso, Texas. He then crossed the border and worked for two years on the Mexican Central Railway. Here he learned to speak Spanish and lived many thrilling experiences he would relate years later to his grandchildren, including Tom. Soon after Joseph's twentieth birthday, he returned to the United States and, through a friend, found a job with the Denver and Rio Grande Railway as a train dispatcher at Leadville, Colorado.

Frates-Slick Links

Leadville, Colorado, often called "Cloud City," was an exciting boomtown in those days. Fortunes were being made in grubstaking, mining, and reselling claims to the gold, lead, silver, and zinc found in the area. By 1880, Leadville had twenty-eight miles of road, an opera house, fine hotels, well-established brothels, dance halls, seasoned gamblers, three volunteer fire companies, and according to the local weekly, the *Carbonate Chronicle*, some 60,000 residents. Amazingly, the town also had one of the nation's earliest semiprofessional baseball teams, the Leadville Blues (Hansen, 1970; Tiemann and Rucker, 1989).

For a few years, Leadville was Joseph Frates's kind of town. In 1889, Joseph Frates married Lula Montez Buck of Leadville, and a year after that, they had a daughter, Berenice. Leadville might have interested Frates as a single man, but the husband and father took a different view of the ladies of the night and the lynch mobs. And he was getting restless again. From Leadville, Joseph, Lula, and the growing Frates family moved on to Fort Worth; El Paso; Las Vegas; New Mexico; Pueblo, Colorado; Sedalia, Missouri; and Vicksburg, Mississippi. In 1891, Frates went to Water Valley, Mississippi, for the Illinois Central Railroad. It was here that Frates would meet B.B. Jones, who at the time was an operator for the Illinois Central. Later that same year, Frates was sent to Tennessee and promoted to chief dispatcher, while Jones remained behind and was promoted to train dispatcher. Jones was instrumental in the story of Tom Slick, Sr.'s, discovery of oil in Oklahoma's famed Cushing Field.

Frates continued his climb in the railroad ranks, and after his excellent handling of the unusually heavy rail traffic for the St. Louis Exposition of 1904, he was appointed the General Superintendent of the First District. To the delight of the Frateses, the railroad provided them with a private car. Life was finally easier.

In 1915, Frates saw the importance of the large amount of freight coming out of the Cushing Field oil boom, obtained a $90,000 loan from a Tulsa bank, built a standard guage railway from Depew to Drumright, Creek County, Oklahoma, and provided the oil lands with the transportation system it so deeply needed.

Thomas Baker Slick, the king of the wildcatters, got to know Berenice Frates during the time her father was building his railroad in Oklahoma. On June 21, 1915, in the midst of the construction phase of Frates's project, Tom Slick married Berenice Frates.

The Town of Slick

Tom Slick, Sr., and Joseph Frates joined forces in many spheres. During 1915, they bought plantations in Yazoo County, Mississippi, and got into several private ventures together. Frates resigned as an administrator of Frisco Railway Company and concentrated on his own businesses. More and more these investments involved his son-in-law, Tom Slick. He entered into agreements covering the acquisition of various Mississippi plantations with Slick. Frates was usually interested in the land, Slick in the oil rights.

From 1916 through 1919, Frates and Slick built tracks to the mines between Quapaw and Pitcher, Oklahoma. In 1920, the two built another railroad from Creek County to Okmulgee County, Oklahoma, to get the business of the new oil fields in the area. It was on this line that the town of Slick (twelve miles from Bristow) was created. In March 1920, Frates and Slick organized the Slick Townsite Company, the Slick Gas Company, the Slick National Bank, and the Nuyaka Townsite Company. All were headquartered in the new town of Slick, Creek County, Oklahoma.

On July 4, 1920, the first train ran from Bristow down the line to the town of Slick. The new town was located in undeveloped, sparsely settled country. The spot—a 240-acre tract of land where the railroad depot was to be built—was sold off in several hundred town lots in a special one-day sale. The town grew quickly, several businesses and residences were completed within a month, and within a year the population of Slick was 2000. At its peak during the 1920s, over 5000 folks lived, worked, went to churches, and sent their kids to schools in Slick. Bank deposits in the Slick National Bank totaled over a quarter of a million dollars, a respectable sum for those days (Frates, n.d.; Miles, 1989). The town of Slick is still on some maps, but today it is a weed-choked ghost town (Gregory, 1984).

When one reviews the history of Joseph Frates, it is apparent that, like his grandson Tom Slick, Jr., Frates possessed keen foresight. In the early 1920s, Frates and Slick, Sr., were involved in buying electric interurban and city street railway lines. By the mid-1920s, however, Frates looked into the future and saw that the increasing use of automobiles would spell the decline of the electric railways. He moved quickly to create the Union Transportation Company, buy some buses, and by the end of the decade was carrying six million passengers annually. In a similar way Frates viewed the business of fire insurance as another untapped field. He organized the Frates Company, and by 1930, it was the largest and most profitable insurance company in Oklahoma (Frates, n.d.).

Close Relatives and a Beloved Granddad

The Frateses and their relatives would remain friends with the Slicks for years. Joseph and Lula Frates had four boys, Joseph Anthony, Jr., Earl Carlton, Clifford Leroy, and Rex (who died as a child); and two girls, Berenice and Ramona, who would marry Arthur A. Seeligson. Berenice and Tom Slick, Sr.'s, grandchildren and Ramona's grandchildren would be tightknit cousins. Both groups of young people would turn up in Tom, Jr.'s, Bigfoot campsites in California during the early 1960s. Ramona's son, Frates Seeligson, as a member of the Board of Directors at the San Antonio Zoological Society, would be instrumental in getting his first cousin, Tom, Jr., the backing of that organization for the yeti hunts of the late 1950s (Frates, n.d.; Slick, C., 1988; Slick, T., 1988; Byrne, 1988).

Years after Joseph Anthony Frates's death, Ramona wrote:

He was an incurable pioneer and adventurer, a man of great physical and mental vitality, courage, business acumen, with a great sense of responsibility, fairness, and duty to his family, friends, and country. His fairness was always tempered with keen perception, understanding, and kindness.

But beware if you were a sham! He was immediately conscious of hypocrisy, self-pity, insincerity, and pompousness of manner. Expecting everyone to do his best under all conditions, uncomplainingly, he had little pity for flabbiness of mind or body. . . . He was a brave man who loved life, but never feared death.

How fortunate the older grandchildren . . . were to know and be with this unconquerable, nature-loving, understanding man, whose character was a great example to them in his daily life. He taught them the delights of nature, the love of the forest, sea, and mountains, with the pleasures, joys, and satisfaction that can be derived from fishing, hunting, and the exhilaration of the sea. They will never forget their "Granddad" (Seeligson, n.d.).

SLICKS AND OIL

Unlike the Frateses, the Slick family has not been able to trace their Dutch roots back beyond the oil fields of Pennsylvania. Born in 1810, probably in February, in Pennsylvania, Tom, Jr.'s, great-grandfather Alfred J.L. Slick lived most of his life in Clarion County. He and his wife Margaret had a son, Johnston (also given as "Johnson," "Jonas," "Johns," and "John" in various records) M. Slick, born on September 8, 1856, also in Pennsylvania. On September 13, 1861, Alfred Slick enlisted in the Union Army and fought in the Civil War until September 1864. He died an invalid and a widower, at ninety-one, on July 7, 1901, in Clarion, Pennsylvania.

In the community of Shippenville, Pennsylvania, there was a miller named Thomas J. Baker (born March 8, 1821; died January 1, 1886), his wife Frances (born May 31, 1824; died April 13, 1886), and their seven children. As the story goes, John Slick, a stranger, walked into the Bakers' mill and asked for a job. He ended up learning the miller's trade and marrying the miller's daughter, Mary, who had been born in 1860 in Shippenville. He mixed a little love with his flour, it was said (Slick, C., 1988).

Interestingly, the Clarion County, Pennsylvania, directory listed J. M. Slick as a driller in 1892 but as a miller in 1904. Somewhere along the way, the miller apparently again became a driller. John Slick is remembered in histories of the area as an oilman, an independent drilling contractor who operated in nearly every oil-producing area of the world. And one reference claims Mary A. Baker came from an "old Pennsylvania family,

connected, like her husband's, with the oil industry in its early days"
(*Encyclopedia of Biography*, 1932; Slick, C., 1988).

Thomas Baker Slick, Sr.

On October 12, 1883, when John was twenty-seven and Mary was twenty-
three, Thomas Baker Slick, Sr., was born in Shippenville. Tom, Sr., would
grow up with an older brother, Jesse, and a younger sister, Flored M.,
but as it turned out, he was the one to inherit most of his father's passion
for oil exploration.

When Tom, Sr., was only seven, his family moved to Clarion, Pennsylvania. He went to public schools and reportedly took classes at the
Normal School, although the present administration there denies this (Miles,
1989). A hard worker, Tom Slick, Sr., enjoyed learning from older and
wiser men. When he was sixteen, he went to the oil fields of West Virginia
with his father, John, helped drill wells, and fell in love with the oil
business. After a year he returned to the Normal School and spent much
of his time experimenting in a laboratory on a better way to refine crude
oil. But the oil fields and the adventure of the quest beckoned, so he quit
the Normal School and found his way to Illinois, then on to Kansas. Tom
Slick, Sr., using a buckboard, began traveling widely through those vast
tracts of the nation then called the Indian Territory. He was buying and
leasing thousands of acres of land for their oil rights, at first for others
and then slowly for himself. Although only a poor boy from Pennsylvania,
he promised himself he would make his first million dollars before he was
thirty. Long after his first million and his thirtieth birthday, Tom Slick,
Sr., remained a driven man.

Dry Hole Slick

Tom Slick, Sr., was an oil prospector who early on established a remarkable
track record for himself. Prior to 1912, he was called "Dry Hole Slick"
and "Mad Tom" because he was forever drilling oil wells that came up
dry. This did not bother him; he realized he was close to something big
and he plodded along. And part of his plan was all of the background work
he would do in a new area. He was friendly and good at socializing.
Landowners trusted him and knew they would share in his good fortune
if he hit it big. Most of the farmers clearly felt he was the right person
to buy their oil rights. At one time Slick owned over 1000 acres of leases
to the rights in Oklahoma alone—territory that had not yet been explored
for oil.

In March 1912, Tom Slick, Sr., very carefully fixed a hold on what would be the biggest discovery of his life—Wheeler Well Number 1 in the Cushing Field of Oklahoma. Bernard B. Jones had backed Mad Tom for several dry holes but withdrew his support for "just one more drilling" at the Wheeler well. Not discouraged, Tom found backing through an old friend and former employer, Charles B. Shaffer. Shaffer granted Slick an $8000 loan. The lease to the Wheeler site was owned by B. B. Jones, so Slick obtained his permission, as well as that of Frank M. Wheeler, the farm's owner, and began drilling (Miles, 1987; Gregory, 1986).

The hard winter weather of 1912 made drilling a difficult task, but Slick kept at it. And furthermore, in his own clever way, Slick did a few other things to prepare for the big day he soon hoped to have. As more and more evidence of oil was found during February, Slick began to make certain no one else would be able to cut into his discovery. When he reached the oil sand indicative of a possibly richer find, he posted guards and roped off the well. A short time later he built a huge wooden fence around the not-so-dry hole.

When the gusher came in at the Wheeler Well on Saint Patrick's Day, 1912, not too many people knew of the giant oil discovery. And Slick wanted to keep it that way as long as possible. Tom Slick rushed into Frank Wheeler's farm early that Sunday morning and cut the telephone wires. As word got out, Slick was ready. First, agents of famed oilmen John T. Milliken and Harry Sinclair showed up. They found Slick had hired out every horse and buggy in the area. When these new leasers finally found someone to rent them a rig, got some oil rights to purchase, and went looking for a notary public with whom to register their claim, they soon discovered that Slick had hired out or paid vacations for all the notaries in the region. While Slick had spent about a dollar an acre for the leases he had obtained around Cushing, Sinclair was forced a few weeks later to pay an average of two hundred dollars an acre for the ones he would obtain. Many say that old Tom's scheme for handling the whole Cushing affair was "slick" indeed, "real slick." From that time on, the discoverer of the Cushing Field was called "Lucky Tom Slick" (Miles, 1987; Gregory, 1984, 1986).

Lucky Tom would make millions from the Cushing leases. But personal matters were to take a front seat. In the midst of the Cushing triumph, word reached Slick that his father, John, was dying in a Pittsburgh hospital. He rushed there on April 11, 1912, and five days later, his father died of stomach cancer. Tom Slick was mentally and physically drained and soon was under doctor's orders to take a break from the oil business (Miles, 1987).

From October 1912 through May 1913, Tom Slick went on an extensive vacation around the world, with an emphasis on the Orient (Miles, 1987,

1989). Tom Slick, Jr.'s, interest in this section of the world can be traced to his father's stories about his travels there.

After the older Slick's return from the Far East, he would go back to Cushing, sell off a good portion of his holdings for two and a half million dollars, and get involved with Joseph Frates's rail interests for a time. Needless to say, this Frates involvement included his marriage to Berenice Frates in Springfield, Missouri, in 1915. Eleven months later, Thomas Bernard Slick was born.

The elder Tom Slick, prematurely white-haired, a chain-smoker and all-night poker player, was by now also known as the "King of the Wildcatters." He had established a reputation for himself of working as an independent, moving into new territory, obtaining some major discoveries, selling out, getting to a state of near physical collapse, then taking a vacation and coming back to start all over again. He did it in 1922 with the Eakin well in Eastland County, Texas, and helped create the boomtown of Pioneer. He did about the same thing in 1926 just before the famous Seminole field opened, and again in 1928 in central Kansas. In 1929, having just made millions of dollars on some shrewd oil field sales, he was buying up leases around Oklahoma City, just ahead of another Oklahoma boom.

Although extremely independent on a corporate level, Tom Slick, Sr., was always very loyal to his employees and friends. During the winter of 1929, he was late to a meeting by a day, and explained his tardiness with: "I've been sleeping on a pine plank for five nights [out in the wilderness with my drillers]" (MacDonald, 1929). When Slick sold off some wells and made thirty-five million dollars during the winter of 1928–1929, he handed his brother-in-law and company vice president, Charles Urschel, and his friend and company treasurer, E.E. Kirkpatrick, each a check for two million dollars for the help they had given him in the sale. But while Tom, Sr., was true to his friends, he was annoyed by "cranks and beggars" who thought he had endless millions to give away. Interestingly, in terms of Tom, Jr.'s, later pursuits, Tom, Sr., specifically noted in 1929 that he had just gotten a letter from a man who wanted him to support a search for the ruins of Noah's ark on Mount Ararat. Slick said he never answered any of those kinds of letters, mainly because he never gave money to people he did not know (Macdonald, 1929).

Some say the King of the Wildcatters worked himself into an early grave. Whatever the cause, on June 27, 1930, Slick went into Johns Hopkins Hospital in Baltimore suffering from thyroid trouble. On August 5, an operation was performed for goiter, and on August 14, he suffered a cerebral hemorrhage. On August 16, 1930, Tom Slick, Sr., died at the age of forty-six (Miles, 1987; *New York Times*, 1930). Left behind were his wife, two sons, and daughter. Also, according to some reports, upward of seventy-five million dollars.

KING OF THE WILDCATTERS REMEMBERED

Tom Slick, Jr., rarely said anything about his father in public. When he did, his family told me, it had to be an important event. They have shared the following example with me. The statement was made on the occasion of a testimonial award at the Cushing Petroleum Festival of September 9, 1952. Tom Slick was accepting the award on behalf of his father and spoke warmly of Thomas Baker Slick, Sr.:

> I expect most sons are proud of their fathers. This is a normal, human emotion. However, the fact that a group like yourself [sic] desire, after these years, to pay respect to my father's services, reinforces my belief in the importance of the things he was able to accomplish during his lifetime.
>
> My father started life as a poor boy back in 1883 in Clarion, Pennsylvania, right in the region where the oil industry was born. His father before him has some connection with the early days of the oil industry as a drilling contractor.
>
> My father left school and was able from that age on to support his family by such devices as selling newspapers and stove polish, buying chickens wholesale from farmers, dressing them, and then selling them retail to the customers.
>
> By the time he was eighteen, he went to work as a "roustabout" in the oil fields in West Virginia, and by the time he was twenty, he moved out to the very early days of the oil industry in Oklahoma—having been promoted, by that time, to cable tool dresser.
>
> After a few years of the hardest work, the most stringent savings, and the most intensive study of all the factors involved in the oil business, he was able to accumulate financial and mental facilities sufficient to permit him to start trying to find oil and financial independence for himself.
>
> His method of operation, with only the most limited of financial resources, was to select a potential area he thought might yield oil, based on whatever crude geological hints my father had available in those days. . . .
>
> He would move out into the selected area, spending time with the farmers so that they would get well enough acquainted with him to have the requisite confidence in him. When this confidence had developed, he would call together the landowners of the community to a meeting where he could tell them of his proposal. His proposal was, that if the landowners would give him the leases on their land, he would guarantee to have a test well drilled for them on their block of acreage, which, if successful, could greatly increase

the value of their royalty. Invariably this young man, admittedly without the money to drill a well, was able to inspire enough confidence that the farmers were willing to give him their block of leases.

With the block of leases in hand, he was able, in turn, to inspire in someone with money, sufficient confidence in the speculative prospects of the block, that the capitalists were willing to advance the necessary capital to drill the first well, in return for a half interest in the play.

On the tenth wildcat well, worked out in this laborious manner, my father, in partnership with Mr. B.B. Jones of Bristow, at the Wheeler Number One, discovered your Cushing oil field—one of the great oil fields of all time.

His health already had been impaired by the strain and hard work, so, a few months later, he decided to accept a major company purchase offer at a price considerably above his previously announced ambition to make a million dollars—an ambition that sounded fantastically high for a young man without any money—but which he well knew was only a small fraction of the true value of his property, in order to retire, to travel around the world, to complete his education, and to "enjoy life."

Unfortunately, he had always had to work so hard that he had never had the opportunity of learning to relax and enjoy life, and, by the time he returned from his trip around the world, he was back full steam in the oil business, fated to go up and down with the usual alternative series of great successes and disappointing failures until his unfortunate death in 1930 (Slick, 1952).

Young Tom was only fourteen years old at the time of his father's death. Tom was close to his father, we have learned from our interviews with his family, and from the pictures of young Tom on his dad's knee. We are not certain of the depth or true nature of the psychological effect that the loss of his father must have had on this boy turning into a man. His lifelong searches, whether for male companionship, innovative ideas, or yetis, we speculate, may have been aspects of the gap that was left in his life by the early death of his father.

Tom Slick, Sr., had left an estate worth millions of dollars. The inheritance was two-thirds to be split equally among Tom, his brother, Earl, and sister, Betty, and the other third went to Tom, Sr.'s, wife, Berenice. The principal to the boys was to be given out in three parts when they reached thirty, forty-five, and fifty-five years of age. All the children were to live off the interest in the meantime. Betty was to never inherit the principal directly, supposedly to save her from men out to get her money. Instead, her share would go to her children. (By 1960, Tom Slick, Jr., had inherited fifteen million dollars.)

URSCHEL AND MACHINE GUN KELLY

Three years after his father's death, in the midst of Tom's teen years, an unbelievable event—the kidnapping of his new stepfather—would interrupt the tranquility of Slick's life.

Tom's recently acquired stepfather was no stranger to him; this man was already a well-known face around the family. Following her husband's death, Berenice Slick married Charles Urschel, Tom Slick, Sr.'s, business partner and manager. Urschel had been Berenice's brother-in-law, but had himself recently become a widower on the death of his wife, Slick, Sr.'s, sister, Flored.

The family moved to 327 Northwest Eighteenth Street, Oklahoma City, Oklahoma. It was there that the incident that changed the moral and emotional fabric of the Slicks' and Urschels' lives occurred. It happened on a roasting dry evening while Tom Slick, Jr., was away from home: Machine Gun Kelly walked into all of their lives.

From the official Federal Bureau of Investigation's report:

On 11:15 p.m. on Saturday, July 22, 1933, Mr. and Mrs. Charles F. Urschel, one of Oklahoma's wealthiest couples, were playing bridge with their friends, Mr. and Mrs. Walter R. Jarrett, on a screened porch of the Urschel residence at Oklahoma City. Two men, one armed with a machine gun and the other with a pistol, opened the screen door and inquired which of the two men was Mr. Urschel. Receiving no reply, they remarked "Well, we will take both of them." After warning the women against calling for help, they marched Urschel and Jarrett to where they had driven their car, put them into the back of the Chevrolet sedan, and drove rapidly away.

Mrs. Urschel, in accordance with the Attorney General's advice to the public, immediately telephoned J. Edgar Hoover, Director of the Federal Bureau of Investigation, United States Department of Justice. Special Agents were sent to Oklahoma City, where an extensive investigation commenced.

At 1:00 a.m., Sunday, July 23, 1933, Jarrett made his way back to the Urschel residence. The victims had been driven to the outskirts of the city, where they had turned right on a dirt road parallel to the 23rd Street Highway and had proceeded northeast to a point about twelve miles from the city. After crossing a small bridge and arriving at an intersection, they had put Jarrett out of the car after they had identified him and had taken $50 which he had in his wallet, warning him not to tell the direction the kidnapers had gone. He stated that after he was released the car proceeded south.

After the kidnaping became known, numerous letters, telephone calls, and other leads were received, many of which were anonymous, indicating possible leads. All had to be followed, although few were of value. Leads of this nature were developed simultaneously in all parts of the United States.

Several days elapsed before word was received from the kidnapers. On July 26, J. G. Catlett, a wealthy oil man of Tulsa, Oklahoma, and an intimate friend of Urschel, received a package through Western Union. It contained a letter written to him by Urschel requesting Catlett to act as an intermediary for his release; a personal letter from Urschel to his wife; and a typewritten note directed to Mr. Catlett demanding that he proceed to Oklahoma City immediately and not communicate by telephone or otherwise with the Urschel family from Tulsa. The package also contained a typewritten letter addressed to Mr. E. E. Kirkpatrick of Oklahoma City, which read in part:

"Immediately upon receipt of this letter you will proceed to obtain the sum of TWO HUNDRED THOUSAND DOLLARS ($200,000.00) in GENUINE USED FEDERAL RESERVE CURRENCY in the denomination of TWENTY DOLLAR ($20.00) Bills.

It will be useless for you to attempt taking notes of SERIAL NUMBERS MAKING UP DUMMY PACKAGE, OR ANYTHING ELSE IN THE LINE OF ATTEMPTED DOUBLE CROSS. BEAR THIS IN MIND, CHARLES F. URSCHEL WILL REMAIN IN OUR CUSTODY UNTIL MONEY HAS BEEN INSPECTED AND EXCHANGED AND FURTHERMORE WILL BE AT THE SCENE OF CONTACT FOR PAY-OFF AND IF THERE SHOULD BE ANY ATTEMPT AT ANY DOUBLE XX IT WILL BE HE THAT SUFFERS THE CONSEQUENCE.

RUN THIS AD FOR ONE WEEK IN DAILY OKLAHOMAN.

'FOR SALE—160 Acres Land, good five room house, deep well. Also Cows, Tools, Tractor, Corn and Hay. $3750.00 for quick sale . . TERMS . . BOX #——'

You will hear from us as soon as convenient after insertion of AD."

The ad was inserted.

On July 28, an envelope addressed to the "Daily Oklahoman," Box H-807, was received. It was from Joplin, Missouri. A letter to Kirkpatrick read in part:

". . . You will pack TWO HUNDRED THOUSAND DOLLARS ($200,000.00) in USED GENUINE FEDERAL RESERVE NOTES OF TWENTY DOLLAR DENOMINATION in a suitable LIGHT COLORED LEATHER BAG and have someone purchase transportation for you, including berth, aboard Train #28 (The Sooner) which departs at 10:10 p.m. via the M. K. & T. Lines for Kansas City, Mo.

You will ride on the OBSERVATION PLATFORM where you may be observed by some-one at some Station along the Line between Okla. City and K.C. Mo. If indication are alright, some-where along the Right-of-Way you will observe a Fire on the Right Side of Track (Facing direction train is bound) that first Fire will be your Cue to be prepared to throw BAG to Track immediately after passing SECOND FIRE.

REMEMBER THIS—IF ANY TRICKERY IS ATTEMPTED YOU WILL FIND THE REMAINS OF URSCHEL AND INSTEAD OF JOY THERE WILL BE DOUBLE GRIEF—FOR, SOME-ONE VERY NEAR AND DEAR TO THE URSCHEL FAMILY IS UNDER CON-STANT SURVEILLAINCE AND WILL LIKE-WISE SUFFER FOR *YOUR ERROR.*

If there is the slightest HITCH in these PLANS for any reason what-so-ever, not your fault, you will proceed on into Kansas City, Mo. and register at the Muehlebach Hotel under the name of E. E. Kincaid of Little Rock, Arkansas and await further instructions there.

THE MAIN THING IS DO NOT DIVULGE THE CONTENTS OF THIS LETTER TO ANY LAW AUTHORITIES *FOR WE HAVE NO INTENTION OF FURTHER COMMUNICATION.*

YOU ARE TO MAKE THIS TRIP SATURDAY JULY 29TH 1933 . . ."

The Bureau's first concern in all kidnaping cases is the safe return of the kidnaped victim. Accordingly, no effort was made on the part of the Bureau to identify the writer of these letters or to interfere in any way with the negotiations until after Urschel was returned.

As a result of the above letters, $200,000 in used $20 notes of the Federal Reserve Bank, Tenth District, was obtained and the serial numbers recorded. They were placed in a new, light-colored leather Gladstone bag. At the same time another identical bag was purchased and filled with old magazines, fearing an attempt at hijacking. As a precaution, it was decided that Catlett would accompany Kirkpatrick to Kansas City. By prearrangement, Catlett sat just inside the rear end of the observation car, while Kirkpatrick sat on the observation platform with the bag containing the magazines. Kirkpatrick remained on the observation platform all night, riding there all the way to Kansas City, but no signals were observed.

Upon arrival at Kansas City Kirkpatrick and Catlett proceeded to the Muehlebach Hotel. Kirkpatrick registered under the name of E. E. Kincaid and waited in his room, where he received a telegram from Tulsa, Oklahoma, as follows:

"Owing to unavoidable incident unable to keep appointment. Will phone you about six. Signed, C. H. Moore."

About 5:30 p.m., on Sunday, July 30, Kirkpatrick received a telephone call from a party who asked if this was "Mr. Kincaid," and upon being advised that it was stated "This is Moore. You got my telegram?" to which Kirkpatrick replied in the affirmative. Kirkpatrick was then instructed to leave the Muehlebach Hotel in a taxicab and proceed to the LaSalle Hotel and walk west a block or two. He requested permission to be accompanied by a friend, which request was curtly refused. Accordingly, Kirkpatrick took the bag containing the $200,000, arriving at the LaSalle Hotel at about 6 p.m. He walked west. After proceeding no more than half a block he observed a man approaching him who, upon reaching Kirkpatrick, said "Mr. Kincaid, I will take that bag," and reached out and took it. Kirpatrick then stated, "I want some instructions. I must telephone someone who is very interested immediately." The man who had taken the bag told Kirpatrick to return to the hotel and Urschel would be returned within the specified time. Kirkpatrick then returned to the hotel and from there proceeded to Oklahoma City. Catlett returned to Tulsa.

Urschel Returns Home

Urschel arrived home exhausted at about 11:30 p.m., July 31, stating that he had been able to sleep but very little during the nine days he had been held in captivity. As soon as he recovered from the shock and regained his strength he was interviewed by FBI Special Agents. A detailed statement was obtained including every movement and action taken by himself, the kidnapers, and those with whom they came in contact during his period of captivity.

Urschel's statement concerning the kidnaping and transactions which occurred immediately thereafter was substantially the same as Jarrett's recollection. Urschel stated that immediately after Jarrett's release one of the men produced some cotton, a short bandage, adhesive tape, and he was blind-folded. Approximately one hour after being blindfolded the car passed through either two small oil fields or the end of two large fields approximately thirty minutes driving time apart; that he could smell the gas and hear the oil pumps working. The first stop was made about 3:30 a.m., when he was taken from the car by one of the abductors into the brush, and that the other man was gone approximately fifteen minutes after gasoline. About one hour later a stop was made to open a gate and approximately three minutes later another stop was made and another gate opened. Within a minute after the last gate, the car drove into what he took to be a garage. In this building the men, from their movements and actions, transferred license plates from the Chevrolet sedan to a larger car, which Urschel believed to be a seven-passenger Cadillac or Buick. A berth had been made up in the back of this car and he was told to lie on this bunk. They left this place immediately and after a drive of two or three hours a stop was made at a filling station, where a woman attendant filled the the car with gas. Urschel overheard one of the men asking the woman about crop conditions and she replied that "The crops around here are burned up, although we may make some broom corn."

Urschel stated that about 9 or 10 a.m. it rained and the road became very slippery, to the extent that on one occasion one of the men was compelled to alight and push the car. In his opinion at no time on this trip did they drive on pavement. At the next stop the car was driven directly into what he considered a garage, and at this point he asked one of the men the time and he replied it was 2:30 p.m. They remained in this building until dark, when he was taken outside, passed through a narrow gate and proceeded on a board walk. He was led into a house and into a room where he was told there were two beds. The bed he occupied was apparently an iron cot and one of the men occupied the other. Shortly after entering this house he heard the voice of a man and a woman in an adjoining room. He stated that his ears were filled with cotton and adhesive tape was placed over them.

Urschel stated that he stayed in this house until the next day—July 24th—when he was taken in an automobile by the two men to a house about 15 minutes driving distance. While in the first house he ate from a small table and he heard barnyard animals outside.

Upon entering the second house he was led into a room where he was told to lie upon some blankets in a corner of the room. He also heard voices of a man and a woman in the adjoining room which did not resemble the voice of either of the two men who abducted him, and that shortly thereafter this man and woman left the place.

Urschel stated that on the first night at the second house a handcuff was placed on one of his wrists and attached to a chair. Next morning the two men brought up the matter of a contact. They asked Urschel if he had a friend who could be trusted in Tulsa, Oklahoma, and he suggested the name of John G. Catlett. The men instructed him to write a letter to Catlett and he did.

In addition to the two men who had kidnaped him, Urschel was guarded by an old man and a younger man. Urschel stated that during the time he was held in captivity one of his two kidnapers discussed freely with him the fact that he had been stealing for twenty-five years, mentioning Bonnie and Clyde, referring to them as "Just a couple of cheap filling station and car thieves," and stating that his group did not deal in anything cheap. He also discussed freely a number of bank robberies, advising that he and his friend had been invited to participate in a bank robbery at Clinton, Iowa, but after making a survey of the place they did not take part in the robbery because the chances of making a "get-away" were unfavorable.

Urschel stated that one of the two kidnapers returned to the house on Friday and brought with him a chain; that thereafter this chain was used to attach to his handcuffs, which enabled him to move about to some extent. He was satisfied there were chickens, cows, and hogs around the place, and he was advised by one of the guards that he had four milk cows. Urschel stated that he was given water in an old tin cup. The well from which this water was obtained was northwest of the house, and the water was obtained from the well by a rope and bucket on a pulley, which made considerable noise. He stated that each morning and evening a plane passed regularly over the house; that he managed to get a look at his watch and determined that the morning plane would always pass at approximately 9:45 and the evening plane would pass at approximately 5:45; and that on Sunday, July 30, when it rained very hard, the morning plane did not pass.

Urschel stated that on Monday, July 31, at about 2:00 p.m., one of his kidnapers returned and told him that he was going to be released, that they had to leave at a certain time, and that another car was going ahead as a pilot car. He was then driven to a point near Norman, Oklahoma, where he was given $10 and released (Federal Bureau of Investigation, 1988).

Don't Shoot, G-Man!

With the clues that Urschel's excellent memory had provided, the FBI was able to find the location of the shack in Paradise, Wise County, Texas. The FBI had been picking up hints that Machine Gun Kelly was involved in the kidnapping and the information that Kelly's wife's family owned the residence where Urschel was held pinned it down.

Machine Gun Kelly was born in Tennessee in 1897 as George Kelly Barnes, and grew up to be a two-bit criminal that was fashioned into something much bigger than life by his wife, Kathryn Thorne, the FBI, and the newspapers. Kelly was not much more than a bootlegger when Kathryn met and married him. She encouraged Kelly to become more deeply involved in robbing banks, bought him a machine gun, and gave him his nickname. For the FBI's part, the nation's Depression had spawned a wave of kidnappings of young children and wealthy men, and it was itching to prevent them. Despite a series of record years of literally hundreds of kidnappings during the early 1930s, it was not until the passage of the Lindbergh Kidnapping Law the year before the Urschel kidnapping that the FBI was allowed to investigate these cases. The Urschel crime was the very first kidnapping case that was to involve the FBI, and it wanted to do a good job. Meanwhile, the media found that kidnappings sold papers. Kidnapping headlines dominated the papers. The kidnapping of Urschel, the intervention of the FBI, and the months of graphic court testimony were all naturals for publicity (Kirkpatrick, 1947; Alix, 1974, 1988; Ellis, 1975; *New York Times*, 1933; Ungar, 1975; Whitehead, 1956).

The FBI's investigation moved slowly but surely. Finally, in the early morning hours of September 26, 1933, the agency conducted a raid on a house in Memphis, and George and Kathryn Kelly were taken into custody by Memphis police and FBI agents. One of the most famous lines in the history of crime-fighting is credited to that incident. Caught without a weapon, George "Machine Gun" Kelly reportedly cried out: "Don't shoot, G-Men! Don't shoot, G-Men!" as he surrendered. The street term, which had applied to all federal investigators, became synonymous with FBI agents. The impact on our culture of this term was immediate. Boys rapidly formed clubs of "Junior G-Men." Lloyd Nolan and James Cagney's crime-busting movie, *G Men*, followed quickly in 1935.

Machine Gun Kelly's kidnapping of Charles Urschel—the *one* event that helped create the modern FBI—was in the newspapers every day for months. This specific incident has made the Slicks overly sensitive concerning publicity, public exposure, and personal safety. Tom Slick was strongly influenced by the kidnapping. In 1933, he allegedly started carrying a gun and was definitely given a huge plainclothes bodyguard called French (Lubar, 1960; Wilson, 1989). Tom would remain shy of media attention for his entire life. What publicity came to him because of his involvement with the yeti was often unwanted and unwelcome. His family remains quiet and withdrawn today, and their actions, such as not sharing information about the Slick-Johnson expeditions for so many years, have frequently been misread. Placed in the context of the Urschel kidnapping, their behavior becomes more understandable.

The sense of adventure so familiar to the Slicks and the Frateses was diminished by the kidnapping. But it did live on in one member of the family: Tom Slick, Jr.

CHAPTER 2

YOUTHFUL TOM
The Loch Ness Monster, Southwest Research Institute, Mind Science, and a Hoat

WE REALLY DO NOT KNOW MUCH ABOUT TOM, Jr.'s, early life. Hints of how it must have been, however, do come through from his family and friends. Tom was born into a family that was forever on the move, from one independent project site to another. Luckily, Tom's strong-willed and determined mother gave some stability to the family by using Clarion, Pennsylvania, as a summer base every year until Tom, Sr.'s, death. By 1929, the family had homes in Clarion, Oklahoma City, and San Antonio. Tom, Jr., demonstrated in years to come that he liked San Antonio the best.

As a boy, Tom listened intently to his father's stories of the Indian Territory wildcatting and the trips to the Orient. He would sit in his father's lap for hours of accounts about those bygone romantic days. Tom, Jr., would accompany his father on the once-a-year hunting trip to Rockport, Texas, and occasionally to the elder Slick's hunting preserves in Louisiana and Texas. Tales of adventure about the Wild West and Old Mexico flowed from the Frates side of the family as well. Tom was surrounded by two rich traditions of adventurers and risk-takers.

Tom found himself very interested in science as a boy. His father, until his death, and then his grandfather, Joseph Frates, were big influences in the realm of natural history, and this interest apparently carried through Tom's teen years. An associate recalled years later: "Tom was one of those rare individuals who seemed to have been born with the notion that scientific research could and would solve most of mankind's problems. Only mature and deep-thinking people know this. When he was of high school age, he was already doing complex experiments in biology; his inquisitiveness was unbounded. While other boys were reading the popular novels of the day, Tom was reading *Scientific American, Popular Mechanics*, and many books on science" (Vagtborg, 1973).

Tom, Jr., spent his first two years of high school at Oklahoma City's Classen High. Tom's father died in 1930, and the next year he went to Phillips Exeter Academy in Exeter, New Hampshire. Dating from 1781 and nestled among stately elms, Phillips Exeter was an old college preparatory school of the highest academic and social standing. The sons of Presidents Lincoln, Grant, and Cleveland attended the school. Politically forward thinkers from Daniel Webster to the current Democratic senator from West Virginia, Jay Rockefeller, also attended Exeter. Cofounder of the Americans for Democratic Action, Arthur M. Schlesinger, Jr., for example, was an upperclassman at the same time as Tom Slick.

While at Exeter, Tom was mainly involved in his studies and with girls, according to a friend who would remain close to Tom until his death. Stewart Strong ("S. S.") Wilson was Tom's closest friend at Exeter and then at Yale. From Oracle, Arizona, Wilson found that Slick and he were immediately drawn to each other because of their common interests in the Spanish language, Mexican food, ranching, and dating. Wilson recalled that Tom was very handsome and rather popular with young women. Tom had time to be a coxswain on the academy's rowing crew team (Slick, C., 1989) and a president of the Southern Club (Exeter, 1934). On campus, Tom Slick wore a long black overcoat and black Stetson hat, relishing the label of Southwestern nonconformist (Lubar, 1960).

In 1934, Slick graduated. Interestingly, Phillips Exeter received several ample gifts during the time Slick was there from the Standard Oil–endowed Harkness family. And, that summer, in one of those bizarre coincidences that often turn up in the lives of individuals like Slick, the adventurer and "bring-'em-back-alive" animal collector William H. Harkness was organizing an incredible expedition for the New York Zoological Society and the Bronx Zoo. The Harkness expedition went to Tibet in search of the legendary and elusive giant panda. Indeed, the giant panda was captured and returned to Chicago's Brookfield Zoo by Ruth Harkness and W. M. Russell* in 1936. This giant panda expedition still ranks, along with the Slick searches, among the most important and media-recognized major cryptozoological efforts of our time (Morris, 1966; Hopkins, 1938; Heuvelmans, 1958; Perry, 1969; Harkness, 1938).

---

*This is the same W. M. (Gerald) Russell who Slick would hire some twenty years later to help him search for the yeti.

The Young Man and The Loch Ness Monster

After the Urschel kidnapping and his graduation from Phillips Exeter, Tom Slick would go to Yale University in New Haven, Connecticut. Here, he was a member of Pierson college, and played sophomore and junior intramural football. He also was involved in squash, went out for crew as a junior, and became a member of the Political Union. Tom's academic record was good; he ranked second or third during his first three years, and eventually graduated Phi Beta Kappa in 1938, as a premedicine biology major (Yale, 1989).

S. S. Wilson, Slick's friend from Exeter, roomed with Slick at Yale. The two buddies were constantly together, and most of their activities overlapped. Wilson managed the Pierson football team on which Slick played. But mainly Slick, Wilson, George Nichols, John Francis, John Nelson, and Rawson Goodwin all were members of an informal group who took weekend trips in Slick's car to Vasser, Smith, and Wellesley (Wilson, 1989).

In addition, Wilson told me that during their Yale years, Slick actually went to Loch Ness and looked for the Loch Ness Monsters, the large humped beasts said to resemble gigantic long-necked seals or waterbound dinosaurs. Since a new road was dynamited around the hills of Loch Ness in 1933, scores of sightings have occurred. During the summer of 1937, Slick, Wilson, Nelson, and Goodwin took Slick's 1934 maroon Buick sedan aboard the *Bremen*, debarked in Germany, and then drove 10,000 miles all around Europe. During August, 1937, the group, at Slick's urging, traveled to Scotland's fabled Loch Ness. They spent a few days talking to residents about the reported monsters and searching the water's surface for signs of the creatures. Slick and his friends stayed for a time in Inverness and Drumnadrochit, a village located on Urquhart Bay, site of the ancient Urquhart Castle and location of numerous monster encounters. Around the time Slick was at Loch Ness, one of the more memorable monster sightings occurred from a tearoom at the Halfway House near Foyers. In August 1937, the Reverend William Graham saw two separate four-foot-high humps the color of an elephant, creating a heavy wake as the creature moved along at thirty-five miles an hour (Whyte, 1957). But the Slick group saw nothing. Yet Slick's search for unknown animals had begun. The Loch Ness Monster really excited Slick (Wilson, 1989). Slick's friends returned with his car to America while Tom went on to Russia just to see what it was like there before going home.

Making a Life for Himself

For a year or so after graduating, Slick lived in Oklahoma City, but in 1939, he established his home in San Antonio, Texas, and remained there for the rest of his life. Soon after moving, Slick married, then quickly divorced, Betty Lewis. His first son, William Lewis, was born after the couple had separated, and thus William was named after Betty's father.

By his late thirties, Tom Slick, like his father, was prematurely white-haired. This did not diminish his good looks, and in his bachelor days he kept the company of many attractive socialites and budding Hollywood starlets. But Tom was not your typical jet-setting playboy. He was as excited by stimulating conversations with his female associates as he was by his allegedly frequent sexual encounters. Nevertheless, Thomas Baker Slick, Jr., was an attractive man, and he seemed to know it. Some five feet, eleven inches tall, he was always fit and trim, never weighing much over one hundred seventy pounds, even into his forties. His sons remember that when he went to the beach with them in the 1950s, he would often go jogging, long before it was the fashionable thing to do. His passion, however, recreationally speaking, was reserved for hunting and fishing. He enjoyed a good game of golf, but he was not a follower of professional sports.

During World War II, Slick volunteered for navy service immediately after the attack on Pearl Harbor, December 7, 1941. Turned down for poor eyesight, he served as a "dollar-a-year man," in the role of a shipping officer of the War Production Board in Washington, D.C. for six months. After that he transferred and served for one year as a cargo officer of the Board of Economic Welfare in Chile. Later, when the navy relaxed its eyesight requirements, he served in Hawaii as a liaison officer to the Oahu Railroad, as a commanding officer of an oil tank farm in Saipan, and with the occupation in Japan. By this time, Tom Slick was engaged to be married again, this time to Patty Nixon.

During Tom's marriage to Patty (they divorced in 1955), they had three children: Thomas Baker, Jr. (not the III; the family name confusion continued), Charles Urschel, and Patty. Slick remained a devoted father despite the fact he lived in a city separate from his former wife and his children. He saw them all frequently, supported them financially, had a friendly relationship with his ex-spouse, and took the kids on mini-trips to some rather out-of-the-way and exciting locations.

Outside the domain of Slick's personal life, Slick made some major achievements. The San Antonio Chamber of Commerce chose him as "Young Man of the Year 1948," and Trinity University gave him an honorary Doctor of Science degree in 1953. Let's take a look at some of these other aspects of Slick's life.

SLICK'S REVOLUTIONARY APPROACH

Slick created a series of research centers to meet the challenge of the betterment of humankind. After graduating from college, he decided to "realize in brick and mortar the nonprofit approach to scientific research that had always fired his imagination" (Beynon, 1983).

Slick often described his thoughts on research to his friends, as in the following heretofore unpublished passage:

Technical progress comes in two ways: the evolutionary and the revolutionary. In the evolutionary method, one little piece of new knowledge, a small step forward from previous knowledge is laboriously added, brick by brick, until a worthwhile accomplishment results. This is the method of university research and of the great research laboratories that have grown up, particularly in America. It is becoming the principal means of scientific advance and probably it is the most certain and safest way towards technical progress. The revolutionary way, on the other hand, is the way of the gifted inventor, or the adventurous explorer. It is the skipping of the small steps and arriving at a radical advance, perhaps more by intitution or by daring trial and error than by entirely logical reasoning. The revolutionary method is the way a Christopher Columbus, reasoning against all the accepted ideas of his day takes a daring try and moves civilization far ahead or by which the Wright Brothers trying a "crazy" idea ushered in the Air Age.

This does not mean that the evolutionary method should be neglected. Actually, it is probably the surer path to progress and the one of the two that will accomplish the most. All that I am advocating is that neither do we fail to encourage and achieve the benefits of the revolutionary method. The evolutionary method is taking care of itself, it is the method today of safe careful conservative work of teams helping each other. It is the revolutionary method of the lone dedicated inventor, the deep genius thinker, the adventurous speculator, the daring explorer in whatever field, that needs encouragement so that society does not lose the fruit of their daring and their dedication. The trend of our society is the other way, towards security instead of daring, towards the cautious instead of the bold, towards protecting what we have rather than advancing. Today the revolutionaries need encouragement (Slick, n.d.).

Essar Ranch

Slick wished to reflect his vision in his creations. And, early in his research career, he wanted a research center involved in agriculture, animal and plant breeding, industrial and economic development, and biomedical research, as well as one that would house a staff, education facilities, and visiting scientists. This was going to take a lot of space, and he found it just west of San Antonio. On June 18, 1940, Slick purchased a piece of land from Leon Creek west to Potranco Road and south of Culebra Road. This property encompassed only 1602 acres, but Slick eventually owned 5000 acres in the area, including the historic Cable House. Slick's Essar Ranch (for the S and R of "scientific research") was the first expression of his desire to encourage the revolutionary approach.

Essar was the location of many of Slick's cattle-breeding successes. He began modestly with a Hereford breeding program, and later, he and his associates orginated the "Brangus," a hybrid that combined the heat resistance of the Brahman and the meat quality of the Angus. Additionally, Slick owned one of the three largest registered Angus herds in the nation.

FAR and SFRE

At the age of twenty-five, Slick set up his first full-fledged research facility. On December 16, 1941, he established the Foundation of Applied Research (FAR), which was later succeeded by the Southwest Foundation for Research and Education (SFRE). FAR was endowed immediately with 1875 shares of the Slick-Urschel Oil Company, with the major share of the Tinsley Oil Field in Mississippi that the Slicks and the Urschels had discovered and developed. Tom Slick used 2500 acres of the Essar Ranch to house FAR/SFRE.

FAR/SFRE was established to provide fundamental research and advanced education, particularly in biomedicine and biochemistry. By 1960, SFRE carried an annual budget of $700,000 and had about seventy scientists working on human heart and arterial disease, cancer, endocrinology, and reproduction research problems.

Today, SFRE is the site of the world's largest colony of breeding baboons, more than 2700. SFRE produces baboons for the entire United States biomedical research community. Besides the baboons, which originally came from Kenya but now are wholly rebred here, SFRE has a menagerie of 3000 rats, 1600 mice, 500 hamsters, 160 marmosets, 150 chimpanzees, 120 opossums, along with miscellenous other monkeys, guinea pigs, rabbits, and chickens. During the yeti searches, Slick told people he would bring the creature back to SFRE to examine it and classify it. SFRE certainly could have met the challenge.

SOUTHWEST RESEARCH INSTITUTE

In 1947, as an outgrowth of the successful SFRE, Slick created the Southwest Research Institute (SwRI), dedicated to effect the best utilization of human and natural resources through applied science and technology. In 1960, SwRI had a staff of 500 scientists, engineers, and technicians conducting about five million dollars' worth of research programs annually. After Slick's death and the ensuing reorganizations, Martin Goland of New York was brought in to take over what he called a "bootstrap operation." In 1970, gross revenue had increased to over twenty million dollars, and by 1986, the total was over $140 million. SwRI employs 2100 people today and conducts more than 1000 projects a year.

With the growth of SwRI, branch offices now exist in Dallas/Fort Worth, Houston, Detroit, and Washington, D.C. Two-thirds of the contracts SwRI gets are from private industry, and the remainder is from the government. The areas of concentration listed in the Institute's brochure reflect the diversity of its research: alternate energy, applied physics, biosciences, bioengineering, chemistry, chemical engineering, compressor system dynamics, electromagnetic systems, electronics, electrical engineering, engine research/development, engineering sciences, environmental/health sciences, explosion hazards, fire technology, fracture mechanics, fuels/lubricants, geosciences, intelligent systems/robotics, materials sciences, mining technology, nondestructive evaluation, nuclear safety, offshore technology, safety on the highways, space sciences, structural research, and terminal ballistics.

The 600-foot tall Tower of the Americas presents a practical example of the kind of problems that SwRI tackles. In 1969, a year after this symbol of the San Antonio World's Fair was built, the city discovered that the architects had forgotten to design a way to clean the huge plates of glass that enclosed the revolving observation tower. As the stream of 200,000 visitors passed through, the layers of grime and grit increased. All kinds of solutions were suggested and tried, but finally the city council turned to SwRI and awarded them a $12,750 contract to use big wipers mounted on magnets. Asked to describe their plans in detail at the time, a SwRI spokesperson declined and said: "The patent is pending" (*National Observer*, 1969).

During Slick's day, SwRI was instantly the second largest research center in the U.S. Today, SwRI is the third largest nonprofit applied research institute in the world, ranking behind only the giant Batelle Memorial Institute of Columbus, Ohio, and the huge Stanford Research Institute in Palo Alto. Known only to a few other scientists in the applied research field, SwRI is a well-kept secret, and few are aware of Tom Slick's early founding role. Unfortunately, Slick's philosophy has given way to a safer and more conservative view of running the Institute. Clearly today, at both SwRI and SFRE "the evolutionary way is seen as the best way forward" (Beynon, 1983).

BUSINESS SUCCESS

Slick's idea that his research efforts were all important never hindered his financial success. He remained an intelligent and responsible business-person throughout his life.

For example, Slick joined his brother, Earl, in founding Slick Airways in January 1946 to fill the void in air cargo freight delivery. Slick Airways and Flying Tiger Lines, during the late 1940s and 1950s, had the corner on the market, and flew many fast-paced and exciting jobs, recalling images from the early scenes in the Indiana Jones movies and John Wayne's 1942 film, *Flying Tigers*. Coming out of the adventurous days of pre–World War II "flying tiger" pilots who "flew the Hump," that is, took cargo over the Himalayas to China, Slick Airways carried on a thrilling tradition. (Frankly, many of Tom Slick's adventures are well worth a George Lucas/Steven Spielberg cinema treatment, and perhaps there are places where the real and the fictional overlap. In *Raiders of the Lost Ark*, Indiana Jones, an archaeological expert on the occult and obtainer of rare antiquities, finds himself first in the South American jungles, then shortly on a Slick Airways–type plane, following German Nazi intelligence and folkloric leads, on route to eastern Nepal. Two of Slick's prized possessions were the German General Staff map of world mineral resources and an ancient Tibetan medical book. Both were examples of some of the artifacts from Slick's quests to eastern Nepal, South America, and elsewhere.)

Slick Airways was a good idea. It was the cargo freight leader of the U.S., and on April 16, 1951, the company became the world's first operator of the highly revolutionary and specialized cargo plane, the Douglas DC-6A. American Airlines and then most of the rest of the passenger carriers soon jumped into the freight business. Opposition from the commercial airlines was probably the reason for the failure of Slick Airways' merger with Flying Tiger Lines in the late 1940s. Slick Airways never regained its central position. The company spurted along through trials and tests in 1959 and 1965 until Airlift finally bought it out in 1966. The holding company, Slick Corporation, still has some Airlift stock, but in the 1970s also had interests in Drew Chemical Company and Pulverising Machinery plant (Davies, 1972).

Slick Airways was not Tom Slick's only business venture, however. Following the lead of at least three generations of Slicks, in 1939, Tom, Earl, stepfather Charles F. Urschel, Sr., Charles F. Urschel, Jr., and his father's creative and clever drilling man, Jim Hewgley and his family, had developed the great Tinsley Oil Field near Yazoo City, Mississippi, on a plantation that Slick, Sr., had bought years before. Soon after, they went on to the Caesar Field in south Texas, and Tom Slick added to it by buying the nearby Medio Ranch. Before long Tom and Earl Slick were drilling fields in Kansas, and the Slick-Urschel Oil Company, later renamed the Slick Oil Company, was rolling.

In 1947, this company purchased the one hundred-million-barrel Benedum Field in west Texas, named after Michael L. Benedum, an old wildcatting foe of Tom Slick, Sr. The field had been a dry hole for Benedum despite the fact that he had spent over a million dollars on it. Young Tom came along, bargained with Benedum and got the site for $250,000. Using Jim Hewgley to direct the drilling, they struck oil in three months. Later Tom sold his interest in the Benedum field and netted over two million dollars. The Benedum discovery and other profitable ventures firmed up the status of the Slick Oil Corporation. Shortly before Slick's death, this company was worth about nine million dollars and Slick owned twenty-five percent of it.

Slick was deeply involved in many other business enterprises as well. Transworld Resources, another Slick-owned company, held mineral rights to locations in Mexico, Alaska, and California. Part of Slick's idea here was to buy up old mines that no longer produced, and with new technological breakthroughs, reap some profits from them. Another corporation of Slick's was Texstar, his hope for consolidating his diverse companies. Through this creation and his buy-out of the Texas Calgary Company, he did obtain an American Stock Exchange listing, but never was able to realize the consolidation of all his interests under one corporate umbrella.

In Tom Slick, Jr.'s, short life he was a partner in Slick-Moorman Land and Cattle Company; Chairman of the Board of Slick Oil Company and of Transworld Resources Corporation; Director at Dresser Industries, Bailey-Selburn Oil and Gas Ltd., Dynamics Research, Inc., Dynamics Iron & Steel, Inc., Quanta Electronics Company, Summit Valley Land Corporation, Guinea American International Corporation, Slick Airways, Inc., Slick Corporation, and Beatrice Perry, Inc.

PEACE AND POLITICS

In the area of world affairs, Tom Slick was supportive of an innovative idea leading to the possibility of international disarmament. Slick wrote two books on the topic. He privately published *The Last Great Hope* in 1951; *Permanent Peace* was printed and distributed fairly widely by Prentice-Hall in 1958 (Slick, 1951a; Slick, 1958). He proposed in these books a plan that promoted world disarmament by way of small national armies slowly decreasing in strength as an international police force backing a global rule grew bigger.

To put his money to work on this idea, Slick founded the Strategy for Peace Conference. The first and second meetings were held at the Arden House in New York in June 1960 and January 1961. The third took place at the Airlie House in Virginia in October 1961. The fourth was scheduled for November 1962, but with Slick's death in October, it is not clear that the last conference ever took place.

Slick was allowed to join the elite circle of internationalists in such organizations as the U.S. Committee for the United Nations—Member Advisory Committee on Education and Public Affairs, as well as the National Advisory Board of the United World Federalists. He joined together such individuals as Cyrus Eaton, Norman Cousins, Albert Schweitzer, Jawaharlal Nehru, Dwight Eisenhower, Henry Cabot Lodge, Jr., Winston Churchill, and John Foster Dulles in his informal group discussions on world peace.

After Slick's death, part of his endowment set aside for world peace was used to support a series of peace-oriented chairs and seminars in various Texas universities. Here too, it appears that Slick's wish for a revolutionary answer to the peace-and-war question has gone the route of the more conservative, evolutionary process.

INSTITUTE OF INVENTIVE RESEARCH

One of Tom Slick's most revolutionary institutes is now defunct. Nineteen forty-four was the year Slick assigned to the birth of his boldest experiment, the Institute of Inventive Research (IIR). Coming out of the earlier Essar Research and Development Company and the Institute of Industrial Research, the Institute of Inventive Research was first used as a name in February 1947. Established to encourage the development of inventive ideas of public value, IIR received more publicity than it or Tom Slick could handle. *Reader's Digest* published an article on Tom Slick and IIR in 1949, and the institute was soon overwhelmed with inventions from all over the world. Lifelong Slick friend and builder of Disneyland, C. V.

Wood, Jr., told me that the response was so large that Slick had to rent a circus tent to create an outside processing center for the incoming inventions. At one point, over 1000 inventions were pouring in per week to IIR. *Fortune* called it "a kind of concentrated chaos" (Lubar, 1960), and before it was over, more than 100,000 inventions were received and processed. Of these, about 114 ideas seen as viable were pursued.

LIFT-SLAB METHOD

The most famous invention to come out of IIR was the lift-slab method of construction. Slick himself was partially responsible for this invention. He had once watched the tedious construction of a food store and thought that there must be a better way. He told his friend, internationally esteemed architect and San Antonio resident O'Neil Ford: "What is all this about —building a wooden building, very carefully, so it doesn't leak, employing all these carpenters for months on end, and then pouring concrete into it and tearing the wooden building down? I have a better idea" (Stacy, 1981). Slick got the notion that concrete could be poured on the ground and lifted into place.

In the midst of working out his "better way," Slick discovered a New York architect, Philip Youtz, who had had the same idea. Youtz had already used hydraulic jacks to lift concrete slabs, so Slick asked him to join forces. The Youtz-Slick Lift Slab method of construction was born and became, quite rapidly, very successful. By 1960, four million square feet of concrete were being used in construction by way of the Youtz-Slick method. Trinity University buildings and the Tower of the Americas were Youtz-Slick Lift Slab constructions in San Antonio; certainly the most famous one now existing, however, is Slick's own home.

An oft-told Slick story concerns the lift-slab method and its involvement in what would be known in some quarters as the "Slick Hilton." In 1958, Tom Slick built his spacious, sprawling, handcrafted single-story mansion on Devine Road, just north of Hildebrand, Texas, for half a million dollars. O'Neil Ford designed it and assisted Slick in finishing it with lots of glass and special Mexican stone. Slick, needless to say, wanted the concrete roof put on using the lift-slab method, and he decided to hold a "raise the roof" party. Over 300 people stood on one of the slabs as it was slowly lifted at a rate of two feet per hour by hydraulic lifts. The dressed-up folks ate and drank, and soon some of the party-goers were almost falling over the rising roof's edge. The host had neglected to devise an easy method of exit, and when the roof reached ten feet, people were yelling for ladders. San Antonio talked about the party for years.

The Youtz-Slick Lift Slab method is still the major way to build heavily molded buildings despite a highly publicized worksite accident, which may or may not have had something to do with this innovative approach. In April 1987, some lift-slab concrete floors in a Bridgeport, Connecticut, apartment house under construction collapsed, killing several workers. The death knell for the Youtz-Slick method was prematurely heard throughout the nation soon thereafter. The present Texstar Corporation President Ralph Geckler told me that the company has some two million dollars' worth of contracts at future construction and off-shore sites using the lift-slab method.

SLICK'S COLLECTIONS: ART, FRIENDS, AND DOGS

Meanwhile, back in 1958, Tom Slick filled his lift-slab-roofed home with his art collection. Some of his selections included Barbara Hepworth sculptures as well as Picasso and Ben Nicholson paintings. He had a keen eye for art and often purchased the work of as yet undiscovered artists. He was one of the early admirers of Georgia O'Keeffe. Most of his art collection today can be seen at the Witte Museum in San Antonio. Slick gathered unique items while traveling, including a leopard skin from the maharaja of Indore and Korean funeral urns.

Filling his house with wondrous pieces that easily stimulated conversation, Slick was very interested in having people around to talk about a wide variety of topics. As a *Fortune* author once put it: "Slick seems engaged in one long conference in which he freely mingles business, philanthropy, and just plain fun" (Lubar, 1960). His sons today talk openly about how many of these people—scientists, inventors, explorers, politicians—seemed at the time like ordinary, mundane business associates, but now they realize the depth and breadth of these people. His brother, Earl, has said: "At dinner, you're likely to find a mind scientist, a financier, and a babe, and they're all getting along fine together" (Lubar, 1960; Slick, C., 1988; Slick, T., 1988).

Was the handsome Tom Slick, with his soft Southern drawl, a typical playboy? No, but he was probably never lonely. As one source told me: "Tom was known to phone up a female friend and . . . would take advantage of the fact he could mention that he was flying in from Zanzibar or some such, and wanted to have dinner with the woman he had called. He was a bit more exotic and a lot more sexy than your run-of-the-mill business traveler, that's for sure!" (Anon., 1988).

Slick's collection of friends and acquaintances ran to extremely intelligent men just as it did to bright and attractive women. And some of the men were adventurers extraordinaire. One of these men, Tenzing Norgay, the conquerer of Mount Everest, introduced Slick to an unusual dog that was as much of a collector's item as anything in Slick's art collection: the Lhasa Apso.

Lhasa Apsos are short-legged, long-haired little dogs with a history going back some 2000 years in Tibet. They were "barking sentinel lion dogs" at the internal gates of monasteries. In 1933 the first pair was brought to the United States by way of a gift from the Dalai Lama to C. Suydam Cuttings, the naturalist who the Roosevelts took with them to Tibet in 1925 and 1928 in quest of the giant panda (McCarty, 1988). In 1948, Norgay received a gift of two Lhasa Apsos from the monks at the monastery Ghanghar in Tibet. He became so interested in the dogs that he began to breed them (Swedrup, 1976). When Tom Slick met Norgay in India and Nepal in the mid-1950s, the Texan became very intrigued with the Apsos. On January 6, 1958, Norgay shipped Pem and Pema La to Slick in the U.S. (Maclean, 1958), adding a rare dog to Slick's household.

Mind Science Foundation

Tom Slick's affection for the uniqueness and mystery of the East is responsible, in part, for the founding of his last institution, the Mind Science Foundation.

During Slick's 1957 visit to India and Nepal, he had a series of startling experiences involving a particular holy man who would suddenly materialize miles down the road from where Slick and his party had last seen him. This individual was also instrumental in getting Slick's check cashed in a small bank in the foothills of the Himalayas—in conjunction with a good deal of earthshaking and seemingly psychokinetic activity in the local banker's office. Slick came back from his trip convinced he had witnessed something worth studying and perhaps harnassing. Levitation, Slick thought, would be a great boon to the building trades if he could channel this form of energy for use in construction work.

Slick took an extremely rational approach to the study of levitation, extrasensory perception (ESP), and other psi phenomena, wanting to test them under strict laboratory conditions. He was especially interested in the ESP experiments that began at Duke University in the 1930s, conducted by Dr. J. B. Rhine. Slick was one of the early followers of Rhine's work, and he frequently traveled to North Carolina to get involved firsthand (Wilson, 1989). Therefore, in 1957, along with two of his levelheaded business partners, C. V. Wood, Jr., and William Rhame, Slick decided to establish the Mind Science Foundation (MSF) for the purpose of studying the mind under the best techniques and methodology of science.

Today, MSF and its staff of nine are kept at a distance from SwRI and SFRE. But Tom Slick, Jr.'s, son, Tom, is MSF's president and remains committed to his father's original mission, as does the director, Catherine Nixon Cooke, Tom Slick, Jr.'s, niece. In 1989, MSF studies include the aging mind and Alzheimer's disease, creativity and problem-solving, learning and motivation, mind and body connection. The latter explores "positive thinking" and healing, and extends the work of people such as Slick's old friend Norman Cousins.

MSF is still, of course, interested in parapsychological subjects, but usually from a very conservative frame of reference. For example, the theoretical physicist Helmut Schmidt, who had in the past been a research physicist at the Boeing research laboratories, a scientist at the University of Durham, and the director of Rhine's parapsychology laboratory, joined MSF in 1976, conducting research into "microdynamic psychokinesis, i.e., PK influences upon electronic random event generators in which randomicity is provided by radioactive decay or thermal noise" (Braud, 1981).

CRYPTOZOOLOGICAL PASSION

The interest and curiosity that briefly surfaced at Loch Ness in 1937 and would more fully emerge almost twenty years later in Tom Slick's pursuit of the hairy hominids of the Himalayas, found another early expression in his securing of the "hoat." On February 10, 1939, the "Ripley's Believe It or Not!" column published a cartoon concerning a cross between a goat and a Poland China hog—front part hog, rear part goat. Within a month, Slick was able to locate the animal, owned by R. B. Grubb of Muskogee, Oklahoma. Grubb had purchased the hoat from a Yellville, Arkansas, preacher, J.W. Usher, who wanted no part of the strange-looking animal that Usher considered a "sign" (*Muskogee Democrat*, 1939). Before contacting Ripley, Grubb showed the hoat as a freak of nature for two days, and 5128 people came to see it. Grubb decided to tell Ripley about the animal because Grubb's job as a postman prevented him from exhibiting it anymore (Grubb, 1939).

During 1988, I was able to track down Grubb, who was ninety-two but healthy, and he remembered Slick, who came up in a nice car and offered him one hundred dollars for the "hoat." Slick put the farmyard monstrosity in his fancy automobile and took it back to Essar Ranch. There Slick tried to breed it with both hogs and goats, but without any luck.

Slick was always trying to solve genetic engineering questions related to animals, and this fact may be one of the keys to why he was so fascinated by the stories of the yeti of the Himalayas. His sister, Betty Slick Moorman, says that her brother was "intrigued by the possibility that the yeti might prove to be the 'missing link' sought by the evolutionists" (Stacy, 1981). In the beginning, just such a thought could have fired Slick's imagination.

Slick's growing awareness of and attention to the accounts of the yeti led him into discussions with some of the early founders of the new science of cryptozoology. Here was a form of zoology that was certainly on the cutting edge of the times, combining biological studies with the revolutionary approach. Tom Slick digested what information he could find on the yeti reports and theories. There was not much, mostly just the work of Dr. Bernard Heuvelmans.

HEUVELMANS'S INFLUENCE

Something about the timing of Slick's first excursions in pursuit of yeti seemed more than coincidental, making me wonder if his ventures were related to an extraordinary book, *On the Track of Unknown Animals*, published in English for the first time in 1958. The author, Belgian zoologist Bernard Heuvelmans, who has since been called "the father of cryptozoology," had been interested in animals since he was a youngster. In the years of World War II, shortly after completing his doctoral thesis classifying the hitherto unclassifiable teeth of the ardvaark, Heuvelmans wrote extensively about the history of science. Then, after four years of research, his book *Sur la piste des bêtes ignorées* was published in French in 1955 by Plon (Costello, 1979). In 1958, Hart-Davis in Great Britian published the Richard Garnett translation, and in 1959, Hill & Wang printed the American edition. As one critic has noted: "Because his research is based on rigorous dedication to scientific method and scholarship and his solid background in zoology, Heuvelmans's findings are respected throughout the scientific community" (*Contemporary Authors*, 1981).

Was this book, therefore, what prompted Tom Slick's pursuit of an understanding of cryptozoology and the yeti? I decided to ask the Belgian cryptozoologist himself. He replied quickly. "You are quite right in surmising that Tom's projects were stimulated by my book *On the Track of Unknown Animals*" (Heuvelmans, 1987).

Other cryptozoologists, such as Ivan Sanderson, George Agogino, and Carleton Coon influenced Slick during the coming years in his quest for unknown animals, but the early and important influence of Heuvelmans can be seen in Slick's fascination with the yeti in particular.

Top: Tom Slick, Sr. (right) traveled around the world in 1912, stopping for several months in China and India. His stories of India intrigued his son and influenced Tom, Jr.'s early interest in the area.

Photograph courtesy of the Western History Collection/University of Oklahoma

Bottom: One significant event in the lives of the Slicks seems to be responsible for their avoidance of the media. The 1933 kidnapping of Tom's stepfather, Charles Urschel, Sr., caused the family to guard their privacy and mistrust publicity. Machine Gun Kelly's negative influence on their legacy contrasts with the positive impact the kidnapping was to have on the FBI's crime-fighting mandate.

Illustration courtesy of the Federal Bureau of Investigation

IDENTIFICATION ORDER No.1205
August 14, 1933

**DIVISION OF INVESTIGATION
U. S. DEPARTMENT OF JUSTICE**
WASHINGTON, D. C.

Fingerprint Classification

23 27 W 0
7 W 0I 14

WANTED

GEORGE R. KELLY, aliases GEORGE KELLY, R. G. SHANNON.

KIDNAPING

DESCRIPTION

Age, 35 years
Height, 5 feet, 9½ inches
Weight, 177 pounds
Build, medium muscular
Eyes, blue or gray
Hair, dark brown
Complexion, medium ruddy
Expert machine gunner

Remarks: Sometimes wears octagon shaped rimless glasses.

Geo. R. Kelly

CRIMINAL RECORD

As George Kelly, No. 1968, received State Prison, Santa Fe, New Mexico, March 14, 1927; crime, violation National Prohibition Act.
As George Kelly, No. 5256, arrested Police Department, Tulsa, Oklahoma, July 24, 1927; charge, state vagrancy.
As George Kelly, No. 2932, arrested Sheriff's Office, Tulsa, Oklahoma, January 12, 1928; charge, National Prohibition Act.
As George Kelley, No. 29962, received United States Penitentiary, Leavenworth, Kansas, February 11, 1928, from Tulsa, Oklahoma; crime, Possession of liquor (Indian Cy); sentence 3 years.

George R. Kelly is wanted for the kidnaping of Charles F. Urschel at Oklahoma City, Oklahoma, on July 22, 1933.

Law enforcement agencies kindly transmit any additional information or criminal record to nearest office, Division of Investigation, U. S. Department of Justice.

If apprehended, please notify the Director, Division of Investigation, U. S. Department of Justice, Washington, D. C., or the Special Agent in Charge of the office of the Division of Investigation listed on the back hereof, which is nearest your city.

Issued by: J. EDGAR HOOVER, Director.

Opposite Top: Belgian zoologist Dr. Bernard Heuvelmans, through his book, *On the Track of Unknown Animals,* and his consultations, greatly influenced Tom Slick and his search for the yeti and orang pendek. Heuvelmans is seen here in 1961 with the young gorilla, Kaïsi. Photograph courtesy of Bernard Heuvelmans

Opposite Bottom: Nepal, a land of mystery, captivated Tom Slick with legends and sightings of the yeti. The Sherpa Buddhist monastery of Thyangboche (background) and the tiny cottages of the lamas (foreground) were the scene of a yeti encounter in 1949. Another sighting, involving Sherpa Sen Tensing, occurred near here in 1950. Photograph by Peter Byrne

Above: Tom Slick was the leader of the 1957 Slick Yeti Reconnaissance. He is shown here on that trek in a montane valley of Nepal. Photograph by Peter Byrne

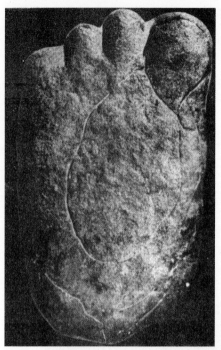

Top: Tom Slick discovered this Nepalese yeti footprint measuring ten by seven inches in the mud during the 1957 Slick Yeti Reconnaissance. Five toes were originally visible, but two blurred in the casting process.
Photograph courtesy of Bernard Heuvelmans

Bottom: Ang Dawa, Gyalzen Norbu, and Peter Byrne found a set of deep yeti footprints at about 10,000 feet during the 1957 Slick Yeti Reconnaissance. Here is one (left) compared to a man's bootprint (right).
Photograph by Peter Byrne

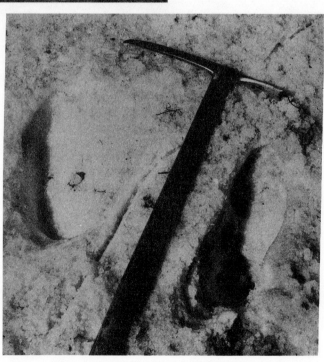

CHAPTER 3

ON THE TRACK OF THE NOT SO ABOMINABLE SNOWMAN

HEUVELMANS'S OPUS CONTAINS A CHAPTER, "THE Not So Abominable Snowman," from which he has given permission to reprint sections here. This selection from his ground-breaking book gives a glimpse into the state of affairs in the quest for yeti right before Tom Slick began his expeditions.

Enjoy this pre–Slick era overview of the search—now frozen in time. It is the best chronology and examination of the important cases most zoologists had about the yeti, just before Slick came on the scene:

Ever since 1899, when explorers still had to disguise themselves as pilgrims or itinerant merchants in order to enter Tibet, strange rumours had been reaching the West about the giants that lived in the icy heights of the Himalayas. In that year appeared Major L. A. Waddell's *Among the Himalayas*, in which he tells how in 1889 he found large footprints in the snow leading up towards the high peaks in the north-east of Sikkim.

These were alleged to be the trail of the hairy wild men who are believed to live amongst the eternal snows, along with the mythical white lions, whose roar is reputed to be heard during storms. The belief in these creatures is universal among Tibetans.

During the first attempt to climb the North Face of Everest in 1921 the rumours became more detailed. On the way from Kharta to the pass at Lhapka-la, Colonel Howard-Bury and his companions saw dark spots moving over the snow in the far distance—there were living creatures in these almost inaccessible heights well above the snow line. Then, on 22 September 1921, when they reached the place, about 23,000 feet up, where they had seen them, they found enormous footprints—more than three times as big, they said, as normal human footprints. The leader of the expeditions attributed them to a large stray grey wolf, but the Tibetan porters thought otherwise. To them there was no doubt that these were footprints of the *metoh kangmi* or "abominable snowman." They trembled with fear as they gave an alarming account of the creature.

From the native reports, which agree in the main, one can compile the following description of the monster. The snowman is a huge creature, half man, half beast; it lives in caves high and inaccessible in the mountains. The skin of its face is white; the body is covered with a thick coat of dark hair. Its arms, like those of the anthropoid apes, reach down to its knees, but its face looks rather more human. Its thick legs are bowed; its toes turn inwards—some even say they turn backwards. It is very muscular and can uproot trees and lift up boulders of remarkable size. The female can be recognised by her long breasts which she throws over her shoulders when she runs.

* * *

Inevitably most of the descriptions of the snowman come from very simple people: peasants and porters, who are terrified of it. The guides who accompany travellers threaten to turn back when fresh prints of bare feet are found. Frank Smythe tells how during the 1930 Kangchenjuna expedition the noise made by a yak bursting in unexpectedly set his porters in a real panic; they thought they were being attacked by snowmen. When he learnt the actual cause of the commotion, one of the Sherpas called Nemu told Smythe that he had several times seen *"bad manshi,"* as he called them in pidgin-English, with his own eyes. He said that they were huge white men covered with thick fur. A Miss MacDonald of Kalimpong also told Smythe how, when she was passing through a defile at a great height on a journey to Tibet, she heard a terrifying roar, unlike any animal's cry that she had ever heard. Her porters were panic-stricken; they dropped their loads and left her there alone. According to the numerous witnesses who have described the snowman's cry—some even trying to imitate it—it is a "loud yelping," often compared to the sad sound of "the mewing of a sea-gull," but of course much louder.

* * *

These legends are found for thousands of miles all over the Himalayan range, from Karakoram to northern Burma, in Tibet, Nepal, Sikkim, Bhutan and Assam, and the creatures have many different names in different countries.

Henry Newman, a very reputable columnist in the Calcutta *Statesman*, seems to have been the first to publish the Tibetan name *metoh kangami* ("abominable or filthy man of the snow"), which he misspelt *metoh kangmi*; Frank Lane says that the Indian peasants on the high plateaux call the abominable snowmen *bhanjakris* (but Mr. M. P. Koirala, Prime Minister of

Nepal, has pointed out that the name *banjhankris*, or "forest wizards," refers to almost unknown forest tribes "credited with great powers of healing"); the Sherpas call the snowmen *yeh-teh* (hence *yeti*) or *mi-teh*, words whose very controversial meaning will be discussed later; Ernst Schaefer asserts that the same creatures are called *migu* around the Green Lake at the foot of Kanchenjunga range, and Frank Smythe quotes the faintly similar names of *mirka* and *ui-go*, all of which are probably misheard variants of the *mi-go* known to linguists; in Sikkim we find the name *sogpa* or *shkpa*, but this is also applied to the Tibetans of the eastern plains and valleys, and even to all the Mongols; finally it seems that in the mountains of Burma the snowman is known as *tok* or "mouth-man."

As one might expect, most naturalists dismissed the legend of the abominable snowman with its ludicrous details. But uneducated Tibetans or Nepalese were not the only people to spread this story. Some decades ago an Englishman called Hugh Knight on his way to Tibet reported that he met a creature whose description agreed with the legendary monster. In order to let his mount get its breath he halted in a sort of amphitheatre surrounded on all sides by mountains capped in snow. Suddenly he heard a sound of stones rolling down a slope and turned his head. Some 30 yards away a sort of large blond gorilla was standing up on its bow legs. When it realised that is had been seen it made off, running sometimes on its hind-legs and sometimes on all-fours. But the most astonishing part of Knight's description is that with one muscular arm the creature was holding a *bow and arrow*!

Be that as it may, Knight is not the only educated man to tell of such an astonishing encounter. In 1925 a Fellow of the Royal Geographical Society called N. A. Tombazi reported a no less startling story in his *Account of a Photographic Expedition to the Southern Glaciers of Kangchenjunga in the Sikkim Himalaya*. About nine miles from the Zemu glacier, at an altitude of some 15,000 feet, he noticed his porters waving and pointing at an object lower down.

> The intense glare and brightness of the snow prevented me from seeing anything for the first few seconds; but I soon spotted the "object" referred to, about two to three hundred yards away down the valley to the East of our camp. Unquestionable, the figure in outline was exactly like a human being, walking upright and stopping occasionally to uproot or pull at some dwarf rhododendron bushes. It showed up dark against the snow and, as far as I could make out, wore no clothes. Within the next minute or so it had moved into some thick scrub and was lost to view.
>
> Such a fleeting glimpse, unfortunately, did not allow me to set the telephoto-camera, or even to fix the object carefully with the binoculars; but a couple of hours later, during the descent, I purposely made a detour so as to pass the place where the "man" or "beast" had been seen. I examined the footprints which were clearly visible on the surface of the

snow. They were similar in shape to those of a man, but only six to seven inches long by four inches wide at the broadest part of the foot. The marks of five distinct toes and of the instep were perfectly clear, but the trace of the heel was indistinct, and the little that could be seen of it appeared to narrow down to a point. I counted fifteen such footprints at regular intervals ranging from one-and-a-half to two feet. The prints were undoubtedly of a biped, the order of the spoor having no characteristics whatever of any imaginable quadruped. Dense rhododendron scrup prevented any further investigations as to the direction of the footprints, and threatening weather compelled me to resume the march. From inquiries I made a few days later at Yoksun, on my return journey, I gathered that no man had gone in the direction of Jongri since the beginning of the year.

*   *   *

Western explorers had no way of verifying the snowman's existence except by studying the strange tracks of bare feet in the high snows. During the summer of 1931 Wing-Commander E. B. Beauman, a pilot in the R.A.F., saw them on a glacier some 14,000 feet up near the source of the Ganges. In 1936 Eric Shipton also saw them 16,000 feet up on his return from Everest. "They resembled a young elephant's tracks except that the length of the stride suggested a biped." When they saw these tracks, the porters refused to go any farther on the excellent pretext that several of their friends had been victims of this Himalayan ogre and that they did not want to suffer the same fate.

A little later the well-known ethnographer and botanist Ronald Kaulback also met them looking "exactly as though they had been made by bare-footed men" some 16,000 feet up in the south-east of Tibet, on the main route between the valleys of Ge-chu and the Upper Salween. As there were no bears in the region as far as he knew, he thought they must have been made by a snow-leopard (*Panthera [Unicia] uncia*). The porters, of course, at once spoke of "Mountain Men." And one of them who had happened to see one from fairly close described it as like a man with white skin, naked, with long hair on its head, shoulders and arms. Kaulback thought that the lack of food at this altitude was enough to refute the legend, but this objection applied equally well to the snow leopard.

In 1937, 20,000 feet up in the Bhundhar Valley, Frank Smythe found footprints in the snow, and followed the trail up to the entrance of a cave. He gives a strange description of the prints.

On the level the footmarks averaged 12 to 13 in. in length and 6 in. in breadth, but uphill they averaged only 8 in. in length. The stride was some 1½ to 2 ft. on the level, but considerably less uphill, and the footmarks were turned outward at about the same angle as a man's. There were well-defined imprints of five toes, 1½ inches to 1¾ inches long and

¾ of an inch broad, unlike human toes, arranged symmetrically. Lastly, there was what appeared to be the impression of a heel with two curious toelike impressions on either side.

* * *

Smythe's photographs of the trail showed that it was indisputably a bear's. The marks of the extra toes were really those of the side toes of the hind-feet, for when a bear is walking it usually puts its hind-feet down in the footprints of its fore-feet. Moreover it turns its feet inwards, so that from the position of the prints alone the trail looks as if it is going in the opposite direction. Then the toes are seen to be on the wrong end of the foot, and so the legend of the men with their feet back to front arose. Since these men lived in the same places as the snowmen, and had similar habits, the character was sometimes transferred from one to the other.

To many zoologists it seemed that the affair of the abominable snowman could now be shelved. But this view was premature: true snowman's footprints never show the same characteristics as a bear's trail. All the same, the idea that its feet were turned backwards seemed to be firmly rooted in local tradition.

* * *

After Smythe's mistake, many other Himalayan explorers found strange footprints in the snow at unusually high altitudes. Among them was a correspondent of *The Times* who signed himself "Balu." In 1937 he was surveying in the Karakoram, in the north of the Himalayan range, when he was brought up short by a perfect row of large footprints, more or less round and about a foot in diameter. They were about 9 inches deep in the snow and 18 inches apart. "Nor was there any sign of overlap," he remarks, "as would be the case with a four-footed beast." The Sherpas, who identified them as footprints of the snowman, unhesitatingly recognised a bear's trail which they found in a valley several days later. They could not have mistaken the two.

In the same year, John Hunt discovered footprints in the Zemu Gap. Then in 1938, H. W. Tilman found them in the same place during a new attempt on Everest.

It was on one of the glaciers of the Menlung basin, at a height of about 19,000 feet, that, late one afternoon, we came across those curious footprints in the snow the report of which has caused a certain amount of public interest in this country. We did not follow them further than was convenient, a mile or so, for we were carrying heavy loads at the time, and besides we had reached a particularly interesting stage in the exploration of the basin. I have in the past found many sets of these curious footprints and have tried to follow them, but have always lost them on the moraine or rocks at the side of the glacier. These particular ones seemed to be very fresh, probably not more than 24 hours old. When Murray and Bourdillon followed us a few days later the tracks had been almost obliterated by melting. Sen Tensing, who had no doubt whatever that the creatures (for there had been at least two) that had made the tracks were "Yetis" or wild men, told me that two years before, he and a number of other Sherpas had seen one of them at a distance of about 25 yards at Thyangboche. He described it as half man and half beast, standing about five feet six inches, with a tall pointed head, its body covered with reddish brown hair, but with a hairless face. When we reached Katmandu at the end of November, I had him cross-examined in Nepali (I conversed with him in Hindustani). He left no doubt as to his sincerity. Whatever it was that he had seen, he was convinced that it was neither a bear nor a monkey, with both of which animals he was, of course, very familiar.

At a reception given at the British Embassy in Katmandu, Sen Tensing confirmed every detail of his description of the animal he saw near the monastery at Thyangboche, adding that "it moved mostly in an upright stance but when in a hurry dropped on all fours."

* * *

After his sixth attempt on Everest, Eric Shipton was exploring the neighbouring Gauri Sanker range with Michael Ward and the Sherpa Sen Tensing. At four o'clock in the afternoon of 8 November 1951 they found a very clear trail of enormous human-looking feet in the powdery snow on the south-western slopes of Menlung-tse. They followed this strange trail for about a mile until they lost it in a moraine of ice. Being unable to follow the mysterious creature any further, they took photographs of its footprints.

Roughly oval in shape, they seemed to have been made by human feet —but by feet more than a foot long. Shipton remarks that they were "slightly longer and a good deal broader than those made by our large mountain boots." A man on this scale would stand about 8 feet high. The big toe was clearly visible, slightly separated from the rest, but there seemed to be only three other toes. Of course it was possible that two toes might be held so close together that they left only a single print in the snow. "Where the tracks crossed a crevasse," Shipton goes on, "one could see quite clearly where the creature had jumped and used its toes to secure purchase on the snow on the other side."

* * *

When Dr. Wyss-Dunant's Swiss expedition made its assault on Everest in 1952 it also found footprints exactly like those that Shipton had photographed the year before. On 18 April, Rene Dittert, Andre Roch and the famous Sherpa Tenzing Norgay set off on a reconnaissance along a glacier. There was a pea-soup fog. When the three men came back they found that at an altitude of 19,000 feet their own trails crossed those of a group of *yetis*, which had perhaps been shadowing them in the fog.

On the clearest footprints one could see a separate big toe and four other toes. In a statement to the Press Dr. Wyss-Dunant declared that they had been made not by a biped but by a quadruped, probably related to a bear and weighing between 12 and 15½ stone.

In 1953, when the successful Everest expedition was at Thyangboche, Sir John Hunt took the opportunity of making inquiries about the *yeti* among the lamas at the monastery which lies some 15 miles south-west of the mountain at a height of 14,000 feet. He learnt from the second senior abbot that the monks occasionally saw snowmen on the heights above their set-tlement, and did not think there was anything mysterious about them. The last time they had seen one, in November 1949, it came out of a large clump of rhododendrons and played for some time in the snow no more than 200 yards away. "It was," Sir John reports, "a largish animal, five feet or more in height, covered with greyish-brown hair. It went mainly upright and occasionally dropped on all fours: it was also seen to scratch itself monkey fashion." The monks made a shindy [a fracas, an uproar] with trumpets and cymbals, which soon drove the intruder back to its lair.

Actually this lama's report merely confirms the main details of Sen Ten-sing's; for he was present on this occasion with several other Sherpas.

The *yetis* were not welcome among the mountain people. Several miles away, on the northern slopes of the mountains, in Tibet, a party of snowmen made themselves thoroughly upleasant by stealing crops, smashing outbuild-ings, fouling linen left out to dry and tearing the roofs off houses. The villagers put out bowls of *chang* (a sort of beer) near their dwellings. When they found the beasts sleeping off their liquor they slaughtered them without mercy. This massacre may seem a little improbable in a country where Buddhism teaches men to respect all forms of life. But the story also relates that after this outbreak the authorities took strict measures to prevent anyone in future from maltreating these simple if savage brutes.

At the end of 1953 Chemed Rigdzin Dorje Lopu, another Tibetan lama, drew a much more attractive picture of the abominable snowman than that of the legend. According to him it was large and harmless monkey, not in the least "abominable," and it never went for human beings unless it was attacked or threatened. This monk's teacher, the lama Tsultung Zangbu, one of the most learned men in Tibet, found himself face to face with a *yeti* one day when he was going to pray in the Chari hills in Assam. The snowman, which was carrying two large chunks of rock under it arms, went on its way without molesting the holy man.

Like all animals, the *yeti* is sacred, and its remains are worshipped as relics in lamaseries. This was how Chemed Rigdzin maintains he was able to examine the mummified bodies of two of these creatures, one in the monastery at Riwoche in the province of Kham, the other in the monastery at Sakya on the road from Katmandu to Shigatse. They were enormous monkeys about 8 feet high. They had thick flat skulls and their bodies were covered with dark brown hair about 1 inch to 1½ inches long. Their tails were extremely short.

What exactly did the lama mean by "thick flat skulls"? It would be impossible to tell if there were not other corroborative accounts of the shape of the *yeti's* head. Sen Tensing said it had "a tall pointed head," and the famous Sirdar Tenzing Norgay confirmed this description when he told Sir John Hunt how his own father had once met a *yeti* "at the yak-herds' village of Macherma" at the mouth of the Dudh Kosi.

The elder Tenzing was driving his herd to pasture in the valley when a sudden disturbance among his animals drew his attention to a sort of little hairy man who was rushing down the mountainside in leaps and bounds. Tenzing was terrified and led his yaks to a stone hut in which they were usually penned, but the *yeti* was furious and leapt on the roof and started tearing off the shingles, which were merely held down with stones. The shepherd was forced to light a fire of dwarf juniper boughs and dried chollies, which gave off acrid smoke and eventually drove away the *yeti*, but not until it had let off its fury in a typically monkey fashion by dashing chattering round the hut, tearing up small shrubs and hunks of rock.

According to the elder Tenzing, the animal walked upright like a man, was about 5 feet high and its body was covered with reddish-brown fur. It had a large ape's features, "but the mouth was especially wide, showing prominent teeth." Its skull was high and conical in shape, and covered with hair so long that it fell down in front of its eyes.

It therefore seems as if Chemed Rigdzin meant by "thick, flat skulls" that the sides were particularly flat, making them pointed and conical in shape.

This was how the snowman's dossier stood at the end of 1953. On the whole it was treated with utter disbelief.

* * *

I had related the legends of Himalayan ogres to [Ralph von] Koenigswald's discoveries [of Gigantopithecus] for some time when in December 1951 the first photographs of clear footprints of the snowman were published. I took the opportunity to write a series of articles on unknown animals which appeared in *Sciences et Avenir* (Paris) in the following January, March, May and August. In the issue of May 1952 I put forward for the first time my view that the snowman was a giant and biped anthropoid no doubt closely related to the Gigantopithecus. At this time scientific opinion almost unanimously rejected the idea that the snowman was an unknown animal. Apart from Sir John Graham Kerr, who gave the *yeti* the benefit of the doubt, all the zoologists who expressed an opinion tried to identify it with some known animal and were not sparing in their sarcasm of those who put any faith in the Himalayan legend. Nobody took much notice of me. (But two years later, on 20 February 1954, a Russian zoologist called Wladimir Tschernezky published an article in the *Manchester Guardian* putting forward a theory identical with mine, down to the details of the argument. A completely revised version of it was included as an appendix to Izzard's *The Abominable Snowman Adventure* in 1955. The fact that we have both independently come to the same conclusions should add weight to our arguments.)

But little by little opinion began to change as the conquerors of Everest brought back the same persistent rumours, Sherpas gave more detailed accounts, a lama claimed to have examined the mummified remains of what he called "big monkeys," and Sir John Hunt himself declared after his interview with the second senior lama at Thyangboche: "There is an interesting problem for an enterprising party to investigate."

By the end of 1953 scepticism was breaking down, and scientists in several countries thought that it was possible that the Himalayan giant might exist and be a new and unknown species. The [London] *Daily Mail* decided to send an expedition to look for the abominable snowman.

* * *

The expedition set off from Katmandu in January 1954. Including the Nepalese porters it consisted of some 300 men. Besides a veteran mountaineer John A. Jackson, the adventurous Ralph Izzard, and a first-class cameraman Tom Stobart, who made the film *The Conquest of Everest*, the team contained several scientists: Charles Stonor, former Assistant Curator of the London Zoo; Dr. Biswamoy Biswas, a young Indian zoologist of the Zoological Survey of India specialising in mammals and birds, and Gerald Russell, an American naturalist who went on William Harkness's expeditions to central Asia in the 1930s and took part in capturing the giant panda in 1936.

Charles Stonor had already set off in December 1953 on a reconnaissance of the route to Namche Bazar, the Sherpa's capital, when he met a Sherpa of about 30 called Pasang Nyima, who said that he had seen a *yeti* three month before when he went to a remote area to take part in a religious ceremony in a sacred place. He heard that there was a *yeti* about and went off with several companions to investigate. When they reached the spot they saw the *yeti* some 200 or 300 yards away on a flat piece of ground sparsely covered with bushes. It was the first *yeti* Pasang had seen. According to him it was the size and build of a small man. Its head, its body and its thighs were covered with long hair. Its face and chest looked less hairy and there were no long hairs on the legs below the knees. The colour of the fur was "both dark and light" and the chest was reddish. It walked nearly as upright as a man and bent down occasionally to grub in the ground for roots. When it realised that it had been seen it gave a loud, high-pitched cry and ran off into the forest, still on its hind-legs, but with a sidling gait. Never once did it go on all fours. As all the villagers insisted that Pasang was speaking the truth, Stonor slyly asked him:

"Is the *yeti* a flesh-and-blood animal, or is it a spirit?"

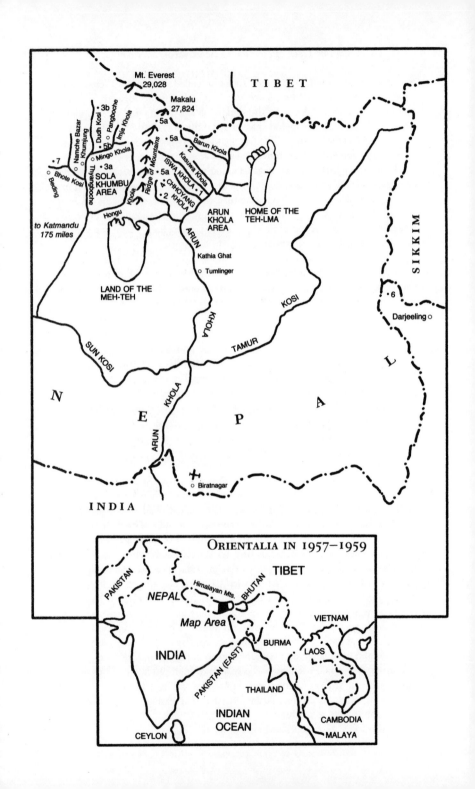

Map of Nepal Showing
Tom Slick Yeti Expedition Locations

- **1.** 1957 Base Camp: tracks discovered near here by Slick and Byrne.
- **2.** 1957 Reconnaissance explores Barun area and south. 1958 Expedition further searches Barun.
- **3a.** 1958 Dyhrenfurth and Ang Dawa search Sola Khumba area. Expedition meets at Thyangboche before ending 1958 effort.
- **3b.** 1958 Dyhrenfurth and Ang Dawa find yeti bed in Dudh Kosi area.
- **4.** 1958 Expedition Base Camp at Moyam near Walung. Da Temba in company with Gerald Russell sees small yeti (*Teh-1ma*) in Upper Chhoyang Khola; Byrnes spend time here using frogs as lures, experience quick glance of possible yeti (*Teh-1ma*).
- **5a.** 1959 Byrnes search entire Arun-Barun area; find tracks in the Barun area; confirm Makula hand is snow leopard.
- **5b.** 1959 Peter Byrne investigates Pangboche hand and imitation yeti skullcaps at Pangboche and Thyangboche.
- **6.** 1958 Kirk Johnson, Jr. searches foothills of Himalayas in India for yeti sightings and signs; spends time at Mount Bisone, site of recent encounter.
- **7.** 1960 Hillary Expedition does most of its investigations in the populated Namche Bazar area; borrows a fake yeti skullcap from Khumjung; buys a bear skin at Beding; examines incomplete hand at Pangboche; fails to reach yeti habitat.

A NOTE ON SPELLINGS: names of locations in Nepal are spelled very differently depending upon the writer, the era, and the context of the item. This occurs because the site names are rough transliterations of various linguistic forms fashioned into English. For the purposes of this map, we have retained the spellings of locations used by members of the Slick-Johnson Expeditions in 1957–1959. Also, the words "Kosi" and "Khola" are used interchangeably, although generally a Kosi is a small river, stream, or creek, and a Khola is a larger river. This map follows information from Byrne (1959b, 1989), Russell (1958a), Slick (1957a, 1958e), Dyhrenfurth (1959), Bishop (1962), Hillary and Doig (1962), and Cronin (1979).

Map design by Nancy Dutting; notes by Loren Coleman © 1989

To which the Sherpa replied with disarming logic:

"How could it have been a spirit since we saw its footprints after it had run away?"

Stonor went on collecting *yeti* lore and soon had several other first-hand accounts of the beast's appearance.

One afternoon in 1947 or thereabouts a yak-breeder called Dakhu who lived in Pangboche saw one some 50 yards away. It walked upright, was the height of a small man and was stocky and covered with hair.

In March 1949 another Pangboche villager called Mingma heard something like a stentorian human cry while he was driving his herd to pasture, then he saw something among the rocks coming down towards him. He took refuge in a stone hut, but was able to see the *yeti* through a large crack in the wall and to examine it very carefully. Stonor reports his description as follows:

A squat, thickset creature, of the size and proportions of a small man, covered with reddish and black hair. The hair was not very long, and looked to be slanting upwards above the waist, and downwards below it; about the feet it was rather longer. The head was high and pointed, with a crest of hair on the top; the face was bare, except for some hair on the sides of the cheeks, brown in colour, "not so flat as a monkey but flatter than a man," and with a squashed-in nose. It had no tail. As Mingma watched it, the Yeti stood slightly stooping, its arms hanging down by its sides; he noticed particularly that the hands looked to be larger and stronger than a man's. It moved about in front of the hut with long strides. . . .

When the beast saw that it was being watched through a crack it growled and showed its teeth; Mingma was very struck by their size.

In about 1950 Lakhpa Tenzing saw a *yeti* sitting on a rock some 30 yards away. It turned its back to him. It seemed to be the size of a small boy and was covered with rather light reddish hair.

And in October 1952 a villager from Thamnu called Anseering and his wife surprised a *yeti* among the rocks when they were going to collect medicinal roots at the upper edges of the forest. The animal was dark brown, smaller than a man and thick-set. It made off, climbing over the rocks on four feet.

All these accounts, and also the elder Tenzing's, Sen Tensing's and Pasang Nyima's, agree most strikingly. But some of the tales Stonor heard seemed to refer to creatures which had little to do with the snowman. So he came to the conclusion that there were two types of *yeti*, the larger being the Himalayan red bear, a fairly rare animal in those parts, but the smaller was the creature they were looking for and that everything pointed to its being an ape. He decided that they should concentrate on it entirely. His theory of two unknown creatures was based on linguistic inquiries. *Yeti*, he found, was derived from two Tibetan words, *yeh* (rocky area) and *teh*— which he did not define. The largest of the *yeh-teh* was called *dzu-teh*, and seemed to be the Himalayan red bear. It went on all fours and had long shaggy reddish hair. *Dzu* meant "livestock" and Stonor thought that *dzu-teh* therefore meant a *teh* that was dangerous to cattle. Then there was the *mih-teh* which was the size of a fourteen-year-old boy but as heavily built as a man. It was covered with light reddish hair and had longer hair on its strikingly pointed head. *Mih* meant "man" and Stonor was uncertain whether the *mih-teh* was so called because it was dangerous to men or because it was like a man. The first alternative seems most unlikely since he goes on to remark:

> There is no certainty about its food, but many people believe it to live on rock-rats (*picas*) and other small beasts which abound in its home. It is not thought to be particularly aggressive towards man, but is very shy and very intelligent.

Let me digress a moment to clear the philological problem of the snow-man's many names out of the way. Prince Peter of Greece, who knows the Himalayas well, was the first to explain what *teh* meant. "It is, I believe, a rather vague colloquial term for 'brown bear' (spelt *dred* and pronounced *t(r)e*)." He added that in the Kalimpong area where he was living *mi-go* (wild man) was the usual Tibetan name for the snowman.

A really thorough philological study of the problem was published in 1955 by an Indian scholar Sri Swami Pranavananda in the *Journal of the Bombay Natural History Society*. He confirmed that *tre* (with the r so softly pronounced as to be almost inaudible, thus making it *te* or *teh*) was indeed the name for the brown bear. He explained that there were three bears known to the Tibetans: the black bear which they called *tom*, the brown bear called *te*, and the *mi-te* or "man-bear" (from *mi*, "man," and *te*, "bear") so called because it walked on its hind-feet like a man. Pranavananda asserted that this is certainly the red bear, adding: "since the *mi-te* walks on all fours and sometimes on hind-legs only, it is but natural that the tracks of footprints are sometimes seen in pairs and sometimes single files."

He went on to say that the name of *metoh kangmi* (from *metah* or *meteh*, "abominable," *kang*, "snow" and *mi*, "man") was an unjustifiable conjunction of different names for the red bear: *mi-te* (man-bear) and *kang-mi* (snowman), the former having been misunderstood and mistranslated. The term *mi-go* usually translated as "wild man" according to this Indian scholar actually meant "beast that walks like man" and was the name for the snowman in Tibetan provinces of Amdo and Kham (which are now part of China) and was also used by the Tibetans on the Indian frontier with Kham. As for

yeh-te, yi-te, yih-dah or yeh-da) it was a quite mythical creature "with the throat as thin as a needle and stomach as big as a mountain, hence a glutton."

Sri Swami Pranavananda's article was welcomed by the sceptics. Newspapers reported that the legend of the abominable snowman had been exploded once and for all. And the distinguished anthropologist William L. Strauss, Jr., of Johns Hopkins University repeated the Indian scholar's conclusions in *Science* with evident satisfaction.

Actually Pranavananda would have done better to have stuck to the linguistic side of the problem, for his zoological conclusions are quite absurd. There are only two known species of bear in the high Himalaya: the black or collared bear (*Selenarctos thibetanus*) and the local variety of brown bear known as the red bear (*Ursus arctos isobellinus*). It is true that in Tibet and Kansu there is another variety of brown bear called the blue bear (*Ursus arctos pruinosus*), but it does not spread as far as the Himalaya. So if the *mi-teh* is a third bear, even more mysterious than Graham Green's *Third Man*, in these great mountains, it must be an unknown species. And if this third bear really walks on its hind-feet as often as its name implies, and does so for miles at a time as its tracks show, it is a truly extraordinary bear, much more extraordinary to the zoologist than a large biped ape.

From Pranavananda's article we can conclude that the people who live in the Himalaya know a creature which they call *mi-teh*, probably because it resembles both bear and man; no doubt it is the same beast which in some areas is called *mi-go* because it walks like a man, and in others *kangmi* because it sometimes leaves tracks in the snowfields; lastly it is often nicknamed *yeh-te*, a word originally meaning an all-devouring demon, just as we sometimes call an actual but particularly savage and voracious beast a monster.

If Pranavananda has really unmasked the snowman he has revealed that it has a much more agreeable face: it was originally called abominable in error and unjustly maligned ever since.

Continuing his reconnaissance Stonor finally found some tracks of the *yeti* 14,000 feet up near Namche Bazar. They were the human-looking footprints so often seen by travellers, but smaller than any reported before: the average length was 10 inches, the maximum width 5 inches and across the heel 3 inches. Stonor was much encouraged.

"My own view," he wrote, "is that we are concerned with some quite unknown and extremely interesting beast."

When the main body of the expedition had arrived and were split into three columns so as to search the largest possible area, more *yeti* tracks were soon found. Jackson and Jeeves went up the Khumbu glacier and discovered one two or three days old which had undoubtedly been made by a biped. The prints were 10 to 11 inches long by 5 to 6 inches wide.

In the upper Dudh Kosi valley Russell and Izzard came upon a second trail, little fresher than the first. The prints were even smaller, having originally been some 8 to 9 inches long by 4 to 5 inches broad. At the edge of a plateau they could see that this usually biped animal had dropped on all fours, no doubt to reconnoitre the ground more cautiously, thus making "smaller indentations" with its hands and knuckles. The two men followed the trail until they were forced to abandon it: but they picked it up again at the top of Lake Lang Boma. Here they were disconcerted to see that it seemed to have been made by a quadruped until it split to go round a boulder, when they realised that it had been made by two bipeds, a second *yeti* had been following in the first's tracks. They followed the trail for some 8 miles and found signs that the animal liked to slide down snowy slopes on its behind, a very playful pastime for a creature that had been called abominable.

Several days later they found a third and then a fourth trail of footprints, very similar in size to the smaller of the tracks they had found before, then they found some more, and yet another trail, so that Izzard wrote to the leader of another column, "You will excuse us if the report of a *single* Yeti's tracks now leaves us rather cold."

Meanwhile members of the expedition also found occasional heaps of excrement along the trails they were following. On his reconnaissance Stonor had twice found a large animal's droppings containing fur, rodents' bones and a certain amount of earth. The natives that he had asked had all unanimously told him that the *yeti* ate small mammals that lived among the rocks (marmots and pikas or "mouse-hares") and large insects, besides consuming clayey earth "perhaps for bulk or for some mineral value." Only a few of the natives thought that the beast also preyed on young yaks, tahr and muskdeer as well as on birds and their eggs. Gerald Russell's analysis of *yeti* droppings left no doubts that it was omnivorous:

> a quantity of mouse-hare fur; a quantity of mouse-hare bones (approx. 20); one feather, probably from a partridge chick. Some sections of grass, or other vegetable matter, one thorn, one large insect claw, three mouse-hare whiskers.

Unfortunately although the three columns moved in pincer movements for 15 weeks the *Daily Mail* expedition did not succeed in seeing a single specimen of the elusive animal, at least not for certain, let alone watching it carefully, photographing or capturing it. But they did not draw a complete blank, as Izzard's and Stonor's books prove.

The most interesting information they collected was about the various scalps supposed to belong to the *yeti*. It will be recalled that the lama Chemed Rigdzin Dorje said that remains of snowmen were venerated as relics in several monasteries and that he had seen two of them himself. Relations with Tibet were so strained that it seemed unlikely that Western scientists would soon be able to check his assertion. But on 9 October 1953 a group of four mountaineers, Rusi Gandhy, J. A. Gaitonde, P. V. Pattankar and Navnit Parikh of the Bombay Natural History Society, stopped on their way back from an expedition at the monastery at Pangboche, 5 miles beyond Thyangboche in the direction of Everest. The monks there told them that there was a *yeti*'s scalp in the local *gompa* (or small temple), and after a good deal of hesitation showed it to them and to Dr. Charles Evans of the successful British Everest expedition, who happened to be passing. An Austrian anthropologist, Professor Christoph von Fürer-Haimendorf, was also present. The Indian mountaineers photographed this oddly conical specimen, and the head lama kindly presented them with a single hair.

* * *

During his reconnaissance Stonor was eventually able to lay his hands on this relic of the *yeti* and learnt that it dated from the fifth reincarnation of San-Dorje, the lama in whose honour the *gompa* was founded. The present lama was the twelfth reincarnation. Every lama was chosen as a child and remained in office until his death, so allowing 50 years for each reincarnation, the scalp would be about 350 years old.

Stonor was not allowed to take this holy relic away. . . . It was 7½ inches high, 9¾ inches long and 6¾ inches wide. The length from back to front over the crown was 17¼ inches. The circumference at the base was 26 ¼ inches. All these measurements are larger than those of a man. Thus the circumference of an adult man's head averages 21 inches and the length of the medial line of the skull rarely exceeds 13 inches. The thickness, ⅛ inch, was also remarkable.

Texture is that of brittle leather: quite uniform throughout, and the skin blackish in colour. . . . The shape at the base is a broad oval: it may be slightly misshapen from age and usage . . . but in view of the very tough texture, I do not think this to be the case.

The outer surface is now largely bare and the skin fairly smooth: but it was quite clearly covered with hair in its original state and is still minutely pitted all over with hair bases. A fair proportion of hair still remains. The hair is foxy-red in general colour, barred with blackish-brown. The individual hairs are a very few inches in length and are extremely stiff and bristle-like. It is impossible to say if there were formerly hairs of greater length. From what is presumably the forehead the hair slopes backward, and slightly downwards along the sides, much as in man: while at the back of the head it slopes almost vertically downwards. This is quite noticeable and I think it to be the natural conformation.

An extraordinary feature is a crest or "keel" which runs from the base of the forehead straight upwards over the crown and down the back. It has a uniform width of almost exactly one inch. It is covered with bristle-like hairs of the same colour as the rest, which are no more than 1.25 in. in length and which slope inwards from each side so as to meet in the centre and form a crest, which is thus triangular in cross-section.

In common with the rest of the hairs much of the crest is gone, but it is distinctly marked as a slightly raised ridge in the skin.

*   *   *

When the expedition visited the Thyangboche monastery, the head lama, with whom they had made friends, told them that there was a second *yeti*'s scalp at the lamasery at Khumjung, 2½ miles away. This proved on examination to be the same size as the first, more battered and with scantier fur. According to the tradition the two scalps had come from a pair, the Pangboche one from a male and the Khumjung one from a female.

Despite much bargaining the monks would not lend either of the scalps to the expeditions, but their friend Sanghi Lama got them a piece of skin 3 inches long by 1½ inches wide which he said had come from an entire *yeti*'s skin that had long belonged to the village of Khumjung but had recently disappeared in mysterious circumstances.

The expedition was subsequently able to examine a third *yeti*'s scalp in the temple at Namche Bazar, but it turned out to be merely a faked version of the other two: it was made of pieces of hairy skin, identical with that of the true scalps, but sewn together to form the same shape as them. Doubtless it had been made to satisfy Namche Bazar's local pride. Izzard suggests that "An impious thought is that possibly the Namche Bazar scalp is the explanation of Khumjung's missing hide."

*   *   *

Ever since the *Daily Mail* expedition the *yeti* has been in the news. In May 1955 the French expedition on Makalu (a 27,190-foot peak 13 miles south-east of Everest) came upon several tracks; one of them, on the Barun Col, had been made that very morning or late on the previous evening. The Abbé P. Bordet, the team's geologist, who photographed the imprints, produced indisputable evidence that the beast was a biped: even where the *yeti* had jumped down into the snow from a small wall of rock there "were no tracks of its forefeet."

I have followed a *yeti* track for more than a kilometre [he writes], and seen nearly 3,000 footprints. They are all of the same kind. They are deep marks made by a foot somewhat resembling a human foot. The sole of the foot is roughly elliptical and rounded underneath. In front of it are the more or less circular marks of four toes (not five), the first on the inside is larger than the rest and perhaps not quite so far forward, the other three lie on the front edge of the sole of the foot and very close to it. These toes are much larger than human toes. There are no marks of claws. . . . In the best imprints there are still little ridges of snow dividing the toe-marks and showing that the toes are slightly separated when the creature walks. The length of the footprints is about 20 centimetres. . . .

The animal walks with its feet almost parallel and only slightly splayed. Its stride was about 20 inches, a little less than my own on this slippery ground. . . . The second track that I saw was that of an animal coming down to a lake, no doubt to drink there. The prints were in a perfectly straight line and the stride was much longer, sometimes as much as three feet.

All the same all these tracks were those of a biped which even in difficult conditions had no need to use its front legs.

Professors Berlioz and Arambourg of the Paris Natural History Museum, whom the Abbé Bordet consulted, admitted "there is no known animal which leaves such footprints, and none which is a true biped as this is." But they refused to draw any conclusions as to what it might be. "Whether it is a kind of bear or ape," Bordet concludes, "it seems too soon to decide, our information being what it is at present." This opinion shows considerable ignorance of the problem and the work that has been done on it. As I pointed out in 1952, one need only look at a track to see if the big toe is on the inside or the outside to decide whether it was made by a primate or a bear. Since the Abbé Bordet tells us that "the first on the inside is larger than the rest," the *yeti* cannot possibly be a bear, even if it is an unknown biped species. Bordet also points out, apropos of the *yeti*'s identity, the odd fact that:

The Indian map of the Himalaya marks the area round Everest as the Mahalangur Himal (the mountains of the great monkeys). As no monkey is known to live there this name may refer to the *yeti*, a characteristic inhabitant in the natives' eyes.

A month later, on 12 June 1955, two members of the Royal Air Force Mountaineering Association expedition to the Himalay, Wing-Commander A.J.M. Smyth, the leader, and Sergeant J. R. Lees, also found fresh *yeti* tracks 12,375 feet up in the Kulti valley. They summoned the transport officer Squadron-Leader L. W. Davies who came and photographed the track and sent a signal about it to the Air Ministry. The official communique gives some interesting details.

There were many prints, each measuring about 12 inches by 6 inches, and indicating that the creature who made them was two-legged, with five toes a quarter of an inch wide on each foot.

The prints were sunk 11 inches into the snow, compared with the one-inch impression made by the R.A.F. mountaineers.

This shows that the creature which made such deep tracks must have been several times as heavy as a man. (A gorilla, by the way, rarely exceeds 40 stone.)

*   *   *

Professor Rene von Nebesky-Wojkowitz, who spent three years of ethnographic research in Tibet and Sikkim from 1950 to 1953, tells several stories about the abominable snowman in his admirably documented book. They agree very well with those that Izzard and his companions heard in Nepal. He draws the following conclusions from the evidence that he had obtained by questioning many witnesses:

> It is a remarkable fact that the statements of Tibetans, Sherpas and Lepchas concerning the Snowman's appearance largely coincide. According to their description a warrant for the arrest of this most "wanted" of all inhabitants of the Himalayas would read as follows: 7 feet to 7 feet 6 inches tall when erect on his hind legs. Powerful body covered by dark brown hair. Long arms. Oval head running to a point at the top, with apelike face. Face and head are only sparsely covered with hair. He fears the light of a fire, and in spite of his great strength is regarded by the less superstituous inhabitants of the Himalyas as a harmless creature that would attack a man only if wounded.

To this description, which confirms in every detail what we know already, he adds some more interesting information about the creature's habitat:

> From what native hunters say the term "snowman" is a misnomer, since firstly it is not human and secondly it does not live in the zone of snow. Its habitat is rather the impenetrable thickets of the highest tracts of Himalayan forest. During the day it sleeps in its lair, which it does not leave until nightfall. Then its approach may be recognized by the cracking of branches and its peculiar whistling call. In the forest the *migo* moves on all fours or by swinging from tree to tree. But in the open country it generally walks upright with an unsteady, rolling gait. Why does the creature undertake what must certainly be extremely wearisome expeditions into the inhospitable regions of snow? The natives have what sounds a very credible explanation: They say the Snowman likes a saline moss which it finds on the rocks of the moraine fields. While searching for this moss it leaves its characteristic tracks on the snowfields. When it has satisfied its hunger for salt it returns to the forest.

This suggests that—as I suspected—the snowman owes the accidental fact that it is a biped to snow beneath its feet, and also that the places where the creature and its footprints are usually seen are not its normal habitat. If its desire for saline food is not the only cause that drives the snowman to venture into open country, where it is more likely to be seen, it is a strong enough reason to explain such journeys: moreover they are strangely reminiscent of the long pilgrimages that elephants sometimes make in search of saline soil.

* * *

We can now even give a detailed description of the giant biped anthropoid of the Himalayas, a shy survivor of the empire of giant primates which once ruled a large part of the earth.

Only four giant ape-men are so far known to palaeontology: the Chinese Gigantopithecus, of which we have only a few molars and a jaw-bone . . . , the Java Meganthropus, represented by a fragment of jaw-bone with its teeth, the Tanganyika Meganthropus, consisting only of jaw and facial bones, and the South African Paranthropus, of which several skulls and a biped's pelvis have been excavated. If I seek to relate the snowman to the Gigantopithecus it is obviously for geographical reasons and because most reports of its size agree with Dr. Broom's estimate of that of the Chinese giant.

It is high time that the snowman was also recognized by a scientific name and since the palaentology of giant primates is so slender, I would give it a new name, *Dinanthropoides nivalis*, or "terrible anthropoid of the snows." If one day its teeth are examined and found to be identical with those of the Gigantopithecus, its name will have to be changed, according to the rule of priority, to *Gigantopithecus nivalis*, the present species being no doubt quite distinct from the Pleistocene primate from Kwangsi. The layman may be surprised that one should give an animal a scientific name on the mere evidence of some footprints and a description of a scalp. In fact this procedure is not only universal in palaeontology, but happens fairly often in zoology. The giant panda and the wolf of the Andes were described merely from skins, the *takahe* [a small flightless bird from New Zealand] was first known only from a skeleton, the first description of the pygmy hippopotamus was based on a skull. And the first (mistaken) name given to the okapi was based on shapeless strips of its skin which were taken for those of some kind of zebra. Naturally the name *Dinanthropoides* risks a similar mistake—firmly though am convinced to the contrary—but zoology cannot go on ignoring an animal which we know far more about than many fossil species.

We have reason to believe that it is a large biped anthropoid ape, from 5 to 8 feet high according to its age, sex or geographic race, which lives in the rocky area at the limit of the plant line on the slopes of the whole Himalayan range. It has plantigrade feet, and the very conspicuous big toe, unlike that of most monkeys, is not opposable to the other toes. It walks with its body leaning slightly forward; its arms are fairly long and reach down to its knees. It has a flat face, a high forehead, and the top of its skull is shaped like the nose of a shell; its prognathism is slight, but its thick jaws have developed considerably in height, hence the disproportionate size of its molars. To this outsize masticatory apparatus are connected very powerful jaw-muscles. On the cranium there is a sagittal crest which is revealed by a thickening of the scalp in the adult male, at least, and the presence of upstanding hair. It is covered with thick fur, which in the smaller specimens varies from fawn to dark chestnut in different places with foxy-red glints, but the face, chest and the lower legs are much less hairy. In the larger specimens the fur is an even dark brown or almost black. It appears to be omnivorous: roots, bamboo shoots, fruit, insects, lizards, birds, small rodents and occasionally larger prey like yaks are all grist to its mill in such barren country. Its cerebral capacity should be about equal [to] or even greater than man's. But the development of the brain must have been affected by the strange shape of the skull giving rise to mental qualities very different from those in which man excels.

The position of this Dinanthropoid in the system of zoology is still uncertain, as is that of the other giant primates, which to my mind do not form a homogeneous group, but are the separate peaks of the evolution of different families of primates: the Paranthropus is the last stage in the evolution of the Australopitheci into giants, the Meganthropus is a giant Pithecanthropus. Just as the Pithecanthropus may be merely a large biped descended from the gibbons, so the Dinanthropoid may have evolved similarly, but on a parallel branch, from the orang-utan. Gates and Remane consider that the Gigantopithecus is a giant of the Ponginia, the family to which the orang-utan belongs.

Of course it is not until an actual specimen of the snowman is examined that my deductions can be checked and its provisional description completed. The *Daily Mail* expedition, alas, was unable to provide one, although four columns of men carried out pincer movements over a vast area.

Actually it is not absolutely necessary to examine a living *yeti*—nor to kill a specimen, which would be needlessly cruel—to clear up the problem once and for all. The lama Chemed Rigdzin Dorje may be right when he says that some monasteries possess mummified snowmen. A study of one of these specimens would settle the question. It might also be possible to get hold of the rest of Khumjung's missing hide. There must be many other relics of the great ape in a part of the world that bristles with temples and is ruled by clerics. Professor David Snellgrove, the expert on Tibet at London University, told the *Daily Mail* team that he understood that at Pangboche monastery there was not only a scalp but also a mummified hand, much larger than a man's. . . .

A quarter of a century ago 32 Nepalese soldiers marching towards Kuti, on the frontier of Tibet, were attacked in the middle of the night by a *yeti* which killed 31 of them. The sole survivor gave the alarm and a patrol of 10 men armed to the teeth were sent off to the place. They found the monster there, sleeping off its meal after eating several of its victims. Ten guns were fired at it at once, but a second salvo was needed to polish it off. The leader of the patrol still kept the beast's head as a trophy.

If an informed zoologist could examine a hand, or better still a skull, he would be able to obtain most valuable information. Even so the diehard sceptics would still suspect that these specimens were in a fossil or sub-fossil state. General incredulity will not be overcome until we can see a good photograph or film a living *yeti*.

The expedition which may one day bring back these trophies will be able to benefit from the lessons of the *Daily Mail* team, who never succeeded in overtaking a *yeti* although their trails abounded. Each time they lost track of the strange ape-man, which could move faster over a terrain to which it was better suited and was no doubt more accustomed to the lack of oxygen at those heights, while its pursuers had to stop for breath more and more often. And, as Izzard remarked, "a party is as conspicuous as a line of black beetles on a white tablecloth." They would probably have done better to follow Gerald Russell's plan. He was a greater expert in catching animals than anyone else in the party, and he thought that rather than keeping on the move, they should have chosen a good strategic position and remained hidden there, if necessary for a week at a time. As it was, Izzard was a sadder and a wiser man for this experience, and concluded that:

> The Yeti is more likely to be met in a chance encounter round, say, a rock, than by an organised search. A reconnaissance party of two or three Sahibs needs about 30 Sherpa porters to support it over a period of about three weeks. We found it impossible to introduce such a large body of men into an "empty quarter" of the Himalayas without disturbing all wild life within it.

We shall find the same situation recurring in most of the problems of unknown animals, and it is this that makes them so hard to solve. It is difficult not to be exasperated when all the pieces of evidence run away as soon as the experts arrive on the scene.

With that Heuvelmans ended his 1950s era analysis of the decades of yeti accounts. This treatment stands as a reflection of the data Slick's expeditions would have had on this mystery animal. Bernard Heuvelmans was to become a member of Tom Slick's select group of yeti consultants.

CHAPTER 4

SLICK YETI RECONNAISSANCE

THE HIMALAYAS BECKONED THOMAS BAKER SLICK.
In those larger-than-life-mountains, Slick met a challenge worthy of his
pioneering way of thinking. Most cryptozoologists and others interested in
Slick's work often believe that he sponsored the yeti expeditions of the last
two years of the fifties from distant Texas. What they often overlook is
his early firsthand involvement in the investigations.

SLICK LEARNS OF YETI AND BYRNE

Tom Slick had been fascinated by tales of India told to him by his father
(Slick, 1951b; Slick, C., 1988). He had furthered this intrigue with the
region by making some mind science inquiries there, and traveled to India
as often as he could. Early in the 1950s, on a visit to Bharat, India, Slick
heard about the reports of half-ape, half-human creatures roaming the
slopes of Nepal, Tibet, and the surrounding region. The 1954 *Daily Mail*
expedition deepened his interest.

As chance would have it, during the spring of 1956, Tom Slick traveled
in the area and asked around about the abominable snowmen reports from
Nepal and Sikkim. When he heard about the yeti sightings coming from
the northern part of the subcontinent, his curiosity was piqued. "Then in
1956," Slick noted later, "I made a reconnaissance of my own into the
fringes of the Himalayas. I talked to caravan people coming out of the
mountains and to other natives who claimed to have glimpsed the yeti"
(Slick, 1958b). Tom Slick's excursions and expeditions into the Himalayas
in search of the yeti commenced in earnest, therefore, in 1956.

The reports of the yeti were not farfetched considering other recent
cryptozoological discoveries in that section of the world. For instance,
reflect upon the fact that the first live giant panda had been brought out

of Tibet in 1936, a short twenty years before Slick got involved deeply with the yeti in neighboring Nepal. As of 1956 only nine Westerners had seen giant pandas in the wild and there was only a handful of giant pandas then in Western zoos (Wendt, 1956; Morris, 1966). Thus, the possibility of bringing back a startling scientific discovery like the yeti seemed very real indeed to Slick.

Through his inquiries about yeti, Tom Slick was to learn of Peter Byrne. The Irish-born big-game hunter Peter Byrne had been searching Sikkim for signs of yeti for some time. Byrne, while on a leave of absence from working as a tea planter in India, had found his first yeti footprint in 1948. He discovered the single track at the edge of a frozen pool in the Green Lake region of northern Sikkim, near the Zemu Glacier where Tombazi saw a yeti in 1925. Excited and interested in more searches, Byrne had to wait to go back. After quitting the British Tea Company and going into the business of big-game hunting in India and Nepal for a few years, Byrne decided to try again, but coming up with financial backing was a problem. He moved to Sydney, Australia, in 1954, and worked as a journalist.

Then in 1955 and 1956, the media began to publish notice of his proposed fall 1956 expedition in Nepal. The *Sydney Sun Herald* headlined their August 14, 1955, story: "Aust. Expedition To Hunt The Yeti." The article reported twenty-eight-year-old Byrne's organizing and fundraising efforts in gaining the support of several Sydney businessmen to finance a yeti expedition. Byrne said the expedition would comprise two or three men traveling as lightly as possible, although he had not yet chosen his companions. When Byrne came to Australia, he had brought a leopard for the Taronga Zoo; now he joked with the press about capturing a pair of yeti for Sydney's zoological park.

The destinies of Tom Slick and Peter Byrne were to meet during the spring of 1956. Byrne had not yet gained the support he needed for a full-scale expedition, so he did some guide work. Between big-game hunting bookings, however, Byrne went up to the Nepal-Sikkim border again as he had in 1948 to try to find signs of yeti. For a month, he looked up to the 15,000-foot level in dwarf scrub for traces of the elusive creatures, but without luck. On the way back, Byrne and two Sherpa were heading over a ridge on the high moorland of Trejablo, near Zemu, when they spied a line of men about 2000 feet below. Byrne's party decided to head down and share camp with them as they all were a bit lonely after the time in the mountains.

Some three and half hours later, Byrne and his group found their way through the foggy cold night to the warm campfire of the men they had seen earlier. Byrne was happy to discover it was old friends Ang Tharkey, Ang Namgyal, and the famed "Tiger of the Snows," the first man to climb

Mount Everest with Sir Edmund Hillary, Tenzing Norgay. They shared hot soup and talked through the night. As Byrne remembered it, the conversation naturally turned to yeti. Norgay told of the story of his father's encounter with a yeti. "Tenzing also told me that he had recently talked to an American named Tom Slick, in Darjeeling, who was interested in projecting an expedition to find one of the creatures. Tenzing's wife, back in Darjeeling, had the American's address" (Byrne, 1975).

SEEDS OF AN EXPEDITION

Byrne immediately wrote Slick, and Slick quickly returned a letter. Tom Slick's first active interest in using Byrne for an expedition appeared in his May 14, 1956, reply to the Dublin-born yeti hunter. Slick was seriously considering an expedition for February to April 1957, but Byrne tried to convince him that a January to March hunt would be better: the harsh winter weather and low food supply would drive the yetis out of the mountains just as it did yaks, goats, and other animals.

The matter of a government permit to search for the yeti stood in Slick's way, though, and he knew it. Following World War II, major changes took place in Nepal and the surrounding region which did not bode well for a smooth running of the government. In 1948, India was freed from British rule; then India decided its northern border was to be defined by the Himalayas. In 1949, revolution swept China, and a year later, the People's Republic of China annexed Tibet. Thousands of Tibetans fled to Nepal. Between November 1950 and February 1951, the royalist troops of Nepal were battling the antiroyalist "freedom fighters." The country was in upheaval. Finally, India stepped in and set up a compromise Nepalese government. Between the ruling King Tribhuvan's death in 1955 and the first democratic elections in 1959, the Nepalese government was in varying stages of chaos. Government officials often worked in isolation, making rules and issuing permits on the whim of the moment. At one instant, the government would decide to require hunting permits or mountaineering permits for certain individuals or for specific seasons, then change the rules. As the conquest of Mount Everest became increasingly important to Westerners during the first half of the 1950s, Nepal found itself playing a central role in trying to regulate the climbing teams. Unfortunately, the political reality that Nepal was not even open to the outside world before 1951 made it difficult for the Nepalese to respond to the increasing interest of foreigners, first in their mountains, then in their yeti (Anderson, 1987; Byrne, 1988).

In a dispatch out of Kathmandu on March 14, 1956, the Nepalese government gave permission to Peter Byrne and his Australian expedition to search for abominable snowmen from September 1956 through February 1957 in the area around Everest.

Byrne, in a letter to Slick dated May 26, 1956, noted:

> Some ten months ago I applied, from Australia, for permission to enter Nepal with a party, to seek out and try to identify the Abominable Snowman. The visa that I wanted took a long time to come through. It evidently arrived, some three weeks ago, when I received a letter from Kathmandu to advise me that I could go into Nepal with a small party next winter and remain in the country for up to six months from date of entry.
>
> As regards this permission that I have been granted, the position is this, while the Nepalese Government have decided to allow a "party" to enter the country, they have not as yet asked me to specify names of particular members of the party. Were we to cooperate, I would have no hesitation in allowing you to use this permission, and the first and most important requirement of the expedition would be in hand (Byrne, 1956a).

Two days after this letter was written, Reuters was carrying notice that an "expedition led by Australian journalist Peter Byrne" was soon going to "try to track down the 'yeti' or abominable snowman, whose strange tracks in the snow have mystified many expeditions to the Nepal Himalayas" (Farrell, 1956). Byrne still had little backing for this expedition, and as time went on, he turned to Slick for support.

Over the summer of 1956, Slick and Byrne kept in touch, and the seeds of the Slick-financed expeditions grew. From all indications, Slick wanted to do something in the autumn, but the Nepalese were not making things easy. In October 1956, Tom Slick was reported to be in New Delhi, India, "with bloodhounds and a helicopter," according to the *New York Times* of October 7, preparing to hunt yeti. Instead he ran into a problem because the Nepalese government enforced new regulations for Slick to be sponsored by "an organization of repute" or the United States government (*New York Times*, 1956). In a November letter to Slick's associate, Cathy Maclean, Peter Byrne let it be known he had discovered the leak in Kathmandu, Narendra K. Saksena, who had sent the information about the helicopter and bloodhounds to the *Statesmen*, a New Delhi newspaper (Byrne, 1956b).

On December 5, 1956, Tom Slick wrote Peter Byrne that he had "just returned yesterday from about a month's very interesting expedition into British Guiana and Venezuela." (This may have been one of Slick's diamond-hunting expeditions.) Slick went on to express his interest in speeding up the process of getting the Himalayan trek going (Slick, 1956a).

ENTER THE ZOO

But Byrne's permit was now useless. Because of Nepal's new regulation requiring some form of traditional backing for Slick's yeti pursuit, he was forced into a position of coming up with an "organization of repute." Tom Slick moved quickly on this, getting the official endorsement of the San Antonio Zoological Society. Slick was on their board, as were friends and relatives, such as State Representative Frates Seeligson and C. F. Urschel, Jr.

On February 11, 1957, R. H. Friedrich, President of the Society wrote a "To Whom It May Concern" letter for Slick's use in Nepal. The San Antonio Zoological Society, as sponsor, requested permission "to go into Nepal to conduct a scientific expedition in interest of Himalayan Zoology [and] Anthropology in search of rare Fauna, including the Yeti and the Himalayan Thar."* The letter also carried this postscript: "Mr. Tom Slick of San Antonio, Texas, and a Director of the Zoological Society, is organizer and leader of this expedition" (Friedrich, 1957a). The society sent another letter with Slick, noting that anything the expedition "obtained for the Zoo was duty free because the Zoological Society is strictly a scientific, educational organization" (Friedrich, 1957b).

Obviously, Slick had been informed before these letters were written that he had the backing of the San Antonio Zoo, and the world soon knew about it. On February 5, 1957, the *New York Times* ran a story out of New Delhi, India, telling of Tom Slick's intentions to hunt the "abominable snowman," a name, the paper noted, "that has saddled all discussions with comedy" (*New York Times*, 1957a). It mentioned the San Antonio Zoo's sponsorship and named the two consultants to the expedition, Professor Carleton Coon (who I interviewed in 1978 about his involvement with Tom Slick) and R. N. Rahul, an Indian national, explorer, mountain climber, and one of India's outstanding specialists on the Himalayan area.

Coon, a well-known American anthropologist and writer, was in India on research projects for the museum of the University of Pennsylvania and the Wenner-Gren Foundation for Anthropological Research of New York when Slick hired him in 1956. Coon's interest in the yeti was deep, and he had been open about his notion that they might be related to Gigantopithecus. He told me when we spoke in 1978 that he thought the gull-like sounds of the yeti were rather well established. Coon also spoke of telling Slick that he firmly believed the yeti was something well worth looking into seriously. Peter Byrne, Jim Greenfield of *Life*, Coon, and

---

*The Himalayan tahr, as it is generally written today, is a rare, strangely maned, bareheaded wild goat.

Cathy Maclean all met in Darjeeling, India, on January 16, 1957. "On the afternoon of that day, we met in the Grand Hotel and had a long discussion on the expedition, the plans and the prospects of success," Byrne wrote to Slick on January 18 (Byrne, 1957a).

(Coon's connection to hairy hominid investigations continued for years after his Slick-era relationships. Examples of his involvement include his review and debates on Sanderson's book, *Abominable Snowmen*; a section entitled "Of Giant Apes and Snowmen" in his own book, *The Story of Man*; and his participation as the keynote speaker at the University of British Columbia's "Symposium on Sasquatch and Similar Phenomena" in 1978.)

In the February 18, 1957, issue, *Newsweek* carried word of Slick being en route to India to organize a search for the yeti; little seemed to be in the way of his goals now that the San Antonio Zoological Society was the official sponsor.

Plans for the Reconnaissance

The proposal that Slick was required to send the Nepalese government gave details of what plans he and Byrne had made. The document is interesting to review in terms of their original objectives versus their actual accomplishments. The name of the proposed project was the "Nepal Himalaya Zoological Expedition" (a name never used) and the time frame was to be February through July 1957. Those who were to be "members" of the expedition, besides Slick, Byrne, Coon, and Rahul, included David Douglas Duncan, a New York photographer; N. D. Bachkheti, the Delhi Zoological Park Superintendent; Dharma Raj Thapa, a Kathmandu historian; and Colonel K. N. Rana, Nepal Bureau of Mines Director. The stated purpose on the proposal closely paralleled the objective mentioned in the San Antonio Zoological Society's letter namely, "A scientific expedition in the interests of Himalayan zoology and anthropology in search of rare fauna, including the yeti and the Himalayan thar (also called sarang)" (Slick, 1956b).

As it turned out, Slick's first yeti "expedition" was more of an extended reconnaissance. This confusion in terminology has led many cryptozoologists, Slick followers, and other authors into quicksand when trying to discuss his activities in 1958 and 1959. Different writers refer to those Slick-sponsored yeti surveys into Nepal as his first and second, or as his second and third expeditions. Of course, Slick conducted more than two expeditions, per se, into the Himalayas, but most writers have not known or have simply ignored this fact. Therefore, for purposes of historical clarification, I will call the March to April 1957 expedition the "Slick Yeti Reconnaissance."

They're Off

The Slick Yeti Reconnaissance entered Nepal via Biratnagar on March 14, 1957, and departed Nepal via Biratnagar on April 18. (Both Heuvelmans [1959a] and Byrne [1975] stated that this spring 1957 "expedition" stayed "three months" in the mountains. Actually, the Slick Yeti Reconnaissance was in the back country for about three to five weeks, depending on whether we count their travel time to and from the Arun area. We can only assume that this unfortunate mistake has been carried forth unchecked for years.)

The list of candidates and consultants was pared down, and only Slick, Byrne, and ("Andy") Bachkheti ever actually went into the field. A group of seven Sherpas* (Gyalzen Norbu, Ang Phenzing, Nima Tenzing, Pemba Sumder, Lhakpa Tenzing, Ang Dawa, and Ajeeba) were also hired for the trek. Forty Nepalese porters carried the party's supplies. Cathy Maclean, listed as the "liaison officer" in some records, met Slick at the airport upon his departure for the Arun and his return.

Almost as soon as Tom Slick and the others left, political trouble began to brew. On March 18 and 19, the Nepalese government forbade all foreign mountaineers from killing, injuring, or capturing a yeti. One account clearly related that this new law would hamper Tom Slick's group, now on its way to the Himalayas. "The expedition is carrying a trap to capture one and two shotguns to be used in case of 'extreme defense' " (United Press, 1957). Another report noted that Slick's three-man party was allowed to carry firearms, and that Nepal had permitted this "on the explicit understanding that these will be used only for personal security." However, this report said Slick had a permit that was "only to trap 'an animal known as the Yeti or the Abominable Snowman' " (*Statesman*, 1957a, 1957b, 1957c).

Tom Slick's expeditions, of course, helped open up the whole debate on the ethics of killing zoological specimens. During the pre-Slick years, the giant panda, for example, was routinely killed and mounted for museums around the world before anyone stopped to consider what effect this

---

*Sherpas are deeply involved in the story of and the search for yeti, the conquering of the Himalayas, and the mood of Nepalese mountain climbing. Sherpa means "people of the East," and refers to their origin in eastern Tibet. Now world-famous as mountain guides, they live mainly in eastern Nepal, and Pangboche is their oldest village. Sherpa village life often centers around its spiritual focus—the local Tibetan Buddhist monastery (Berzruchka, 1985).

would have on the breeding population. Pandas were killed first to provide evidence that they even existed, then as prized natural history exhibits, and finally captured alive as animals of choice for zoological gardens. Today, the giant panda is a symbol of endangered species, and no one would even consider killing one for a museum or any other scientific purpose.

Slick entered the field of cryptozoology when the rules were just beginning to be redefined. His goal, as he saw it, was to collect a specimen, alive or dead, to prove to the scientific world that the yeti existed. By the late 1950s, the era of hunting and collecting was beginning to end. Slick grew out of that era, and he naturally designed his first efforts around killing or capturing. Between 1957 and 1962, Slick's thoughts on killing began to change, to reflect the times, and to mirror his own notions on the creatures' right to survive. But over thirty years ago, Tom Slick was prepared to continue in the tradition of the Roosevelts (killing pandas) and James Audobon (killing birds), and get a yeti. Even back then, though, he had the foresight to engage photographers, as well as hunters, to record anything, even what might be merely seen from a distance but not "collected."

Tom Slick received a good deal of bad press about his very Texan approach to the yeti hunt, especially from British writers in England and India. The notion that Slick was only out to kill a yeti may have influenced at least one of the early British cinema treatments of the abominable snowmen. (See the Appendix A for more.)

The Arun Valley

The Slick Yeti Reconnaissance used the Arun Valley in northeastern Nepal as its base of operations. This decision would influence all future Slick yeti searches and those of others in the coming years as well, such as the Cronin-McNeely expedition of 1972–1973 (Cronin, 1979). How did Slick and his associates reach the conclusion that the Arun would be the best location to look for yeti?

Peter Byrne explained:

We had a particular reason for choosing the Arun Valley area for our hunt and this reason had been greatly strengthened by a visit, while in Kathmandu, to Colonel Rana, head of the Geographical Survey of Nepal. Colonel Rana, a widely travelled and highly intelligent man, had toured all over the eastern parts of Nepal and although he had never actually been in any of the great valleys [called kholas in Nepalese] that we intended exploring, he was able to provide us with considerable information concerning them. He was familiar with the yeti legend and with the many stories of the yeti of eastern Nepal being much larger than those elsewhere in the country. In conversations with Sherpas and Nepalese we found this intriguing suggestion cropping up again and again. Accounts of meeting up with the eastern yeti invariably told of a creature at least seven feet tall, whereas the yeti spoken of by the Sola Khumba people seldom measured more than four and a half to five feet in height. Through Colonel Rana we were able to meet a man who had encountered a yeti in the Arun Valley several years before. The man had been a foreman of one of the Colonel's surveying parties and told us that a yeti had appeared one afternoon above the camp where he was employed. There were more than forty men with him at the time and they all saw the creature clearly. Apart from the usual description he emphasized that the ape-like creature stood well over seven feet in height and Colonel Rana told us that this was the usual height mentioned by people in the Arun Valley area who had seen yeti.

Our meeting with Colonel Rana in Kathmandu, the stories of the larger yeti that the eastern sector was said to contain and the wild unknown qualities of the area, were the deciding factors in our plan to enter the northeastern valleys (Byrne, 1988).

Getting to the Arun Valley was not an easy task in 1957, and an early incident in the Slick Yeti Reconnaissance's travels almost killed Tom Slick. On the afternoon of March 14, the party had gone from Biratnagar to Dharan by bus when the whole affair nearly came to an end. The bus stopped for a while on a hill in Dharan, so people could sleep. All of a sudden, the vehicle started rolling downhill, backward, with no brakes. Everyone panicked. Peter Byrne recalled: "At first we couldn't figure out if it was going to be better to stay on the bus or attempt to get off. Then, quite quickly, we decided to jump. I got out okay, but Tom landed heavily, on his knees, and then fell and rolled" (Byrne, 1988). The bus was a mess, their supplies were here and there, but at least they were safe. By early afternoon the next day, they were ready to march for the Arun Valley.

Tom Slick's injury, however, was to haunt him in more ways than one for years to come. The bang on his knee hurt temporarily, and continued to trouble him chronically. But more importantly this one incident is the key to why Slick never went on another trek in the Himalayas. The accident caused his extremely strong willed mother to request that he avoid being in the field and on such dangerous trips. Although Tom Slick was over forty years of age, the early loss of his father and his respect for his mother's wishes made him reevaluate his upcoming plans for the yeti hunts. He never again returned to Nepal.

The Slick Yeti Reconnaissance made quick time, and went via Dharan,

Dara Pan ("The Place of Clear Water"), Dhankuta, and Pokribas into the Arun region. Once there, they traveled through Legua Ghat, Tumlinger ("The Place of Five Hills"), and crossed the Arun River at Kathia Ghat. By March 20, they were often splitting into different parties or teams and then regrouping. The next afternoon, for example, one group went on a side trip to the village of Tamkoo and camped near the Sangkua Khole (*khole* means river). On March 22, Slick visited the village of Kampalung, where he was able to interview some people who had seen yeti. Here, he gained insights into the differences between the *shookpa* (yeti) and other varieties of abominable snowmen, the *chutay* and the *metay*. The villagers were positive the yak-killing chutay were not the shookpa. These village interviews were the origin of Slick's ideas about there being three types of yetis, and they gave him much to ponder.

By the time Slick, Byrne, and the others had established a camp on the ridge between the rivers Chhoyang and Iswa, several days had passed; it was March 23 or 24. At this 10,000-foot-altitude camp, Tom Slick discovered snow leopard pugmarks. Slick's party set up another camp at 12,000 feet. They made treks to the 13,000-foot and 16,500-foot levels through the end of the month and into April. It was on these explorations that what they believed were yeti footprints were found.

Tracks, At Last!

Tom Slick, working at 12,000 feet, near the snowline but separately from Byrne, found a set of footprints thirteen inches in length, five-toed, and obviously bipedal. Slick discovered the prints in earth, not snow, made photographs of them, and then made casts of the tracks.

Peter Byrne found a different set of prints at about 10,000 feet on April 2, 1957. He shared his personal record of that discovery with me:

> By eight o'clock we had been climbing steadily for about two hours. Ang Dawa and I were together, with Gyalzen close behind, and the carriers swung out in a long line behind us. Ajeeba was ahead, breaking trail and we were deep in a grove of twisted rhododendrons when he suddenly stopped and pointed at the snow directly ahead. Tracks! Tracks that looked like the tracks of a man. Tracks in a place where there were no men but ourselves.
>
> Running diagonally across our route was a set of deep footprints in the snow, footprints that looked at first to be those of a man. I came up quickly with Ang Dawa and Gyalzen and at a glance saw they were not the tracks of a human being, but footprints exactly similar to those that I had now come to regard as belonging to the yeti.

Until we had examined some twenty yards of the tracks the Sherpas were inclined to be conservative in their opinion of what made the prints. Gyalzen, a cool-headed man, was particularly reticent about stating his mind. But after a thorough examination, they unanimously declared that the tracks were those of a yeti; the Sherpa yeti, the half-ape, half-man creature that walks upright and leaves a five toed print at the end of his broad, flat foot.

The tracks were still fresh. They had been made that morning, probably only an hour before our arrival and though I was keen to start following them at once, I decided to await the arrival of the Walung village men and see what their reaction would be.

One by one they came in and dropped their loads. I called them up to see the tracks. As each one approached, I pointed to the footprints and said, "Look, a *thom* has been here." *Thom* is the Sherpa name for a bear. Together they examined the tracks and then without exception declared, "No sahib, these are not the tracks of a *thom*. A yeti made these tracks. See, there are no claw marks and if a *thom* had made these, there would have to be claw marks."

I realized that there was no time to waste. The tracks, although not completely new, had been made early that morning and I realized the tremendous possibility that a quick follow-up of the prints presented the chance of coming face to face with the creature that had successfully concealed its identity from the world for more than seventy years. I took some quick photographs of the tracks, in line from the side and from above by climbing a small rhododendron tree. I used all of one [roll of] film and reloaded the camera with another. Meanwhile, Ang Dawa had broken out the gun and was stuffing shells into his pocket. I arranged for Gyalzen to take some of the Walung men and backtrack the footprints in the hope of finding some droppings or, perhaps, even the lair where the creature might have spent the night. I asked them to carefully examine any bushes or branches close to the trail that the creature may have brushed against, for hairs or fur. After dispatching a man down the hill to Andy for plaster of paris, I set off with the shotgun, camera, and binoculars and Ang Dawa. The remainder of the party were to camp on the spot and await my return.

The tracks led off downhill on the deep snow and after a few hundred yards, I realized that the follow-up was not going to be easy. They carried on for most of the time in a straight line, crashing through bushes or bamboos that were in the way. In steep places, the creature appeared to have sometimes slipped in the snow and gone slithering down in deep, ploughed furrows, scattering snow in all directions. In other places, the surface had given way and its foot had gone right through. Once, where it had crawled under a mossy branch above a steep slope, it had reached up and gripped or hung on the branch for a moment. The moss was torn off on an area about the size of a large man's hand. In another place, where it had gone over a huge fallen log, it had leapt a considerable distance off the log and landed on two feet. The tracks were, continuously, the tracks of only two feet and nowhere did I find anything to suggest that the creature had gone down on all fours. I took careful photographs of most of the markings.

We had been going for about three hours and the time was about midday when we came to a steep ridge that forms one of the shoulders of the Sangkua Chhoyang divide. Here, the tracks led upwards into great broken masses of dead bamboo and thorn, never faltering in their determined plodding step. On the steep side of the ridge, the winter snow had slipped away in places, leaving patches of bare ground where the prints virtually disappeared. Ang Dawa and I had trouble in finding them again and we found that as we climbed the ridge, they started to zig zag in a rather disconcerting manner. This slowed us down considerably and when the sun disappeared and grey mist began moving up the mountainside in the early afternoon, I had a sudden premonition that whatever we were following was a long way ahead of us and moving faster than we could ever hope to over that difficult ground. At three in the afternoon, we were roughly four miles from where we had started and I decided to call a halt. It had taken us all of five hours to cover those four odd miles. I wanted to go on and even though the deep snow and the endless falling into drifts and the thin air of the high altitude had tired us considerably, I think I might have done so. But the thought of getting caught out on the mountainside for a night, without tents or sleeping bags, made me change my mind. I was very reluctant to leave those tracks and spent another half an hour on the top of a hillock, searching the slopes for any sign of movement. But nothing stirred in the frozen air and after a short rest we started back to join the others.

On arrival, we were greeted by Gyalzen and Ajeeba, who were just about to trek out to look for us. They told me that they had spent all the morning backtracking the footprints to where they led into dense dead bamboo thickets. There they had lost them. But they had found some droppings and one black hair, snagged on a thorn back in the line of the tracks. They had also found three brownish-black hairs on another bush, but Gyalzen was not too sure about these as they were not quite on the track. The late arrival of Nima with the mailman concluded the day. It had been an exciting, if a disappointing one for me (Byrne, 1957b).

Byrne continued to search in the next few days for further signs, but the creature had apparently moved too far. The reconnaissance was coming to a close, and the teams regrouped to begin their descent.

SLICK'S FINDINGS

On the way down, going quickly from 12,000 to 7000 feet, Slick's party stopped at the village of Kampalung, as well as others along the route, and talked to more Nepalese about yeti. They then retraced their steps back to Biratnager.

Slick felt they had discovered much.

> In the course of the trip, we came upon three sets of tracks with very considerable evidence that they were of the yeti. . . . From discussions with the natives, as well as from previous reports, we believe that there are at least two types of ape-like animals in this area and perhaps three or more types. The large type is known as the Yeti. From eyewitness accounts, of which we have fifteen, this animal would seem to average about eight feet in height, to be generally similar in appearance to a gorilla, to have long black hair. . . . Two reports describe a white band around the middle. The face is similar to that of a gorilla but the head is very pointed in shape. The animal apparently normally walks erect on two legs and there were no reports of it being seen on four legs. It is fairly definitely tailless, according to eyewitnesses (Slick, 1958c).

Heuvelmans would note years later that Tom Slick's "most important contribution . . . is his belief that there are two kinds of yetis: one with blackish hair and about 8 feet high, and the other reddish and smaller" (Heuvelmans, 1972).

This description may seem commonplace now, but when Slick was detailing his findings, these ideas and his discoveries were ground-breaking. No one had gone into the field with such vigor, talked to locals in such a nonjudgmental way, and tried to do real community-based research. Remember, the *Daily Mail* expedition consisted of over 300 men in the field. Slick's work was superb, but the modern memory has become foggy and vague. He geared his methods in the field to a very low-key approach to the subject, despite the publicity he seemed to have received at the time. A case in point is his design for achieving the best objective results from his interviews with Nepalese on what exactly a yeti looked like.

> In the course of the trip, we talked to some fifteen eyewitnesses who have seen the Yeti. Besides the description that they gave us, as recounted above, we gave them a group of about twenty photographs which had been selected as being of animals that some of the scientists think might be confused with the Yeti. We asked these people to select the photographs that most resemble the Yeti.
>
> It was quite impressive that there was a unanimous selection [of these photographs], in the same order, with the first choice being a gorilla standing up, the second choice an artist's drawing of a prehistoric ape-man, *Australopithecus*, and the third choice an orangutan standing up, which they liked particularly for the long hair.

When they came to the picture of the bear, which many authorities have thought may be the explanation of the Yeti, every one of the observers immediately said that this was a bear and not a Yeti.

Similarly, when they came to the picture of the langur monkey, which some other authorities have thought may have been confused with the Yeti, they immediately recognized this as a monkey rather than a Yeti. All in all, the eyewitness descriptions and the selection of photographs were most impressive evidence of the existence and nature of the Yeti (Slick, 1958c).

The Slick Yeti Reconnaissance was important for other reasons as well. We know from a private report prepared by Slick that they had achieved new routes for future explorations, namely, one down into the Chhoyang Khola from the Sangkua Chhoyang ridge, and two separate routes to Peak 6 and Namche Bazar (near Mount Everest), both via the Sangkua Khola. They had found ways to get to the historic cave of Kampalung, and the pilgrim center of Sawane Kampalung (Slick, 1957a). The Arun Valley had never really been open to Westerners before the Slick party ventured there in March and April 1957; now it was.

We also learn a little more about Tom Slick the person because of his firsthand involvement in this effort. For example, on the first night out in the cold snowline area of the Arun, Slick was shocked to discover the custom was for the team leaders and some Sherpas to sleep in tents while the porters slept outside on the ground. Slick would not have that, and sent men back to buy huge tarpaulins for use as makeshift open-air tents. That was the kind of man Slick was, people told me, and the Sherpas and porters did not forget his kindness.

The world was waiting for results from Slick's mini-expedition, and he decided to hold a news conference in New Delhi on April 24, 1957. The *Times of India* headlined its story: "Tom Slick Convinced of Snowman's Existence—Move to Capture Yeti Alive on Next Expedition." Slick told of what his group had found—the three sets of footprints, hair, and droppings (which were probably from a snow leopard)—and outlined his theory of the three types of yetis (one of which he believed to be a bear). The media chose to report that Slick planned to put together a full-scale expedition in September that "would try to catch" a yeti. (We know the Nepalese government did not wish to have anyone kill a yeti, but we remain uncertain about how they felt at the time about its capture.)

Meanwhile, at about the same time as Slick's news conference, the Russians were releasing statements to such outlets as the *New York Times*, saying Slick was behind a move to subvert the Chinese. They felt the snowman-hunting expedition was the source of a 1957 border incident between China and Nepal. Such news items were not worth Slick's time, and he never commented on them. In fact, Slick had been actively consulting with the Soviets for some time through their Snowman Commission. The Academy of Sciences in the U.S.S.R. set up the commission in 1957 to examine all reports of manlike creatures, analyze them, and produce some findings. Slick's money and world leader status opened many doors for him. He traveled to Moscow on his way to Nepal in 1957. Slick's ideas about various types of yeti fit closely with the Soviets' beginning understandings of the "snowman problem," as they called it. They were always interested in his thoughts and his searches (*New York Times*, 1957b; Sanderson, 1961a; Shackley, 1983).

EVIDENCE DISAPPEARS

What happened to the evidence Slick brought back in 1957? Some reports indicate that the hair and casts went to the Delhi Zoo with Andy, and Slick's letters seem to confirm this, up to a point. However, I have also seen evidence that at least one copy of a footprint cast and an alleged yeti hair were shipped to *Life* magazine. On August 14, 1957, Peter Byrne shipped one plaster cast weighing one kilo from India to Ken MacLeish, *Life*, Time-Life Building, New York, via Pan American World Airways' Clipper Cargo Service. *Life* had been at one of the first meetings between Byrne and Coon, and Slick later told Heuvelmans that the magazine had offered a million dollars for a picture of a yeti. Slick's letters mention *Life*'s "consultants" throughout 1957, so it is rather certain they had a role in the expedition (Slick, 1957b; Heuvelmans and Porchnev, 1974; Byrne, 1988). In a letter dated September 20, 1957, Slick asked *Life*'s Mary E. Barber to get some analysis done on the materials sent by Byrne. "We would, of course," Slick continued, "like to have the information held confidential since *Life* is not presently involved in the project" (Slick, 1957).

Does *Life*'s archives hold yeti treasures? Are some artifacts from this first Slick effort hidden deep in one of the research institutes he founded? Such questions still surround the Slick searches. We simply do not know.

As 1957 progressed, Slick kept tabs from the United States on what was happening on the yeti front. There were reports that never went anywhere of a "preserved head." He heard from Byrne in Nepal during late May of a Sherpa report about a yeti showing up at a salt lick. Still, Slick was generally discouraged. By June, he knew he would never return to Nepal, and any efforts on his behalf were now dependent on external forces such as the required Nepalese permit, which he did not expect to obtain. Slick kept in touch with Byrne during the remainder of 1957 but Byrne generally stayed in New Delhi and waited for the next big push in the yeti search. By autumn, things did begin to fall into place for another quest. On September 13, Peter Byrne's visa was granted by Nepal for his reentry into the country. Tom Slick was preparing to support another effort to find a yeti.

The full investigative team of the 1958 Slick-Johnson Snowman Expedition in Nepal. Top row (from left to right): Passang Temba, Pemba Norbu, Sona Gurmey, Da Temba, Pushkar Shumshere, J. B. Rana (Government Liaison Officer, Nepal), Norman Dyhrenfurth, Gerald Russell, Peter Byrne, Bryan Byrne, Gyalzen Norbu (Foreman of the Sherpas), Gonden. Bottom row (left to right): Ang Dawa, Nima Tenzing, Lakpa Gyalbo, Ajeeba, Tashi, Ang Namgyal, Nim Dorjee, Karma Ongchu, Phu Tharkey. In the foreground: a German shepherd loaned by expedition friends in Darjeeling and three hounds from the Lees of Arizona. (Names supplied by Pem Pem Tshering and Peter Byrne.) Photograph by George Holton

Opposite Top: 1958 Slick-Johnson Snowman Expedition encampment. Bryan (left) and Peter Byrne dig out after an overnight snowfall.
Photograph by George Holton
Opposite Bottom: Peter Byrne leads part of the 1958 Slick-Johnson Snowman Expedition through the Nepalese rain forest, into the territory of the man-sized form of yeti.
Photograph by George Holton

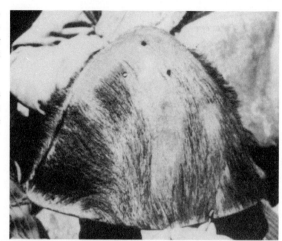

Top: At the Pangboche monastery, the 1958 Slick-Johnson Snowman Expedition examined and photographed, for the first time, this skullcap made in imitation of the yeti. Hillary was to use an even worse imitation in 1961 as the cornerstone of his drive to debunk the yeti. Photograph by Peter Byrne
Bottom: One of the most significant finds of the 1958 Slick-Johnson Snowman Expedition was this yeti bed discovered by Ang Dawa and Norman Dyhrenfurth in the upper Dudh Kosi valley, Nepal. Photograph by Norman Dyhrenfurth

Top: Bryan Byrne examines yeti tracks found at 10,000 feet in the Arun Valley of the Himalayas in March during the 1959 Slick-Johnson Snowman Expedition. Photograph by Peter Byrne

Bottom: F. Kirk Johnson, Sr. (right) was the "Johnson" of the Slick-Johnson Snowman expeditions. The Fort Worth oilman was able to get his old fishing and hunting buddy and business partner actor James M. Stewart (left) to assist in the transporting of the Pangboche hand out of India. This photograph was taken in the late 1950s or early '60s. Photograph courtesy of the Deborah Johnson Head Collection

CHAPTER 5

THE 1958 SLICK-JOHNSON SNOWMAN EXPEDITION

AFTER THE HUNT FOR YETI IN 1957, TOM SLICK worried about financing the next expedition. Despite his millionaire status, his money was not always easy for him to use, especially when it was wrapped up or tied down in research institutes, oil wells, beef ranches, and other nonliquid resources. Slick turned to a friend in the oil business, F. Kirk Johnson, Sr., of Fort Worth, Texas. Little is known about their discussions, except that their arrangement, late in 1957, left Slick mostly in charge of all the decision-making aspects of future explorations. The Slick-Johnson expeditions were born.

What should the expedition be called? At one point, stationery with the heading "Slick-Johnson Himalayan Zoological Expedition" was created, but apparently it was used only a few times. Most of the expedition's members called it various names: Slick-Johnson Snowman Expedition, Slick-Johnson Nepal Snowman Expedition, and Slick-Johnson Expedition. No one seemed to be interested in using the term "yeti" as much as it had been employed with the 1957 trek. I have not been able to discover why. For the sake of simplicity, I will use the name, "Slick-Johnson Snowman Expedition" for the 1958 search.

DEAD OR ALIVE

Excitement for the quest ran high, and Slick wrote of that year's expedition: "I believe today, next week, or several weeks from now a report may come out of that ancient wilderness [of the Upper Arun Valley, Nepal] telling that an expedition member has at last come face to face with a fierce and hairy apeman, eight feet tall" (Slick, 1958b).

Although it may be difficult for us to believe today, in the context of the times and of Slick's rapid discoveries, he felt he was truly on the threshold of encountering a yeti. These high expectations show in a February 5, 1958, letter from Slick's personal secretary, Jeri Walsh, on Tom Slick stationery, to expedition members:

In order to take advantage of the winter weather Mr. Slick feels if there is any sizable delay in sight an advance party should be sent into the area and when the equipment is all ready the others can follow. . . .

Since the actual capture of the animal is uncertain, he would like it to be photographed first, and he feels the photographing would not actually get in the way of the capture. Actually these operations can be simultaneous if one man is assigned to getting the photos while the others move in on the animal and after he gets his pictures then he can assist with the capture. But bear in mind that if you are not successful with the actual capture at least the photographs will prove the animal, so this is important. If you try to get it with the capchur [nonlethal tranquillizer] gun first and then miss, we will lose our chance to prove the animal.

There isn't time to obtain any more capchur guns and Mr. Slick suggests you get whatever additional cross bows are needed over there in India and have arrows made up like the ones sent. The size of the hypodermic needle should be judged by the ones for the capchur guns. . . .

Mr. Slick would like you to kill the animal only if it is absolutely necessary—with extreme justification—and he definitely prefers drugging it to killing it. Killing it should be a last resort only. If it does become necessary to kill it for self-preservation or chance of losing it altogether, then be sure you have enough formaldehyde to preserve the entire body. If you capture it you should plan to hold it indefinitely and not release it at all.

We are sending four traps which should be set in a ring and you could possibly have your "hole up" party watch them. They do not injure the animal if he is caught—in fact the inventor has been practicing catching himself in them. . . . If you have a way of luring the animal (salt licks perhaps) to the traps, then the inventor claims these should hold him without harm till you decide what to do with him. . . .

Mr. Slick thinks he would probably come into Nepal and might also send some zoologist and/or anthropologists to see the thing if you get it—dead or alive.

Regarding the guns—he would like any of his guns that are in worthwhile condition brought back and he would also like the capchur guns brought back to him. . . .

We eagerly await word on the "mail system."

Good luck and God Bless! (Walsh, 1958a).

Tom Slick reinforced some of these ideas in a March 3, 1958, letter to the team soon after they had left for the Arun:

We, of course, would love to have the animal captured alive, but, on the other hand, the main thing is to definitely prove the animal. . . . If one has to be killed in self-defense we certainly want to save the entire body. . . . If you should be able to get one of the animals, or definite proof, or outstanding information, let me know confidentially as rapidly as you can. If you get the actual animal alive, I will almost definitely be over there immediately (or even if you get a preserved body). You probably should keep it in secret in the mountains until I can get in there (in the meantime trying to catch more or some of the other type). . . . I am with you in trying to make this thing a success, which could be of great importance to everybody.

Get along good, good hunting, and catch the bastard! (Slick, 1958d).

HIDDEN AND STRATEGIC

Tom Slick had decided to field an expedition using a technique not employed for yeti hunting before, namely to go after the animals as if they were animals. Most casual inquiries in search of yeti traces had been conducted as mere afterthoughts of mountain climbing expeditions. One specific effort to look into the mystery of the yeti had used enormous numbers of people, as if the hairy creatures could be caught in some massive dragnet of men and equipment, but Slick rejected this approach. From his own knowledge of natural history, and from his trusted consultants' advice, Slick realized that a yeti would be caught only if it was pursued as a highly intelligent animal that did not want to be seen or caught. Knowing that professional animal collectors employed small probes into new territories and a close relationship with the local population, Slick planned to have his men break up into small groups. These teams would stay in strategic locations, hidden from view—like successful animal gatherers—and would wait for their quarry. They also would try to strike up friendly associations with the locals. These simple ideas were revolutionary at the time.

As the previous *Daily Mail* expedition and other less grand international mountaineering efforts to find yetis had involved large numbers of men, the animals were more than likely scared away from any area that had been searched. Ralph Izzard, you will recall, compared the 1954 expedition's three columns of men moving through the mountains to a line of beetles traveling across a white tablecloth. They were that noticeable against the Himalayan landscape.

Members of the Expedition

Along on the *Daily Mail* expedition was one man that would have a large
influence on Slick's deliberations concerning the plans for his own 1958
expedition, the American naturalist W. M. (Gerald) Russell, then living
in France. In the past, attempts (such as in 1954) to find a yeti had been
dominated by mountain climbers and big game hunters. By contrast, Russell's expertise was as a professional animal collector. He had been involved,
mostly uncredited, with collecting the first giant panda in Tibet in the
1930s. For months, Russell, as well as the Harknesses, looked in the wild
for a live giant panda to exhibit in an American zoo. Then, tired and
frustrated, according to some versions of the event, they came into a village
and discovered a local individual who had a cub as a pet. They were
delighted and yet, in some ways, not surprised (Morris, 1966; Perry, 1969).
The native people of an area are the best resource for finding local animals.
This giant panda was purchased and taken out of China, triumphantly
(Perry, 1969; Heuvelmans, 1959a). Such luck and local interactions are
the stuff of some major cryptozoological and zoological discoveries. Nevertheless, in 1954, yeti hunters had ignored Russell's ideas about hiding and
waiting for animals.

But it was not to be so with Slick. Using Peter Byrne as a foundation
member of the team and adding Peter's brother Bryan, another hunter,
for good measure, Slick put a major imprint on the Slick-Johnson Snowman
Expedition by choosing Gerald Russell as its leader. Ivan Sanderson, in
his 1961 book, *Abominable Snowmen: Legend Come to Life*, spares no praise
for this decision, for he saw "the extremely fortuitous bringing together
of Gerald Russell* and the brothers Peter and Bryan Byrne" as "the hap-
piest event that had until then—and still has been until the time of
writing—happened to ABSMery. For the first time in history the leadership
was not given to mountaineers or hunters, but to persons with collecting
experience who believed that the quarry was real, was multiple in form,
and that, in all its forms, it lived in the forests as opposed to on the upper
snowfields" (Sanderson, 1961a).

Additional members of the expedition included George Holton, an American still photographer living in Guatemala; Norman G. Dyhrenfurth, a
Swiss-born American mountain climber, filmmaker, and photographer;
Gyalzen Norbu, once again returning as sirdar, or leader of the Sherpas;
and Captain Pushkar Shamshere Rana, Nepalese liaison officer.

---

*Gerald Russell, Ralph Izzard, and Ivan T. Sanderson were classmates at Cambridge Uni-
versity. Sanderson and Russell were co-leaders of the Percy Slade animal collecting expedition
to Africa in 1932.

By February 17, Russel was in Kathmandu preparing to depart. *Newsweek*, in its February 24, 1958, issue, reported that the Slick-backed "abominable snowman" hunting expedition had just departed from the village of Biratnagar with seventy-five porters and fifteen Sherpas. "How the hunters plan to capture whatever it is they are after—if they find it," the newsmagazine commented, "remains an expedition secret" (*Newsweek*, 1958).

Two different techniques were employed to search for yetis during the course of the Slick-Johnson Snowman Expedition. The first method was used by Byrne and Dyhrenfurth. Peter Byrne's team used the village of Walung as its base of operations. From there they fanned out—sometimes with dogs—into the high isolated valleys of the Arun area. In a similar vein, Dyhrenfurth and Rana made a trip to Cepua, near the Tibetan border, to follow up on a report of a yeti skin there. Although the results were negative, this party used the trip for other investigations of yeti traces.

Gerald Russell, the group's acting leader, along with his Sherpa guide, Da Temba, planned to set up an observation post in a montane valley site, stay there for as long as a month, and let the yetis come to him.

GOING TO THE DOGS

Correspondence to and from Slick shows there was a good deal of conflict about how the expedition should be run, and the splitting into various teams made it possible for any member to gain control of the situation. The letters and tidbits of information in a few articles on this phase of the search mentions Russell as either "field director," "acting leader," or merely "leader." Byrne called himself the "chief guide and general organizer." Dyhrenfurth has been referred to as the "deputy leader." As Byrne put it: "Once every two weeks all of the members of the group came together and compared notes" (Bryne, 1958a). We speculate they yelled at each other a lot, as well.

Tom Slick tried to be a peacemaker. For example, in a March 3, 1958, letter to Gerald, Peter, Norman, Bryan, and other members, Slick wrote:

> I think that it is most important that everybody get along well together. I sense, from some of the letters, certain differences of opinion, certain possible personal frictions or criticisms or questions of judgment, which is probably only to be expected under the circumstances that have existed so far, but I urge you all to be reasonable, considerate, and to get along even though everyone may not agree with everyone else, otherwise the results of the expedition will suffer. I think I can count on all of you for that. . . . The main thing is to get the results (Slick, 1958d).

And then there were the dogs. Slick was personally tied to the notion that bloodhounds would tree a yeti as well as they would a bear or puma. Early in 1958, Tom Slick obtained three hounds from the famed Lee Brothers of Tucson, Arizona. The Lees were specialists in the guiding of big game hunts for jaguars, mountain lions, and bears by using trail hounds in Arizona and Central and South America. Perhaps Slick was also aware that they had successfully been tracking the cryptozoological felid, the onza, a legendary animal of northern Mexico. Author and investigator Robert Marshall, *Sports Afield*, and Dale Lee were discussed frequently in the late fifties by individuals interested in the onza mystery (Marshall, 1961).

The three hounds obtained by Slick were a bluetick female, Mary; a red female, Lou; and a bluetick male, Blue. I have reviewed the reams of 1958 letters written by the Lees to Dyhrenfurth, Slick, and Byrne; I was also able to talk to Dale Lee before he died in 1988. Frankly, I am surprised the dogs lasted as long as they did with the Byrne-Dyhrenfurth faction. Despite being excellent trackers, the dogs were very delicate animals. Gail Lee detailed in a four-page, single-spaced letter to the expedition members the special requirements for the dogs: lightweight jackets for the cold; lanolin to be put on their feet daily; penicillin and other drugs, plus hypodermic needless and syringes for medical needs; double headed snaps, leashes, chains; and food. Lee summarized the family's long-distance yeti-hunting insights nicely: "If you were hunting bear or lion, it would be easy to advise you from here. But obviously, these hounds have never trailed a snowman before" (Lee, 1958a, 1958b).

Initially, the Lees thought Dyhrenfurth was going to lead the dogs, and they worked hard to teach him how. As it developed, Peter Byrne received this duty, and he had a great deal of trouble with the hounds. They did not lead. They got loose and ran off. They were cold sometimes. Tired others. They did not cross rivers well. And they were overwhelmed by the heat of the Nepali valleys. Finally, Byrne discontinued the use of the dogs. In some village in the Arun Valley today there are probably offspring of these canid members of the expedition.

LENGTH AND RANGE OF THE EXPEDITION

Various estimates have been given for the length of time the main body of the Slick-Johnson Snowman Expedition remained in the field. But a check of the expedition payment records indicates that the longest time period the expedition employed any Sherpa was from February 15 to June 29, 1958, with the majority of the Sherpas working from February 22 to June

15. Most of the Sherpas were, therefore, paid for 113 days of expedition time; this seems to be a good way to get a handle on the expedition's length. Other sources confirm this record. *Newsweek* and a few press outlets claim the expedition went into the field some time between February 17 and 24, 1958. Dyhrenfurth stated that most of the expedition left Biratnagar on February 24 and camped in Bumling on March 4. The New York newspaper dispatches from the Himalayas were carried from April 20 to June 22, and Gerald Russell filed his report on the expedition on June 27, 1958.

During March, Russell and Da Temba went to the Chhoyang Khola, while Holton and the Byrnes explored the Barun area. Dyhrenfurth and his Sherpa friend Ang Dawa searched the Iswa Khola, crossed a twentythousand-foot pass toward the Barun Khola, and then returned to their base camp at Moyam in the Iswa Khola valley, where all members regrouped on April 6. During the three weeks in their various sites, the expedition's teams had stayed in caves for observation purposes, and discovered some tracks.

During April, Russell went back to Chhoyang, the Byrnes to Irkhua east of Arun, and Dyhrenfurth to Dima Khola to the north with a quick side trip to Cepua to follow up on that rumor of a yeti skin.

By May, with Holton and Russell gone, the expedition broke into two parties. The Byrnes took over the promising Arun/Chhoyang Khola valley from Russell, and Dyhrenfurth searched for the yeti in the Sola Khumbu. This division also reflected the split in reports of a smaller yeti in the first area, and a larger one in the second.

The two groups met on May 29 at the lamasery at Thyangboche, did some work in the area, and on June 4, started homeward. Peter Byrne's dysentery forced him and his brother directly back to Kathmandu, whereas Dyhrenfurth went via Thami, Rolwaling Khola, and Lichenku, reaching Kathmandu on June 15.

More casually, apparently, the Byrnes, from their own reportage, continued the hunt throughout the rest of 1958. An article in the *Daily Mail* of September 9, 1958, marked Peter Byrne's recent return from the yeti expedition supported by Tom Slick.* At the very least, it seems that Slick sent the Byrnes on additional exploratory missions.

After all this time in the field, what did the parties discover?

*This article is by Ralph Izzard whose book on the 1954 expedition is a classic. Izzard wrote me that he had met Slick in the mid-1950s but was not much impressed by him. Izzard commented: "He struck me as a bit of a showman, anxious to promote a big American prestige success. He seemed particularly interested in the possible presence of an Abominable Snow-*woman*. It was the first time I had even considered such a possibility but it dawned on me at once that a big breasted woman would arouse much more public interest than a man" (Izzard, 1988). This is an interesting comment in terms of the Chorvinsky appendix.

LITTLE YETIS AND FROGS

Different members of the expedition concentrated on diverse aspects of
the yeti question. Gerald Russell appeared to be associated only with the
investigations of the smaller type of yeti, often called metay, meti, or tehlma. He had found droppings of these little creatures in 1954, and had
always kept a keen eye out for evidence of them. Russell's never-before-
published "Report on the 1958 Slick-Johnson Nepal Snowman Expedition"
reflects his hunt for these specific beings.

The members of the expedition met at Bumling from whence I left on my
first "sortie." On the fourth day after leaving Bumling on the way to Chaun-
rikhara I came across tracks of the small yeti in the snow at an altitude of
approximately 8,500 to 9,500 feet. I made camp a few hundred feet above
the tracks. This was the most difficult moment of the expedition: to look at
a low altitude instead of going high. About ten days passed during which
no mammal of any kind was seen when a local man, who at one time had
seen a small yeti, called and suggested we (Da Temba, Sherpa, and self)
look lower down, along a stream, where we might see the yeti. Camp was
moved nearly 1,000 feet lower, well below the snowline, and a blind built
on a rock in mid-stream with a view up and down stream. No mammals
whatsoever were seen here. Just before our departure for the main base,
Moyam, near Walung, a man who had at one time seen a small yeti, called
and said if we pitched our camp by the stream, just below a waterfall, but
still lower down, and stayed about a fortnight we might see the yeti. Before
leaving for the base-camp a site was chosen near the stream, below the
waterfall and a few hundred feet lower down. After a conference at the
base-camp, instructions were sent to build the blind. A few days later we
returned for our second "sortie" and watched near the bottom of the waterfall
for about ten days during which a pair of porcupines and some monkeys
were seen. A man, who had at one time seen a small yeti, called and said
the yeti came to the stream at night to hunt for frogs. Within an hour
another man called and said he had seen a small yeti the night before while
looking for frogs, using a local torch. It was arranged that Da Temba and
he should go that night (I had had the 4 A.M. morning watch) at the critical
frog time which is supposed to last one hour. After patrolling up stream
then down stream without seeing anything, and about to turn off from the
stream to the camp about 30 yards away they noticed a wet footprint on a
stone and soon after saw a small yeti in the torch light 10 yards away. The
yeti took one step towards them whereupon they ran and spent the night in
a small settlement a few hundred yards away.

On the following night all three of us sat up and saw nothing. Yet, in
the morning, yeti tracks were seen in the gravel by the stream. It is interesting to note that the man saw a yeti two nights running and tracks on the

morning after his third night. On the next night, our third night, Da Temba and I sat up and saw nothing, and no tracks in the morning. On the fourth day some herdsmen camped just below us about 50 yards from the river: their large flock of sheep over-ran all the stream and country nearby. We sat up: nothing. Following morning there were tracks. That evening Peter arrived and we stayed up that night: nothing, and no tracks. Following morning I left and Peter took over (Russell, 1958a).

The sighting took place in the Chhoyang river valley in April 1958. Peter Byrne arrived on the scene and immediately "spent one night near the pool, huddled in the hollow of a big rock. . . . I took with me a 12-gauge shotgun. The rain was cold and persistent and the roar of the waterfall drowned out all sounds" (Byrne, 1958a). Into late May and June, Peter and Bryan Byrne continued the hunt near the Chhoyang river. They used frogs as lures, found four-inch footprints near a half-eaten frog, but never saw, photographed, or caught a yeti.

Da Temba's encounter confirmed for Russell the descriptions he had gathered of the smaller yeti:

Excluding Da Temba I spoke to seven people ranging from 14 to 40 years old who had seen the small yeti. When possible I made them act out what they were doing when they saw the yeti, what the yeti was doing when they saw it and what each did when each saw the other. The most striking feature was the slowness with which the yeti moved and the hunched shoulders.

I showed the animal photographs in the order arranged by you [Tom Slick] to six of the men. Five of them picked out the photo of the imaginary drawing with the pointed skull, and nearly all showed fear on seeing it! One picked out the drawing with the white "belt" because that is a characteristic of the Yeti's hair growth. The most observant one said that if the brows and lips of the gorilla were placed on the face of the pointed skull, and if the hair on the head and body were not sparse and long but thick and shorter, and if there was a white "belt," it would be exactly like the yeti. A few, who had seen the animal close up, said the foot in both drawings was too long. All, with one exception, were agreed on a height of three feet (Russell, 1958a).

Tom Slick quoted Russell's conviction that the smaller yeti existed in reasonable numbers. "He has estimated that perhaps as many as 4,000 might exist in the whole of the Himalayan area," Slick wrote in a confidential report (Slick, 1958e).

THE YETI CAVE

Norman Dyhrenfurth and Ang Dawa conducted a ten-day search in May of the upper Dudh Kosi valley, where the 1954 *Daily Mail* party had discovered so many footprints. It was there that Ang Dawa found a cave where a yeti had been living for some time. Many droppings and rodent remnants were inside.

Here's the way Dyhrenfurth described the discovery to cryptozoologist Gardner Soule: "We found a cave and in it a bed of juniper branches, pulled out of the ground to make the bed. You'd have to be immensely strong to pull those juniper branches out of the ground. We tried. We couldn't. The yeti must be stronger than a man." Inside the nest, Dyhrenfurth examined the droppings: "They contained the finely ground up bones and hair of mouse hares. There were mouse hares in the area nearby" (Soule, 1966). To this day, Dyhrenfurth is convinced of the reality of yetis (Dyhrenfurth, 1959, 1988).

OF SCALPS AND HANDS

Dyhrenfurth and the Byrnes were instrumental in bringing to the awareness of the world the so-called "yeti relics." Shamanistic relics play an important part in the rituals of Nepalese Buddhism and are kept in significant Buddhist centers, representing the linkage the Buddhists have to their surroundings. Because of their importance in the community and involvement in festivals, the Buddhist monks sometimes fabricated items in imitation of segments of the natural world. Such was the case with some yeti skullcaps.

Rivalry between different Sherpa villages appears to be another basis for the making of some of the items generally called "relics" by Westerners. The Sherpas sometimes gave religious authority to myths, legends, and rare accounts of creatures seldom seen, but they did not do so with deception in mind. The Sherpas, tied to Tibetan Buddhism by their ancestry, gain strength from these spiritual tools, be they amulets, prayer flags, or yeti relics (Anderson, 1987). This concept has been difficult for Westerners to understand.

At the lamaseries of Thyangboche* and Pangboche, the members of the

---

*During February of 1989, the shocking news of heavy fire damage at the Thyangboche monastery in Nepal reached the West. Besides being the site of an alleged yeti scalp, this monastery is the location of a much-discussed November 1949 yeti sighting. The animal was chased away by monks blowing trumpets and banging drums. Also near Thyangboche a yeti was seen by Sen Tensing.

1958 Slick expedition were allowed to photograph the two 350-year-old alleged yeti scalps. The 1954 British expedition had been shown one of these, but Slick's group was the first to examine them so closely and photograph them so extensively. We now know that these relics likely were made in imitation of the yeti, but at the time they became a source of great debate. Slick's support of the expedition was able to thrust this discussion into the light of day, where the evidence could be observed and the relics investigated. Despite what would happen two years later when the Hillary expedition declared the scalp at another lamasery (other than the two Slick's men visited) a fake, the possibility of proving that yetis actually existed seemed imminent to Slick's people.

Slick's expedition also revealed for the first time that the lamas possessed "yeti hands." Slick proved that a hand, wrist, and forearm at Makalu were actually those of a snow leopard. But the Slick-Johnson Snowman Expedition did obtain the first photographs of a very old and mummified yeti hand found in Pangboche. This discovery gave Slick's associates much to ponder, to analyze, and to seek well into 1959.

Tom Slick decided to keep the ultimate quest alive. He thought he could catch the smaller yeti at the lower altitudes, and he was excited by the possibility of learning more from the "hand." Slick moved on to the next expedition.

CHAPTER 6

THE KIRK JOHNSONS
AND JIMMY STEWART

THIS BOOK, OF COURSE, IS MAINLY ABOUT TOM Slick and his search for the yeti, but the Slick-Johnson expeditions involved some financial and strategic support from some folks named Johnson and their friend, the actor Jimmy Stewart.

The Johnson in the Slick-Johnson expeditions was a man who was known affectionately to his family as "Big Daddy" and, indirectly, that man's son. Sportsmen and oilmen, the Johnsons of Fort Worth had much in common with Slick. As early as the fall of 1957, two Texans, F. (for Francis) Kirk Johnson, Sr., (F K J Sr.) and F. Kirk Johnson, Jr., (F K J Jr.) joined Tom Slick in his pursuit of the abominable snowmen. Through 1959, the Johnsons donated at least $100,000 to the search for yeti.

F. KIRK JOHNSON, SR.

F. Kirk Johnson, Sr., was a director of the Fort Worth National Bank and a national director of Project Hope, a People-to-People organization that shared some international objectives with Slick's peace conferences. Johnson owned ranches in Texas, California, and South Dakota, as well as several radio and television stations in Texas and Oklahoma. He was a director in Overseas Motors, and, almost until his death, held controlling stock in Central Airlines. Slick, of course, owned Slick Airways. The two men traveled in the same circles and had overlapping interests.

A native of North Bend, Nebraska, F. Kirk Johnson, Sr., was a noted big game hunter and had gone on several African safaris, bringing back trophies for himself and live animals for the Fort Worth Zoo. His wife recorded one trip to Africa in her privately published book, *Safari Diary/*

Africa, 1961. (Big Daddy's granddaughter, Debbie Johnson Head, lent me this and other Johnson family diaries and related material for my research.) Often Jimmy Stewart would accompany F K J Sr. on hunts, as he did during the summer 1961 safari. Bess, F K J Sr.'s wife, wrote that she and her husband "had the excitement and the thrill of sharing with Gloria and Jimmy Stewart their first safari. We had been with them in Assam on shikar and had assured them they would like Africa. This proved to be the understatement of the year. They adored it and are already signed up for next year" (Johnson, 1961).

F K J Sr.'s association and friendship with Stewart went back many years. Johnson was the chairman of the boards of Ambassador Oil Company and Ambassador Irish Oil Company. Stewart appears to have been a business partner of long standing. "Mr. Johnson and his associate, James M. Stewart, and others had organized Ambassador Oil Company," wrote George B. Collins in his book on the oil business in Ireland, *Wildcats and Shamrocks.* "Mr. Stewart, better known as Jimmy Stewart, is the popular movie star" (Collins, 1976). Furthermore, Johnson and Stewart were co-owners of Live Oak Stable, located in several states.

F K J Sr. took his interest in animals seriously; he was president emeritus of the Fort Worth Zoological Society in the 1960s, and donated $5000 to the construction of the ape house. His membership in the Mount Kenya Safari Club (co-owned by the actor Bill Holden and Ray Ryan) was one of his favorites. Bess Johnson's book mentions that Jimmy and Gloria Stewart would be put up in the Holdens' suite while staying at the Club, and how glad they were that Artis Holden had a hair dryer in her dressing room.

Naturally, when Slick was looking around for someone else to assist him in financing the yeti expeditions he turned to Kirk Johnson. When he needed an important piece of yeti evidence taken out of Nepal, Slick asked Johnson for help. And Johnson came through by way of his friend, Jimmy Stewart, who was to be involved in one of the most important events in the history of yeti research.

JIMMY STEWART AND THE YETI HAND

James Maitland Stewart was born in Indiana, Pennsylvania, on May 20, 1908. Growing up, he enjoyed visiting his parents' hardware store and daydreaming about becoming a big game hunter and explorer. After an education that prepared him to be an architect, he spent a summer with his friend Josh Logan, who ran a summer theater. Jimmy Stewart was on his way to becoming a stage and film artist, and along the road to stardom he made friends with Henry Fonda, Burgess Meredith, Benny Goodman, Margaret Sullivan, and other famous entertainers. After years as the most eligible single man in Hollywood, Stewart married Gloria Hatrick McLean on August 9, 1949.

Stewart seemed hardly the kind of guy who would be open to getting involved with yetis. His career in movies gave him the image of everyone's favorite hometown boy in the early years, and the thoughtful man-next-door as he matured. Interestingly, during 1958 and 1959, when he assisted and watched the yeti mystery unfold, Stewart did a movie about the supernatural (*Bell, Book and Candle*) and another that has become a Hitchcock classic (*Vertigo*). Jimmy Stewart, mild-mannered Mr. Middle America, however, was the person to whom the Johnsons and Tom Slick turned to get a yeti hand out of Asia and into England.

F. KIRK JOHNSON, JR

Like his father, F. Kirk Johnson, Jr., was involved in the oil business, and was president of Murjo Oil and Royalty Company, as well as a director in Overseas Motor Corporation and Universal Volkswagen, Inc. The younger Johnson was a vice president of Ambassador Oil Company until his father's death, when Ambassador was sold to Anadarko Production Company.

F. Kirk Johnson, Jr., like Big Daddy, was an African game hunter and adventurer. Unlike his father, who merely financed the effort, F K J Jr. also went hunting for the yeti himself. Some time around late 1957 or early 1958, Johnson sent a team of four men to western (*not* eastern) Nepal. This sector was said to have yetis of a much more aggressive and larger variety. The Soviets were especially interested in these yetis because they were similar to those reported just across the border of their country. Very few expeditions or chance European expedition encounters have occurred in western Nepal, but it would be informative to learn more about this exploratory party someday. Tom Slick, of course, had sent expeditions only to eastern and northeastern Nepal.

During November and December 1958, the younger Johnson was supposed to be en route to join the Byrnes in Nepal as part of the Slick-Johnson expedition. Instead, he went on his own mini-expedition to India in search of the "abominable snowmen." He started in earnest on November 14. That night he had dinner in New Delhi with Andy Bachkheti of Slick's earlier parties. F K J Jr. then learned what he could about the yeti from locals and interested individuals. That same night he talked to Peter Byrne, back briefly from Nepal, suffering from malaria.

On November 19, after a three-week wait, Johnson's permit finally came through. He later said that the permission he had been granted was to hunt sheep and goats in India, not yetis. "India doesn't recognize the yeti," he commented. (It is still not clear why Johnson stayed in the Himalayan foothills of India instead of going into Nepal, but that is what he did.) His diary of the quest reflects a loneliness that is often overlooked in fanciful accounts of such searches. He would walk for hours on end, set up camp, try to get warm, and finally write a few words in his journal. He would trek from 9:45 A.M. to 2:00 P.M. out of Ghuttu, set up his camp, and then go hunting. He "saw a big animal they call a thar" but no yetis.

For six weeks Johnson thrashed about the Indian foothills around Mount Bisone. He had heard reports of the little yeti coming out of that region and wanted to follow up on them. One porter of his, for example, claimed to have seen a five-foot yeti covered with black hair. Did Johnson believe the people he was interviewing? "You talk to too many people, even children, who have seen it. And the country is so remote. I thought there would have been one yeti brought out by now," he wrote in his diary at the time (Johnson, 1958).

Finally, word reached Johnson that a man from Dehra had just sighted a yeti. The man had seen the creature sitting in a tree, edged toward it for a better look, and apparently frightened it off. The thing had grabbed a limb with both hands, swung down, and trotted away. The yeti stopped several times to peer from behind the trees and tall grasses at the man. Johnson hurried to the site and spent two weeks there.

From Mount Bisone on November 28, at about 11,500 feet, Johnson wrote: "The guide showed me the tree he saw the snowman jump from so if he is here I am in the right spot. The mt. up here looks good and not too thick. It should be better hunting than lower down. . . . We got here at noon and no huts. . . . It started to rain with some snow. . . . Might have to leave as the men can't sleep in the open with one blanket and sweater, all due to more bad advice. . . . I sat in a tree from 3:30 'til dark in the rain but saw nothing" (Johnson, 1958). He would continue his routine of searching the area on foot during the days and spending twilight at a set spot trying to see the tree-incident yeti. He had no luck, but came away from his trip to the Himalayan foothills more convinced than ever that yetis existed.

While F. Kirk Johnson, Jr., failed to find yeti in India, he continued his adventures after the Slick-era yeti hunts. In the late fifties, he organized a dive off the coast of Quintana Roo, near Cozumel, Mexico, and recovered 200-year-old treasure from a sunken Spanish ship. He showed up in California at the Byrnes' campsite and looked for Bigfoot with Peter during the early 1960s. Kirk, Jr., was there in the spring of 1968 at the Sacred Cenote of Chichen Itza when his personally sponsored expedition recovered evidence of hundreds of human sacrifices and artifacts that redefined the history of the Mayans.

Deaths of the Johnsons

The deaths of both of the F. Kirk Johnsons of Fort Worth came suddenly. The senior Johnson, sixty-seven at the time, was on a business trip to Los Angeles with his wife and Mr. and Mrs. Earl Baldridge. On June 11, 1963, he died of a heart attack in his hotel room shortly after arriving.

F. Kirk Johnson, Jr., died swiftly and mysteriously a short five years after his father's death. Soon after a routine physical, Johnson, then forty, was acting like his old self. On the evening of August 14, 1968, he reportedly poured himself a drink, tried to swallow it, and died of pneumonia brought on by the liquid coming from a small slit in his esophagus incurred during the physical. Details of this accident are still unknown, as the family avoids discussing the matter in depth. Johnson died in the Ochsner Foundation Hospital in New Orleans. The Johnson family still refrains from pointing a blaming finger at anyone. F. Kirk Johnson, Jr.'s memory is not worth a series of dirty investigations, they feel.

The legacy of the Johnsons lives on in the work they did and the adventures they sponsored. They extended the exploratory efforts of Tom Slick and joined him at a critical time to support the search for the yeti.

CHAPTER 7

THE 1959 SLICK-JOHNSON
SNOWMAN EXPEDITION

By the end of 1958, Tom Slick had been in the yeti-hunting business for some time, and his expeditions became better supplied with equipment and useful information. For example, Slick and the Southwest Research Institute had invented a very unique capchur tranquilizer crossbow just for the search. And in June 1958, at the end of the first formal expedition, Slick said: "We didn't capture an abominable snowman, but I believe we have added significantly to the knowledge about this elusive creature" (Slick, 1958f). He clearly saw the little yeti as the most catchable and wanted to employ methods and obtain traps to get proof. He had to sort through the evidence that had been collected thus far—prints, droppings, and the hands—and make some sense of it all.

The Hunt Resumed

After the effort of 1958, Slick was gearing up for the next segment of the search. He dashed off a telegram to Bryan Byrne at the Maidens Hotel in New Delhi, India, asking him to check on the availability of some reported Kathmandu photographs of a "yeti skull and teeth." Slick noted that he "would like [to] secure these [reproductions of the] apparently humanoid" items. His message also noted that the "northern skull [was] most important" to obtain (Slick, 1958g). This may be the "Mustang animal" referred to in some items from the time. Mustang, a small region near Bhutan, was the site in 1958 of the killing of a "yeti" that turned out to be a sloth bear. Whatever became of the clues that Bryan Byrne was able to track down has been lost for now.

Meanwhile, in October 1958, Peter Byrne received some traps that Slick was interested in his using. They were a new invention by Roger

Allen Cook of San Antonio. Cook had forwarded eight traps designed to catch and hold, as humanely as possible, animals weighing in the range of 100 to 1000 pounds. They were a complex assembly of steel cable, spring cartridges, grooved spreader rings, split tabular shield, a piece of canvas, and pins to set it. From drawings I've seen, the thing looks like three circles of cable all set together with a spring off to the side. It was to be placed in a depression, and yetis were supposed to step into it unknowingly. The traps were heavy and cumbersome, though, and Slick's man did not find good sites, regularly traversed by yetis, for them. No yetis were caught.

Slick asked Peter and Bryan Byrne to conduct a very subtle Slick-Johnson Snowman Expedition in 1959. They went off by themselves, with little equipment, no food, and no tents. Sometimes they were with Nepali or Sherpa. Often they were alone. They lived off the land, bought from villagers, slept in caves when in snow and wooden shelters in the valleys. This expedition was Slick's attempt to get his men as close to the land as possible. Only this way, he felt, could a yeti be captured. For nine months the Byrnes trekked a thousand miles around the Arun valley, interviewed villagers, looked into the reported relics of Pangboche and elsewhere. Again, although they found some tracks, they came away without a yeti,* but still convinced that there were yetis in the mountains.

YETI STOOLS

A large collection of scientific consultants were confidential members of the Slick-Johnson effort in 1959 (see Appendix C). Two key members of the consultation group were zoologist Bernard Heuvelmans, who led some elements of the European examinations, and anthropologist George Agogino, who coordinated individuals in the United States and England. Agogino was in charge of distributing to his contacts the alleged yeti droppings picked up by Byrne during the 1959 expedition. Early in 1959, Agogino sent sections of a stool labeled to indicate its supposed yeti origin to five individuals in the United States and to Izzard and Hill in England with instructions to discover its zoological affinity.

In April, Osman Hill got back directly to Byrne with his initial analysis: "Macroscopically it has every evidence of being vegetarian, but microscope studies may extend this. Maybe some parasites will be revealed which will give further clues" (Hill, 1959a).

---

*The Byrnes did collect some animals. In September 1959 they sent two Himalayan black bears to the Taronga Zoo in Sydney and the San Antonio Zoo. These were followed by a leopard to the Taronga Zoo in November 1959.

On May 4, 1959, Izzard wrote back, saying he was "not adequately equipped here to analyse so small a specimen." Still, he ventured a guess that a hungry wolf could have been responsible (Izzard, 1959a).

Agogino took Izzard's casual comment to heart. In July, he wrote Slick: "I still believe it was a hungry wolf." By November, Agogino was critical of Slick's teams, which did not have "trained men in zoology and in physical anthropology" in the field. He specifically pointed to the stools, "which didn't seem associated with a primate" as an example (Agogino, 1959a, 1959b, 1959c).

F. G. Wallace at the University of Minnesota on May 27, found that the sample was "not human; is most improbably primate; is most probably from a sheep or other herbivore" (Wallace, 1959). This analysis was cautiously seconded by G. A. Matson in his July 9 letter accompanying Wallace's: "There is a question in my mind as to the validity of these findings even though it could have been shown that the specimen was of human origin." Wallace had found parasite eggs in the stool sample, which he felt were outside the human range, and at least one might have been a sheep parasites' egg (Matson, 1959). Heuvelmans disagreed with these conclusions later because Wallace had found three, not just one, egg sizes that could have been used to link them to sheep. Heuvelmans would comment in a letter to Ivan Sanderson that Wallace's work had been less than adequate (Heuvelmans, 1960).

Heuvelmans, meanwhile, through Dr. A. Fain of the Tropical Medicine Institute of Anvers, had discovered that the droppings found by Byrne contained the egg of an unknown species of the parasitic worm Trichocepale of the genus *Trichuris*. Heuvelmans wrote: "Since each species of mammal has its own parasites, this indicates that the host animal is also equally an unknown animal" (Heuvelmans, 1961). These results, originally written in French, have never been published in English before.

An analysis by Dr. Anne Porter of another late 1959 stool sample showed a combination of vegetable tissues and animal tissues in the stool. The animal material included mammalian hairs from some small rodent or insectivore, parts of a caterpillar and a grasshopper, and earthworm setae. She wrote on April 9, 1959: "The findings are not inconsistent with the theory that the provider of the sample included frogs in its diet. Although no vertebrate tissue, other than mammalian hairs, are included in the sample, it is feasible to assume that the insect and other invertebrate tissues were from the alimentary contents of the prey, still remaining undigested in the predator's gut" (Porter, 1959).

The Footprint Cast

Between May and July 1959, Slick's consultants examined closely one of the first yeti footprints that Slick had collected in 1957. This print, about ten inches long, was broad and compared favorably with the track found by Sir Eric Shipton in 1951. A good cast of Slick's 1957 yeti footprint was taken (see photograph following p. 32) and analyzed by Slick's experts.

Here is a selection of the comments from various investigators as recorded in Slick's confidential report:

Coon 5/13/59: If it is a primate, it is an exceedingly unusual one.

Agogino 5/18/59: Most interesting thing was the discovery of hair imprints between the two smallest toes. This creature had hairy feet—not on the undersurface but between the toes and perhaps above.

Coon 5/20/59: Thinks this is the most important thing to have come out of the area so far. Now thinking of a completely unknown animal—close to primate or halfway between bear and primate.

Hausman 5/20/59: Footprint is much like Bushman footprints.

Schultz 6/11/59: Most likely a new local species of giant panda.

Coon 6/22/59: Says Schultz is most excited about the footprint and feels it is a new type of giant panda.

Ulmer 6/22/59: Has a panda and says its footprint is not the same as that of the cast. Feels it is more human—even with the small broad toes (and only four showing).

Izzard 6/27/59: Looked at foot imprints of a giant panda in the London Zoo and feels Schultz is incorrect in his assumption that the yeti is a giant panda.

Agogino 6/27/59: A recently extinct type of giant panda was known to have existed in upper Burma. Maybe in Nepal an allied genus still survives.

Ulmer 7/11/59: Surprised at Schultz calling the yeti paw print that of a giant panda. Is acquainted with giant pandas from his days at the Academy of Natural Sciences, collected three for the museum group. The toe imprints of the foot cast are far too big for any panda. Cannot get over Schultz calling it a panda. This is preposterous (Slick, 1959).

In September 1959, Slick noted that the cast "has stirred up interest as well as differences of opinion" (Slick, 1959). The last record of the cast showed it on its way to Izzard and then to Agogino. No one can determine where this cast is now, and all that exists today are some poor copies of photographs.

THE MAKALU HAND

I have already noted that Slick decided the Makalu hand and forearm was from a snow leopard, but a brief examination of how his consultants reached this conclusion merits our attention. Slick's people assembled to study the gathered evidence. They wanted to discover a firm basis for the yeti which could be presented to the scientific community. They did not blindly accept every tidbit that came along, and clearly were not embarrassed to tell Slick when they found something that was not worthy of further efforts.

The Slick-Johnson Snowman Expedition of 1958 brought the Makalu hand to Slick's and his consultants' notice. Peter Byrne was to eventually take photographs and X rays of the humanlike hand and forearm vaguely claimed by some Makalu villagers to be that of a yeti. No terminal phalanges were attached to the hand, so the full structure was in doubt. Materials on the hand were distributed to the consultants, and Slick waited for opinions.

Osman Hill was the first to report. On February 2, 1959, Hill told Slick he was convinced the Makalu hand was not human, nor even primate but pertained to a carnivore, almost certainly a feline and therefore probably a snow leopard (Hill, 1959b). Frederick Ulmer, Curator of Mammals, Philadelphia Zoological Society, wrote Slick on March 6 that the hand looked like part of a carnivore, possibly a wolf (Ulmer, 1959a). The next day, Slick received word from Carleton Coon that he also thought the Makalu forelimb was from a wolf or other carnivore (Coon, 1959). George Agogino noted on May 7 that he had received several letters about the Makalu artifact and his opinion was that it came from a leopard. At first, Agogino said, he thought that it was from a wolf, but after looking at the X rays, he favored the leopard theory (Agogino, 1959a). Ulmer wrote again on May 13, stating that he definitely thought the limb was more felis than canis and might be a snow leopard or something like that (Ulmer, 1959b). Hill got in touch again on July 5 deciding that the hand belonged to a snow leopard (Hill, 1959c).

The Slick-Johnson Snowman Expedition can be credited with dismissing the significance of the Makalu hand. In a confidential report, Slick put an end to the investigations with these words: "Makalu hand is probably of a snow leopard—abandon any further work on this one" (Slick, 1959). He relayed this verdict to Peter Byrne, who then concentrated on the Pangboche hand.

THE PANGBOCHE HAND

As 1958 was ending, Slick started feeling the pressure to do more about the Pangboche hand. Osman Hill wanted Slick to get more solid evidence on it. He had examined the expedition's detailed photographs and decided the hand was not from a gorilla, orangutan, or chimpanzee. "Therefore an unknown anthropoid is the mostly likely conclusion at present," Hill wrote in a confidential memo to Slick on October 14 (Hill, 1958a).

Peter Byrne was able, early in 1959, to obtain parts of the yeti hand so desired by Slick's consulting anthropologists and primatologists. At the time, there was great secrecy surrounding the acquisition. Byrne wrote Slick on February 3:

> I shall not go into details here of how we got the thumb and the phalanx of the Pangboche hand. The main thing is that we have them, and that the lamas of the monastery *do not know* that we have them. Because they do not know it is of the utmost importance that there is no news releases on this or any publicity for some time. . . . The Pangboche hand is still complete, as far as the lamas are concerned. It still has a thumb and an index procimal phalanx. What they do not know, and what they *must never know*, is that the thumb and the p. phalanx at present on the hand are human ones, which we switched (Byrne, 1959a)

Byrne had obtained from Hill some human hand parts and had pulled off a delicate exchange when he was allowed to examine the Pangboche hand privately.

Only through the efforts of Jimmy and Gloria Stewart did these pieces of the yeti puzzle reach London. Slick had to solve the problem of transporting these important parts of the Pangboche yeti hand past customs and out of Nepal and India. As he recalled, Byrne found removing the relic's bones from Nepal simple; one of the expedition members put it in his pack and took it across the border. The problem they faced was getting it out of India, where custom inspections were more thorough. As Peter Byrne wrote in 1975, the difficulty was solved by friends of the Kirk Johnsons who were passing through Calcutta after a visit with an old friend of Kirk's, the maharaja of Baroda. Baroda arranged for Byrne to meet with these Johnson associates at the Grand Hotel and transfer the yeti relic to them for their return to England (Byrne, 1975). These folks, of course, were Jimmy and Gloria Stewart. Byrne recalled during my interviews in 1988 that they were very amused with the grisly trophy. He then added a scary detail to the story. When the Stewarts arrived in London, their luggage was lost. For many anxious hours, the couple waited to see if their bags would turn up, and if so, whether customs officials had found the piece of yeti hand tucked in their underwear. Finally, they were happy to discover that the suitcases had been delivered right to their hotel room unopened and safe.* The Stewarts passed the hand on to F. Kirk Johnson, Jr. Johnson delivered the hand parts to Hill on February 20.

Osman Hill was quick to get back to Slick with his initial overall analysis of the parts he examined. He wrote on February 26, 1959, "*Pangboche Hand*: This proves from examination of the thumb and phalanx to be human" (Hill, 1959 d).

The seriological analysis of the skin from the hand, however, indicated that it was not human, gorilla, old world monkey, beef, pig, goat, horse, or bear: "I regret my inability to make a positive identification," wrote zoologist Charles A. Leone on July 16 (Leone, 1959).

Down through the years, others who examined the specimen would disagree with Hill's quick conclusion. Anthropologist George Agogino did not think it was simply a mummified human hand. He told researcher Gardner Soule:

> I did notice that the hand had very flat metacarpals, far flatter than is normally expected in a human being, but something which is very characteristic of the giant anthropoids. Many people who have examined this hand feel that it is a human hand with very primitive characteristics. It is so close to the border line it could be a non-human hand with very advanced characteristics and still be little different than it is currently. I do not feel that this hand is a normal human hand at all. The flat metacarpals, particularly in the top surface, just do not occur among human beings very often, if at all. Feel at the back of your own hand [for the bones between your fingers and your wrist]. It is highly characteristic, however, of all the giant anthropoids (Soule, 1967).

Other Slick consultants would have similar reservations as to the true nature of the Pangboche hand. Fred Ulmer noted that the metacarpals "are considered massive even for a mountain gorilla. Metacarpals are extremely wide and flat on top. Hand is massive" (Ulmer, 1959a). Later, Ulmer wrote that it looked like "a strange human hand" (Ulmer, 1959b). Anthropologist Stanley Garn found the "relative lengths of segments of digits to the metacarpals is somewhat out of order for the normal man" (Garn, 1959).

Hill seemed to modify his quick opinion later in the year. On July 5,

*James Stewart confirmed this story in a letter to me, June 19, 1989.

1959, he was no longer convinced that the Pangboche hand was fully human (Hill, 1959c). By 1960, he apparently had rethought his verdict on the Pangboche hand further and was beginning to wonder if it might have come from a Neanderthaler (Sanderson, 1961). The question of the Pangboche hand's affinity remained open during Slick's time (as it does today), and Slick noted that his analysis of the Pangboche hand was incomplete (Slick, 1959).

I strongly disagree with the tactics of mutilating this sacred relic and with the apparent theft of the hand's parts from Nepal. But I also understand this event in the context of the 1950s and the strong notion that by proving the existence of the yeti, the Slick-Johnson Snowman Expedition personnel hoped to establish the yeti's place in zoology. But lingering worries persist. Were investigators examining the reconfigured Pangboche hand after 1959 sidetracked by the human parts now attached to the yeti hand, and did they use this as grounds to debunk the whole skeletal relic? Photographs taken by Byrne and George Holton of the hand before it was changed (see photographs of the hand between pages 104 and 105) show clearly that the index finger is one joint long and that the thumb is massive. Photographs of the relic by Professor Teizo Ogawa after Byrne took the bones from the Pangboche hand definitely show a nice long complete human index finger and thumb. I believe this bewilderment among post–Slick expedition investigators resulted in the Pangboche hand being discredited in 1960–1961. Even Ivan Sanderson, who must not have been fully aware of the switch, would write that "two very old mummified and obviously hominid hands" at Pangboche were worthy of investigation (Sanderson, 1961a). He apparently was confusing the pre-1959 hand with the mutilated post-1959 hand. They looked different enough for this cryptozoologist to claim there were two Pangboche hands!

What other means have overzealous yeti hunters used in their pursuit of these animals? Have other yeti relics been mishandled? And today, where are the parts of the Pangboche hand that took the combined efforts of Peter Byrne and Jimmy and Gloria Stewart to get out of the Himalayas? We do not know. And that's too bad.

ON TO AMERICA

The Slick-Johnson expeditions' search for the yetis of the montane valleys and slopes of the Himalayas was viewed as a success by Slick, Johnson, and the others involved with the surveys. Cryptozoologists who remember Tom Slick acknowledge that these expeditions supplied the first indications of data we now take for granted on the so-called "abominable snowmen" of Nepal. These naturalists, adventurers, and explorers discovered several new pieces of the puzzle, including the possibility of two types of yeti; their exact descriptions, habits, and food choices; and the location and close examination of several relics.

But Slick and the Byrnes were becoming weary of the extended chase in the remote, sometimes permit-granting Nepal. Slick was beginning to think about bringing the search back home. In November 1959, he talked to George Agogino about his determination to seek out the "California Yeti or whatever it is," as Agogino put it (Agogino, 1959c). Slick had been gathering the reports that started coming out of the Bluff Creek area of northern California since 1958, and he wanted to move on them. It was time for the Byrnes to come to the Pacific Northwest of the U.S.

Yetis would remain in the Himalayas, Slick figured, but why not first catch one in your own backyard? He could go back to Nepal in the future, he told friends. On the horizon, though, was a massive publicity circus that would kill the Himalayan yeti as no gun Slick or Byrne ever carried.

CHAPTER 8

HILLARY'S ASSASSINATION
OF THE YETI

DESPITE A GROWING BODY OF EVIDENCE THAT
pointed to the possibility of a species of unknown anthropoids existing in
the Himalayas, Slick did not seek and did not receive much publicity from
results of his yeti expeditions. He had, more often than not, labeled reports
and letters from his consultants and expedition members "confidential."
Most of the information from his investigations was never shared with the
public. Slick processed his findings as a scientist. He felt he should gather
as much data as possible, analyze it, obtain more concrete proof, and
publish it later. This policy was in direct contrast to the approach taken
by the *World Book* and Sir Edmund Hillary.

THE GERMINATION OF A PUBLICITY STUNT

During 1959, Hillary was in New York City to give a speech on exploration
at a function sponsored by the men's magazine, *Argosy*. Field Enterprises
Educational Corporation, publishers of the *World Book Encyclopedia*, then
asked him to Chicago to give a similar talk. In discussions with Hillary
over dinner, the beginning of a massive media campaign took shape in the
mind of the Field Enterprises Public Relations Director John Dienhart.
Hillary, who was interested in doing some high altitude acclimatization
experiments and climbing some peaks, told Dienhart he wanted to "search
out the Abominable Snowman and find out if he was a myth or monster. . . . John Dienhart seemed to find it rather fascinating. . . . It would
be very good internal public relations and they'd be making history and
not just recording it" (Hillary, 1975).

Field Enterprises liked the idea and contributed $125,000 or $200,000
(depending upon the source) to pull together the World Book 1960 Scientific

Expedition to the Himalayas. Hillary, who would later describe himself as "always . . . a little sceptical about the existence of the Yeti" led the expedition (Hillary, 1975; Haas, 1962).

The other major personality chosen for the expedition was the fifty-five-year-old television star and zoo director, Marlin Perkins. In fact, the first person to ask Perkins if he wanted to go with Hillary to investigate the abominable snowman was Don Meier, a television producer at NBC-Chicago and creator of *Zooparade*. In their 1959 interchange, Perkins recalled, he told Meier he knew "not really too much" about the yeti. *Zooparade* had just been cancelled during the summer of 1959, but Meier and Perkins quickly developed the concept for their next program, *Wild Kingdom*. The timing of the Hillary expedition seemed just right to keep Perkins in the public eye until *Wild Kingdom* premiered in 1962. Perkins, therefore, decided to get some exercise and agreed to go (Perkins, 1982; Meier, 1987).

The origins of the Hillary–*World Book* expedition are deeply interwoven with the media, public relations, and television production. What happened once this excursion to the Himalayas discovered it could not bag a yeti in three months is no surprise. For indeed they were ready, just as Slick was, to kill a yeti. Regular firearms were part of their equipment. As Perkins told a reporter before they left: "If we see the Snowman, we'll make every effort to capture it alive. We don't intend to harm it—but we can't predict what will happen until we know what we are looking for, and how big the animal is" (Earle, 1960). Perkins illustrated with that comment his continued lack of information about his quarry.

SLICK'S INVOLVEMENT

Slick took Field Enterprises at its word. He thought they would open-mindedly examine the yeti question, and he decided to share information with them. Early in the spring of 1960, Slick journeyed to Chicago to spend time with Marlin Perkins at the Lincoln Park Zoo. Slick handed over data to Perkins on the findings from his yeti expeditions. Perkins's chapter "In Quest of the Abominable Snowman" from his 1982 autobiography, *My Wild Kingdom*, does not mention his meeting with Slick. We know about their sessions only through a news report of the time, subtitled "Oilman Hands Snowman Data to Zoo Chief Here." Slick is quoted therein as saying: "I wish them the best of luck and will give them all possible cooperation" (Haas, 1960).

Hillary also talked with Slick at some point. In a letter to me in 1988,

Hillary wrote: "I met Tom Slick only on one occasion, I believe, and it was quite clear he was very much convinced of the existence of the Yeti. When I expressed my modest doubts, he was completely unaffected and was obviously very determined in his beliefs. . . . He seemed determined to carry on the search until a firm conclusion had been reached. If it hadn't been for his premature death then he might still be looking" (Hillary, 1988).

THE DEBUNKING BEGINS

Soon, the World Book 1960 Scientific Expedition to the Himalayas was on the march. Hillary, Perkins, and others left in late 1960 for Nepal to discover the truth behind the "abominable snowman." Many treatments of what they have said they did and discovered have been written (Hillary, 1962; Bishop, 1962; Hillary and Doig, 1962; Perkins, 1982; and more). As Hillary noted: "The search for the Yeti had been an interesting and entertaining part of our expedition but it was not our major undertaking"* (Hillary, 1975). A member of the reading public certainly would not have reached that conclusion at the time.

How and why the Hillary expedition virtually destroyed the belief in the yeti held by so many following the Slick-era searches is worthy of review. Ivan Sanderson's *Abominable Snowmen: Legend Come to Life* offers a good summary. Sanderson's three reasons for the expedition's failure:

> First, that the group had hardly gone, before it was back; second, it went right through the real habitat of ABSMs—namely, the montane forests; and third, it is stated to have consisted of a small army [600 men, in one report] that might well have scared even human beings into moving over into the next valley. Failing to obtain any truly concrete evidence that any ABSM exists, it was apparently decided that evidence of their nonexistence might be demonstrated by the old method of debunking one of its aspects (Sanderson, 1961a).

---

*One item that the American press accounts did not mention at all had a very Cold War flavor to it. Desmond Doig noted in an article in the *Sunday Times* of London, November 13, 1960, that two rocket experts were members of the expedition. Tom Nevison of the United States Air Force and Peter Mulgrew of the Royal New Zealand Navy were closely watching and gathering evidence of the Chinese firing rockets from Tibet. Doig, Nevison, and Mulgrew witnessed just such a launching when they were camped at Tolam Bau glacier (Doig, 1960).

Without the body of a yeti, what was this overpublicized expedition to do? What the Hillary group did was borrow the obviously fake Khumjung "yeti skullcap," known to be made in imitation of those at other village monasteries, and take it on tour throughout Europe and America. The overly photographed set shots of Hillary or someone else with the skullcap on his head created a media storm. And every story about the skullcap mentioned its escort Khumjung guardian Khumjo Chumbi, who the press accounts variously identified as a guide or an elder. Hillary took the relic around to zoologists, who fairly quickly figured out that it was not primate in origin. Then, as a rabbit out of a hat, Hillary and associates revealed an exact twin that had been made from the hide of the goatlike serow. Hillary wrote about this fake skullcap: "It certainly never held the cunning brain of the elusive Yeti" (Hillary and Doig, 1962).

DOIG'S SKINS

The *World Book* folks also bought, through journalist Desmond Doig, first one and then two other alleged yeti skins. Hillary and Perkins quickly showed these were bear skins and scored more media points proving that something else said to be from a yeti wasn't. Slick and his associates had determined late in the fifties that a skin owned by Doig was that of a Himalayan blue bear. As researcher Mark A. Hall has pointed out to me, a dispatch from Reuters for September 13, 1959, reported Doig's return from Bhutan with a blue bear skin that he said he had bought from a lama. Peter Byrne, in a letter of September 20, 1959, told Slick that "Desmond Doig has backed out of his original terms for the 'yeti skin', and he now wants Rs 4000.00 [about $528] for the skin outright and full publicity rights." Byrne, in the same letter, also noted: "I am more than ever convinced, although not absolutely sure, that the skin is that of a Blue Bear" (Byrne, 1959b). Furthermore, Ralph Izzard wrote Peter Byrne on November 23, 1959, that Doig had attempted to sell a blue bear skin to Slick for 300 pounds but that Slick had turned down the offer as not a fair market price (Izzard, 1959b).

What is the truth behind the tales of the blue bear skins? Doig wrote often about his alleged October 1960 hagglings to obtain one of these chuteh skins from an old nun at Beding for $45 during the *World Book* expedition (Hillary and Doig, 1962; Bishop, 1962). The *Chicago Daily News* wire service used the purchase to announce on November 2, 1960, that the expedition was going to be extended for a few weeks because of this "exciting discovery" (*Chicago Daily News*, 1960). Who was fooling whom?

Doig had a blue bear skin in 1959; did he really purchase one from "an old nun" in 1960? Were Hillary and Perkins hoodwinked or part of a scam? Later, two other blue bear skins were supposedly acquired on Hillary's expedition (Perkins, 1982). How many "rare" blue bear skins did Doig have? Doig knew the true origin of these so-called yeti skins, so we can conclude only that he was spinning a good story for his latest dispatch out of the Himalayas. All retellings of the *World Book* incidents omit Doig's knowledge that the chuteh skins would easily be proven to be blue bear skins. Here again, this event led to the further debunking of the yeti, although the claim that these were yeti skins had never really been made.

HILLARY'S BELITTLING OF A WITNESS

It may be a shocking revelation to members of the hero cult surrounding Sir Edmund Hillary that he was capable of fighting dirty in order to save face regarding his rather rigid disbelief in yetis. In supporting his position, he has had to explain away the reports of individual sightings, often by presenting the individuals themselves in an unflattering manner.

Take, for example, the case of the Sherpa Sen Tensing. Tensing had told Sir John Hunt, Hillary, and others in 1951 of his sighting of a yeti near Thyangboche. Hillary had to discredit this account in 1960. "He [Sen Tensing] had been attending the three-day Mani Rimdu ceremony at Thyangboche—a most important annual occasion and one that I knew by experience ended in a carnival atmosphere with much drinking of beer and spirits . . . [Description of the encounter is given with Tensing] quivering in fear. . . . Sen Tensing is a shrewd and capable man—I am sure that he saw something, but I doubt if he was in a suitable condition to judge precisely what it was" (Hillary, 1975). Hillary appears to be using the old reasoning that none of the Loch Ness Monster sightings have really occurred because, after all, everyone knows that all the lake residents drink Scottish whiskey. Hillary's jump in logic from beer at the Thyangboche festival to Sen Tensing's drunkenness is tenuous at best, insulting at worst.

PANGBOCHE HAND REVISITED

Then there's the matter of the Pangboche hand. Doig, Hillary, Perkins, and others have used this as a building block in their case against the yeti. But examine their words. Doig observed:

The Pangboche monastery also boasts a 'Yeti' hand, which more than one expert (examining photographs and a flake of skin) has declared to be human or part human. The hand is skeletal; heavy, markedly squared phalanges are wired together and the palm partly covered with brown, leathery skin. It is possible that some of the bones are not human, but almost certainly the best part of the hand is. It is a large but slender human hand, a woman's perhaps, but more possibly a young lama's (Hillary and Doig, 1962).

Hillary stated: "This is essentially a human hand, strung together with wire, with the possible inclusion of several animal bones" (Hillary and Doig, 1962). And, of course, from Perkins, we get something simple: "This turned out to be human" (Perkins, 1982).

Now the whole problem with the Hillary party's examination of the Pangboche hand is that, as noted in the last chapter, the hand was changed and incomplete. Byrne had taken off the thumb, a phalanx, and skin from two locations. He had replaced what he took with human bones. Hillary, Perkins, Doig, and their medical staff unknowingly made judgments on something that was, indeed, part "human" and part "animal" (read "non-human" here, as humans, of course, are animals). The "best parts," such as the index finger and the thumb, of the hand would of course look human; they were human. It would look somewhat faked being "strung together with wire," for indeed it was. These very portions were the human bones wired to the original by Byrne. The Slick-Johnson Expedition was responsible for adding the "human" part; was the portion labeled "animal" by the *World Book* expedition sections of a yeti's hand?

Hillary was able to debunk the whole Pangboche hand based on what can be seen today only as a mistake in judgment on the part of the Slick-Johnson effort. As far as is known, members of the *World Book* expedition never realized they were examining a badly altered hand.

OTHER HILLARY CONCLUSIONS

The *World Book* expedition, with its regular dispatches in the *Chicago Daily News*, sent the serious study of the yeti back into the Dark Ages, into the pre-Slick years of an unenlightened public and an overly critical scientific community. Besides the findings on the skullcap and the Pangboche hand, the group ticked off their other conclusions one by one:

1. They believed alleged yeti tracks were made by the sun melting the footprints of a fox in the snow. They ignored all mud tracks discovered

right after yeti sightings. They never dealt with the reasons some yeti footprints showed distinctive primate toe marks. They could not name what fox inhabits the upper montane levels.

2. They said that all the skins described as coming from chutehs were from blue bears. (Slick had strongly suspected the chutey or chuteh was a bear back in 1957.)

3. The small tehlma sounded very much like a rhesus monkey, their expedition reported, completely neglecting descriptions from witnesses.

4. They said that they could not fully explain the noise of the yeti that "many Sherpa claim to have heard." Interestingly, in the one area that his expedition could not fully come forth with a debunking explanation, Hillary seemed personally to believe in what his fellow mountaineers and Sherpa friends had heard. Had Hillary also heard the whistle of the yeti? (Hillary and Doig, 1962).

(As recently as 1989, on the BBC/PBS program, *Search for the Yeti*, Hillary was still repeating some of the same old tired, unsupportable arguments for why yetis do not exist. Often his remarks reflected the notion that the Sherpas are somewhat foolish for believing there's something real behind it all.)

Media Blitz

When the expedition returned, the damage had been done. Or should I say it had only begun? The *World Book's* claim that the yeti belonged in the field of mythology buried Slick's mostly unpublished work under a pile of press releases. Through a *Life* article, news items in numerous papers, changes in the encyclopedia's public presentations and its entries on the "abominable snowman," along with expedition members' books, this one short project had a lasting and devastating effect on the field. Early in 1960, the *World Book* sent out a two-page supplement on the "abominable snowman" to new customers. The text was extremely open-minded, with quotes from Izzard, Stonor, and others. I got one myself. Two years later, the encyclopedia's annual yearbook and then its later editions discussed the mythical nature of the yeti. The turnaround was complete.

National Geographic and most national newsmagazines published skeptical articles on the "abominable snowman." The premiere of *Wild Kingdom* used film from the *World Book* expedition to "explode myths and superstitions" about the yeti and other unknown animals. A subsequent installment of *Wild Kingdom* featured an entire show devoted to debunking the yeti. Even school-age children could pick up their *Weekly Reader* and find articles like "His Tracks Are There—Yeti Can't Be Found." Perkins, Hillary, and Hillary's wife toured the country presenting a slide show, "In Search of the Abominable Snowman." Waves and waves of appearances, articles, television shows, books, and radio programs drove home the message that yetis did not exist, no matter how flimsy the negative evidence.

Reopen the Study of Yeti

The study of yeti has never fully recovered from this blow and regained the status it had during the Slick era. Slick's yeti evidence has largely been ignored and left neglected. The curious yeti hand has never been fully examined with new technologies. Except for the 1972 Cronin-McNeely search, yeti expeditions since Hillary's day have continued to look in the wrong places. The possibilities of other relics in Tibetan locations have not been pursued. The bright beginnings of the Slick-Johnson Snowman Expeditions should be rekindled once again, especially in light of the glaring holes in the Hillary expedition's case against the yeti. Tom Slick's quest should be renewed.

CHAPTER 9

THE PACIFIC NORTHWEST
EXPEDITION

TOM SLICK WAS ALWAYS ON THE MOVE. HE OR
Jeri Walsh periodically kept members of his yeti expeditions informed of
his whereabouts. Alaska one week, Venezula another. Slick's money and
his way with people opened doors and cut through red tape. A quick trip
to Paris to see Heuvelmans, an easily arranged stopover in Moscow to visit
the Soviet Snowman Commission, a talk in India with Nehru about yeti.
Slick's multipurpose trips were often romantic, frequently exciting. In
1956, for example, he found himself hunting for diamonds in the jungles
of British Guiana. He was flying to a remote river location when the plane
developed problems and had to make an emergency landing. For two weeks
he spent time among the helpful Waiwai tribespeople, who shared their
parrot meat with him. Eventually, he got back to civilization and speculated
that diamond smugglers had put sugar in his gas tank (Lubar, 1960).

But after his near fatal accident in Nepal, the resulting painful knee
infection, and his desire to keep his mother's blood pressure in the normal
range, Slick started to pick his journeys carefully. Still he was frustrated
and wanted to continue his personal involvement in the yeti hunts. Events
in 1958 brought his quest within range once again.

CREW'S ENCOUNTER: THE STIMULUS

It all really began on August 27, 1958. Jerry Crew was one of a group of
men bulldozing a road through an unexplored section of forest on the
Native American reservation of the Hoopa, near the Bluff Creek in California. That morning he was returning to his earth-moving equipment,
which he had left overnight at the worksite. He found that something had
visited the area during the night, leaving footprints showing on a hill,
down a road, and across a creek. They were no ordinary tracks. Although

they looked human, they measured some sixteen inches in length, seven in width. Crew and the men continued to work, finding occasional footprints into September. Finally, Crew asked a taxidermist friend, Bob Titmus, about how to work some plaster of paris on tracks, and he decided to make a cast. On October 1, 1958, Jerry Crew found a quarter-mile-length of giant prints and made a cast of one. A member of the road crew had dubbed the creature "Bigfoot," and when Jerry showed the cast to Andrew Genzoli at the local *Humboldt Times* in Eureka, the name stuck.

Genzoli's "RFD" column published an item about the reports of something big-footed in the area. As Genzoli recalled in 1961: "The column brought in Jerry Crew of Salyer, who had with him a plaster cast proof of the tracks. Rather hesitatingly, the story [complete with a photograph of Jerry Crew holding the cast] was placed on the Associated Press wires. This was like loosening a single stone in an avalanche, letting go a torrent of earth and snow. Editors from many parts of the United States demanded more, more, more about Bigfoot" (Genzoli, 1961).

Reports of giant hairy creatures were not new in the Pacific Northwest. Canadians had been following them in the British Columbia area for a few years and had a special name for them: Sasquatch. The October 6, 1958, Associated Press dispatch noted that in 1956 there had been reports of full fifty-gallon drums of gasoline being thrown around at a logging camp. Sightings went back for years, but had been treated very locally. The Bluff Creek incident, however, brought Bigfoot into the consciousness of Americans in a way that none of the older reports had. Maybe the name did it. Maybe the time was right. Whatever it was, the story caught on. Canadian newspapers, for example, which had quietly published items on the Sasquatch for years, shouted on October 6: "New 'Sasquatch' found—it's called Bigfoot" (Green, 1980).

When Slick began hearing the first reports of Bigfoot he decided to try and trap one. Slick's yeti consultants quickly informed him as to the potential for finding an "abominable woodsperson," as Ivan Sanderson liked to call them, in California. The possible genetic relationship between the yeti and the Bigfoot excited Slick. He had based his initial interest in the Himalayan search on thoughts that yetis were a possible "missing link." In a similar vein, he felt that the anthropological and genetic importance of Bigfoot could not be ignored. Slick told a California news reporter early during the American search that he thought there was "considerable possibility the creature reported in the Humboldt-Del Norte wilderness [near Bluff Creek] could be closely related to that searched for in the Himalayas" (*Humboldt Times*, 1960a). In Slick's opinion, "if the creature is what it appears to be, its capture could be one of the most important scientific events of all time" (*Humboldt Times*, 1960a).

Slick's Footprint Cast

A newspaperman out of Harrison Hot Springs, British Columbia, John Green, and his associate, Rene Dahinden, had investigated old Sasquatch reports for some time. Bluff Creek gave them a chance to investigate one that had just happened. Dahinden, who was having visa trouble, could not make the first trip, but Green hopped in his car and went to California. Along the way he interviewed Jerry Crew and stopped to see Bob Titmus. At Bluff Creek, Green saw some of the old tracks from the October incident.

On November 2, 1958, Bob Titmus, along with his friend Ed Patrick, found some perfect prints on a Bluff Creek sandbar and called Green, who arrived on the scene two weeks later. This Bigfoot was a different one from the Crew Bigfoot; it left fifteen-inch-long tracks with more uniform toes and a strange double bump in place of the normal ball of the foot.

Throughout the end of 1958 and most of 1959, Bluff Creek's Bigfoot population left more prints. Titmus now knew what to look for and was able to find them on other sandbars in the area. On November 1, 1959, Titmus found more of the fifteen-inch footprints, plus knuckle marks, on a Bluff Creek sandbar, and later showed them to Green and Dahinden. More importantly for our story, these are the prints that brought Tom Slick into the search. I am very certain of this because I now have the cast of this print that was in Slick's possession for years. This is one of the casts Slick showed to friends and enemies when challenged about his interest in Bigfoot. This probably is the cast Slick was holding and showing to his friend Sir Victor Sassoon when *Fortune* photographed them in 1960. Southwest Research Institute had the cast until 1988 when Chief Architect Norman I. Turner gave it to me.

On the back of the cast is this note:

These tracks were made on Bluff Creek, Del Norte County, California, during the night of Nov. 1, 1959. I made these casts on November 5, 1959, after several days of hard rain had fallen on the tracks.

Consequently these are very poor casts with a great deal less detail showing than the 1958 casts of the same individual's tracks.

This is the 15 inch track—Not to be confused with the 16″ track.

> Bob Titmus
> Anderson, Calif.

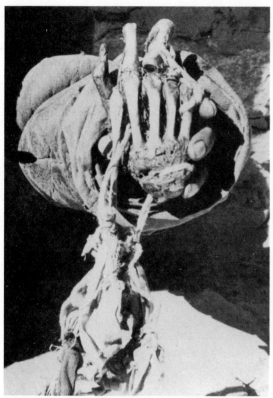

Top: The Pangboche hand, 1958. The first photograph of the hand by Peter Byrne of the Slick-Johnson Snowman Expedition, before sections had been removed.
Photograph by Peter Byrne

Bottom Left: Pangboche hand, 1958. The hand is shown intact, with a watch for size. Wrappings visible in Photo #1 have been discarded, and are in the background.
Photograph by Peter Byrne

Bottom Right: Pangboche hand, late 1959. Unknowingly, Professor Teizo Ogawa of Tokyo University examined and photographed the hand after Peter Byrne had removed and replaced the thumb and phalanx of this alleged yeti hand with those of a human. The *World Book*/Hillary Expedition of 1960–1961, therefore, based their analysis of the Pangboche hand on this mutilated post-1959 object.
Photograph by Teizo Ogawa

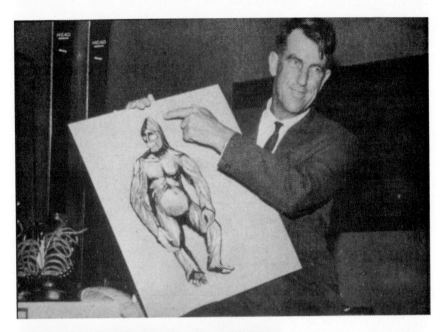

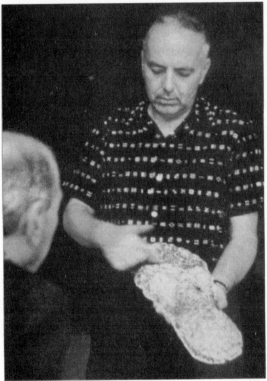

Top: Sir Edmund Hillary, before the *World Book* expedition departed in 1960, during a press conference with a drawing of the yeti based on eyewitness accounts. The sketch was adapted from one in Heuvelmans' *On the Track of Unknown Animals*.

Photograph from the Coleman Archives

Bottom: Tom Slick in 1960 showing his friend Sir Victor Sassoon his footprint cast of the California Bigfoot.

Photograph by Roy Stevens for *Fortune*

Loren Coleman holds the November 1959 Bigfoot cast, formerly in Tom Slick's collection and, until given to Coleman, in the possession of Norman Turner, Chief Architect of the Southwest Research Institute. Photograph by David Parnes

The 1957 film, *Abominable Snowman of the Himalayas*, may have been loosely based on Tom Slick's search for the yeti. The main American character, played by Forrest Tucker (center), is named Tom Friend, and appears to be a cinematic version of Tom Slick. From the Coleman Archives

BIRTH OF THE PACIFIC NORTHWEST EXPEDITION

November 1959 was the month Slick got involved in the California quest. The Titmus tracks of November 1 to 5 mesh nicely with George Agogino's November 4, 1959, letter regarding his conversations with Slick about pursuing the California "yeti."

Agogino was a friend of Ivan Sanderson. Sanderson was in California during August 1959 doing research for a major Random House book on the natural history of North America (*The Continent We Live On*, 1961b). He used this West Coast opportunity to collect data on Bigfoot for a later article in *True* and for his forthcoming abominable snowmen book. Sanderson traveled to San Antonio during this same tour and he had also been in touch with Green about the Sasquatch. All of the players in the American Sasquatch/Bigfoot drama were assembling in California.

John Green and Rene Dahinden went to California to look at Bob Titmus's November 1 prints. Green wrote in his excellent 1978 book, *Sasquatch: The Apes Among Us*: "On that trip, in some manner the details of which I no longer recall, negotiations started involving Bob, Ivan, Rene, myself and Tom Slick, a San Antonio millionaire. . . . We made another trip to California to meet with Tom a couple of weeks later, and the 'The Pacific Northwest Expedition' was organized" (Green, 1978).

Tom Slick liked to be in charge, and he saw this American expedition as an opportunity to get involved in a firsthand way and be active in field operations again. Correspondence and photographs of the time tell us that Slick took his children to the campsites, and Kirk Johnson, Jr., showed up also.

MEMBERSHIP AND MADNESS

The record of the Pacific Northwest Expedition is anything but clear. Three people who were there—Green, Dahinden, and Byrne—have written about it. This triad has been able to say more nasty things about the episode than about any other Bigfoot event, perhaps because so many strong-willed individuals were in the act. After all, it takes a special kind of person to look for unknown animals and deal with the ridicule of the public, family, or friends. New conflicts seemed to arise with each new month of the expedition.

Slick may have added to this problem, or may have been trying to solve it, by placing several teams of men in the countryside at the same time, all reporting to him. Or maybe he was just trying to catch a Bigfoot. Green reported that three search parties were active in 1959 and 1960. Bob Titmus, the field leader for the first few months of the expedition, found several sets of tracks, some hair, and fecal matter.

Because of the hostile nature of the personal accounts, only some news accounts of the time, supplied by, among others, Warren Thompson and Jim McClarin, help to reconstruct the group's membership. As Dahinden reported it, some of the members were members in name only. All were to live in the bush and search for Bigfoot. Dahinden wrote that there were some who never as much as slept out overnight (Hunter and Dahinden, 1973). Others just abused Slick's trusting nature.

A case in point was John La Pe. On December 10, 1959, the *Humboldt Times* of Eureka, California, reported that a hunt headed by John La Pe and George Gatto of Eureka and ten other heavily armed men was under way. Charles Burgens, helicopter pilot, and Bob Titmus, were to join them. Not until the next day did the *Sacramento Bee* leak the news that Slick had flown into one of the search parties' camps by helicopter during the previous week, and that he was behind La Pe's hunt for Bigfoot (*Humboldt Times*, 1959a; *Sacramento Bee*, 1959).

Slick had trouble with La Pe and Gatto early on when they refused to produce proper receipts and refused to follow orders from Slick and Titmus. Slick thought La Pe was taking him for a ride and sent him a telegram firing him and telling him that he had a "legal commitment to release no news material" (*Humboldt Times*, 1959b). La Pe walked over to the *Humboldt Times* and spilled his guts. He was disgusted with Titmus, he told the paper, and could not understand why Titmus was starting a search for a "nine-foot salamander" as well as Bigfoot. The same paper that carried La Pe's sad story in its December 16, 1959, issue carried a small item in the March 25, 1960, issue, which also told much about what Slick had discovered. "Erstwhile Bigfoot hunter John Albert La Pe, forty-three, is in custody at the county jail on a bad check charge," the tidbit read (*Humboldt Times*, 1960b).

The expedition's cast of characters also included Ray Wallace and Ivan Marx, both of whom may have gotten into the hunt on the serious side of things, but from all accounts traveled down a dark path of greed and deception before their involvement was over.

Several diverse factions were breaking out in the Pacific Northwest Expedition. Slick had pulled out of Nepal altogether and along with both Kirk Johnsons was now pouring money into the Bigfoot hunt in the United States. Bringing the Slick-Johnson personnel from the Himalayas only created more administrative problems for some of the original American-Canadian team members. Something had to give. Dismayed by what was happening and seeing a slowdown in California reports in the early 1960s,

Titmus, Green, and Dahinden took their investigative efforts back across the border to Canada. They concentrated on the Sasquatch phenomenon and left the California expedition to the others.

THE BYRNES

The quests in Nepal for yeti were winding down. Peter and Bryan Byrne were living in a cave in the upper Chhoyang river valley. It was late in 1959 and they were reportedly tired, ragged, and rather bored with the yak's milk and yak's milk cheese they were living on. Then one night while sitting around the warm fire in their cold cave:

> A Sherpa runner arrived from Dharan, the British Army Gurkha Recruiting Depot in southern Nepal, 140 miles away. The runner, who had completed the trip in four days, came pounding in out of the dripping gloom of the Himalayan night and handed us a rather crumpled letter from Tom Slick.
>
> The letter contained instructions for us to terminate the three-year hunt for the Snowmen and come out. We were to proceed to Kathmandu, the capital of Nepal, where we would find further instructions awaiting us. In the time that it took us to march down, the letter continued, we were to give consideration to coming to the United States to take over a new expedition that would search for something called the Bigfoot, a giant primate not unlike the Yeti. It, or they, apparently lived in the Pacific Northwest of the United States and their habitat was the thickly wooded coastal ranges of the northern states of Oregon and Washington.
>
> Tom's letter was persuasive, and Bryan and I agreed to give the expedition a try. It took us one day to pack, pay off our local Sherpas, and begin the trek down to Kathmandu.
>
> Three weeks after leaving Kathmandu I found myself installed in a tiny motel in a little town called Willow Creek, in Humboldt County, in northern California (Byrne, 1975).

The Byrnes did their best to organize their part of the North American expedition, but such items as money, equipment, and men had been lost, according to Peter Byrne's version of the story. Various associates of the expedition, some good ones, some bad, had left for various reasons. Slick turned over the expedition to Peter Byrne who felt he did the only kind of job he could do, considering everything.

The Byrnes, along with their associate Steve Matthes, never saw a Bigfoot, but in one year alone, 1960, they stated that they found twelve sets of footprints (Byrne, 1975). Peter Byrne continued the Pacific Northwest Expedition through 1962. (After Slick's death, Byrne would not return to the Bigfoot hunt again until 1971, leaving the search entirely in 1979.)

British Columbia Expedition

Meanwhile, in 1961, Tom Slick decided to sponsor men in British Columbia as well as in California. He called it the "British Columbia Expedition," but it seemed to be merely an extension of the Pacific Northwest Expedition.

In July 1961, Titmus, Geoff d'Easum, and Green were on the northern coast of British Columbia for Slick. They came across a set of large tracks on the beach of an island located in a bay off British Columbia. They were bigger than Green's size eleven shoe, but the expedition members were not sure if they were from a barefoot human or Sasquatch.

Later, in October, when Titmus found a fresh series of thirteen-and-a-half-inch prints with a four-foot stride on a little island near the large island of the earlier find, he was convinced they belonged to something unknown. Titmus had been caught in a storm on the way over to the island and was trying to get his boat anchored and settled. In a report to Slick, Titmus wrote:

> I climbed atop the [boat's] cabin for a look at the water and weather outside past the bar. It seemed to be quieting down just a little. It was while I was standing up here that I scanned the sandy beach on the island to the right and saw this string of large tracks with a long stride. I felt certain that these were what we'd been looking for and an inspection with the binoculars confirmed it.
>
> Although I was little more than a hundred feet off the island there seemed no way to get ashore without swimming; eventually I screwed up my courage, stripped off and did just that. The tracks came out of the water angling toward the timber and the undergrowth; paralleled the growth line for about 125 feet and then entered it. . . . Some of the impressions were quite deep although the creature was only walking (Green, 1973).

The British Columbia Expedition never consisted of more than—as Green somewhat critically put it later—a leader, deputy leader, co-deputy leader, and a cook. However, this small party very much reflected Slick's way of supporting an effort by fielding a mini-expedition, instead of a massive one. Furthermore, Slick assisted the hunt with two 30.06 guns (one a Browning semiautomatic), by sending Titmus to the University of Washington Hospital to study embalming techniques, and through the transporting of embalming fluids to his people off the coast of British Columbia (McClarin, 1975). Slick was serious about the quest.

THE END OF THE ULTIMATE HUNT

I have known for almost three decades John Green, Peter Byrne, Rene Dahinden, and other figures who were involved in the Pacific Northwest Expedition. I have talked briefly to Bob Titmus and touched base with a few other important players on the telephone. I have spent many months interviewing scores of people who knew Slick and both Kirk Johnsons. Some of these men have become very emotional when telling me about the impact Slick had on their lives. Although today the majority of the Bigfoot/Sasquatch searchers belongs to one camp or another, Slick gave them a mission, way back then, and they won't forget him for that. One of the Pacific Northwest Expedition members described Slick as "a man of vision, a gentle man, sensitive to the feelings and needs of others." Yet another told me that he "loved Slick and if he were alive today, I would do anything for him." Others said things as revealing.

Some have said that Slick was taken advantage of for his lack of street smarts or because he had money. This may be true, but Slick was a rather shrewd guy. I wonder if he didn't take advantage of the sense of adventure he found in the men and women with whom he associated. He harnassed their fire, at least briefly.

Upon Slick's death, paranoia, distrust, and rivalry reigned among the current and former expedition members and associates. Slick's efforts on North American soil were never fully chronicled, analyzed, or understood in their context. Slick appears to have been learning and growing with cryptozoology. The California effort was in its infancy, just beginning to walk, and a look at the psychological makeup and reactions of its membership as well as the latest hot report would have been a logical exercise. However, some lessons were lost. Field disorganization and craziness seemed to be the main products of the Pacific Northwest Expedition. Yet no one ever examined what occurred during and after the actual field operations. Slick's death happened too suddenly and the work simply collapsed. Byrne wrote: "Our efforts were terminated by the death of Tom Slick" (Byrne, 1975).

Dahinden observed:

> The Pacific Northwest Expedition ended abruptly in 1962. . . . All of Slick's records concerning the Sasquatch had been sent to his research institute in San Antonio. This material has never been traced and it has been speculated that Slick's family and/or associates, embarrassed by his participation in the hunt, were quick to get rid of anything smelling of involvement (Hunter and Dahinden, 1973).

Green added

> Many sets of tracks were found as well as some hair and fecal matter that could never be positively identified, but everything that was collected, including pictures, had to be sent to Tom's Southwest Research Institute at San Antonio. Later he was killed when his private plane blew up in the air, and this material can no longer be traced. Presumably Tom's associates, who were not in sympathy with his researches of this sort, lost no time in disposing of it (Green, 1980).

George Agogino has in the past confirmed some of these statements. He was the American coordinator of the various materials obtained for analysis, and had most of the "missing materials" obtained during the expeditions in California at the time of Slick's death, he has said privately. He then "sent them back to the Slick foundation and to where they went at that point, I do not know." Almost ten years after the fact, Agogino recalled that he did analyze some stool samples "with parasites we could not identify. Outside of that there was a whole series of obvious dishonesties involved." Agogino told about moose hair and moose droppings (even though there are no moose in California) that were presented as Bigfoot specimens. "One thing that did disturb me was the fact that many of our cameras set up on the trail were tripped and the film removed from the camera. Now I could see a possibility of a Bigfoot tripping a camera, but I can't see the afterthought of the Bigfoot removing the film from the camera. Obviously what was happening at that time was clandestine enough that the individual who was caught 'in the act' took the liberty of removing the film from the camera. This happened on more than one occurrence when we were supposed to be hot on a Bigfoot trail" (Agogino, 1971).

Slick had always been secretive about what evidence he was finding for Bigfoot. In a 1960 report on his role in the Hillary–*World Book* hunt for yeti, Slick was asked about his search in the Pacific Northwest for "Snowman-type creatures." The *Chicago Daily News* writer noted that Slick "declined to discuss results of that search so far" (Haas, 1960).

Yet I was able to pull together scores of photos and reams of material I never thought I would be able to find. Perhaps there's a series of reports detailing the chaos of the American search for Bigfoot. We could learn from that also, improve our techniques for field study, get a good manager on the job, and maybe catch a hairy hominid. Slick was trying. But then suddenly Slick was gone from the scene and the hunt ended.

CHAPTER 10

RHINOS AND ORANG PENDEK
The Sumatra Expedition

FEW PEOPLE KNEW AT THE TIME, OR EVEN REALIZE today, that Tom Slick and F. Kirk Johnson, Sr. backed a separate crypto-zoological effort in the late fifties to discover more about another Asian hairy humanoid, or anthropoid.

To find out more about this expedition, I had to dig deeply, and read between the lines. Indeed, very few printed references to this search exist. In 1962, a Texas newspaper mentioned it in passing. The report noted that "in 1959, they [Tom Slick and F. Kirk Johnson, Sr.] sponsored an expedition in Sumatra in search of a similar creature, called in the Malayan language the 'orang pendek,' or 'little man' " (*San Antonio Express*, 1962a).

HEUVELMANS AGAIN

The timing of Slick's yeti searches was more than coincidental, and, as it turns out, this Sumatran expedition figured into that temporal picture. Both ventures had much to do with Bernard Heuvelmans's book, *On the Track of Unknown Animals*. When I discussed the matter of Slick's interests with Heuvelmans, he specifically noted that his book "was even instrumental in the particular case of the Orang Pendek. If I remember well it was my late friend Peter Ryhiner, whom he [Slick] commissioned to investigate the case in Sumatra, while the latter [Ryhiner] was trying to capture specimens of the small hairy rhinoceros (*Didermocerus sumatrensis*) on this island" (Heuvelmans, 1987).

Who was Peter Ryhiner? An animal collector almost since his January 1, 1920, birth in that great animal trading capital, Basel, Switzerland. And he also was a friend of the other noteworthy cryptozoologist of the

1950s and 1960s, Ivan Sanderson (Hall, 1987). Interestingly, Ryhiner had coauthored a book that Slick may have seen when it came out in 1958, *The Wildest Game*, written with Daniel P. Mannix. But more about Ryhiner in a moment; let's first turn to orang pendek.

ORANG PENDEK

Chapter Five of Heuvelmans's *On the Track of Unknown Animals* was entitled, "Orang Pendek, the Ape-Man of Sumatra." The simple, straightforward chapter gathered all that the cryptozoologist could find on the little hairy men. His overall description of the animal was based on the locals' observations and European sightings, the latter having begun at the start of the nineteenth century but becoming rather concentrated since 1916.

> The orang pendek, according to reports, is a very shy biped which speaks an unintelligible language. It is between 2 feet 6 inches and 5 feet. Its skin is pinkish-brown and, according to most versions, covered all over with short dark brown to black hair. It has a head of jet-black hair forming a bushy mane down its back. It has no visible tail. Its arms are not as long as an anthropoid ape's. It hardly ever climbs in trees, but walks on the ground. . . . It eats young shoots, fruits, fresh-water molluscs, snakes and worms, which it finds by turning over stones and even, with herculean strength, the trunks of fallen trees. It is very partial to durian fruit. And sometimes it raids banana or sugar-cane plantations, or the natives' gardens. This man-faced beast is known all over southern Sumatra below the equator (Heuvelmans, 1958).

Heuvelmans carefully chronicled the sighting and footprint evidence for the orang pendek. For example, he detailed Dr. Edward Jacobson's 1917 recording of a native encounter with one of the animals in the forest at the base of Boekit Kaba, followed by the doctor's discovery of a broad and short humanlike footprint near Mount Kerintji. Examining all of the evidence at the time, the physician concluded that an unknown anthropoid existed on Sumatra.

Heuvelmans noted many other reports from European plantation managers, surveyors, and new residents of Sumatra. *On the Track of Unknown Animals* brought into the English-speaking consciousness a wealth of material from the records of Dutch settlers. And Tom Slick was one of the book's most avid readers.

Slick, perhaps through his oil contacts (Sumatra was an important oil-producing site) or his cryptozoological friends, soon learned that the way to get to the orang pendek was very much tied to the search for Sumatran rhinos and to the colorful characters of Peter Ryhiner and Harry Gillmore.

RHINOS AND GILLMORE

The pieces of the Sumatran adventure, of course, are difficult to reconstruct after all of these years, but the fact that the record regarding the search for the rhinos is relatively clear helps. Harry K. Gillmore is a central figure connecting the Sumatran rhinoceros drama with that of the orang pendek. Gillmore, born in 1917, came to Sumatra to work for Standard Vacuum Oil Company. He is long dead, having been crushed by a buffalo in Liberia almost thirty years ago.

My task was to search for someone who might have known Gillmore in Sumatra. After tracking the various links between the former Standard Vacuum Oil Company and its current entities down through a series of blind alleys and well-lighted paths, I found that a Mr. Otto R. Irrgang in Washington State had much to tell me about Gillmore.

I first met Harry in Manila, P.I., in 1946 when he was working for the Manila Engineer District of the U.S. Army, and I was working for an architect-engineering firm from San Francisco. We were enlarging an airfield in Manila and building Clark Air Force Base to the north.

Shortly after my family and I arrived in Sumatra in 1957, we were invited to a 'Plop' party at Buatan by a Dutch contractor, and traveled down the Siak river with a group of people on a small riverboat. When we arrived at Buatan I looked up at the dock and there was Harry, who called me by name and asked how I happened to be there. Since we were old friends, we soon became quite close, and Harry used to send a speedboat up the river to Pakanbaru on Fridays, and we would travel downriver to Buatan and return Sunday evening. This would happen every other weekend for some time. Several times Harry would visit us in our camp at Rumbai, near Pakanbaru. We tried to make life a little better for him; Nina, my wife, for example, made at least three sport shirts for Harry. He was constantly acting as a doctor for the local people, and spent a great deal of money to buy penicillin on the black market to treat many of the jungle people for yaws.

He was a kindly and too-generous person who spent most of his pay helping the local people and paying for traps, a tree house, etc., in his pursuit of animals. Harry did not have a gun, and to my knowledge, never killed an animal. Jungle people brought him two clouded leopards who were two weeks old, for example. He had many other animals as pets. Every one of them had a name (Irrgang, 1988).

One of Gillmore's pets was a baby Sumatran rhino named Dimples. The animal was first sighted from a tree house that the Irrgangs and Gillmore had built.

My son and I saw Dimples and a male rhino twice her size. Just before dark the two animals came crashing through the jungle to visit the muddy area around the saltwater well. (The location of the saltwater well, the tree house, and our sightings of these and other animals is approximately twenty kilometers off of the road and pipeline from Liric field. Buatan is on the right bank of the Siak river just downstream from the entrance of the Mandau River.) We could hear the sucking sound of their feet in the mud even after it became dark. Harry (who was away on a supply run) said I must have seen a pair of large tapirs. At the first sign of daylight next morning Harry was down the ladder and over to the well, where he soon was shouting with glee that indeed there had been two rhinos there. As soon as possible he had a corral of heavy posts built around the well with a trap gate. He baited this with durian, a thorny, odoriferous, and very delicious fruit much loved by all animals. That is how Dimples was captured (Irrgang, 1988).

Enter Ryhiner

Since Gillmore kept many animals of his own, he was the person animal traders naturally contacted if they were looking for rare animals of Sumatra. And it was to Gillmore that Peter Ryhiner turned during the great rush of the late 1950s to capture the island's rhinos. According to a 1964 story published in the *Saturday Evening Post*, Ryhiner decided some time after the summer of 1958 to capture a male and a female pair of Sumatran rhinos for a European zoo. Soon Ryhiner had dispatched a telegram to Gillmore asking for his help. About Gillmore, the article notes, Ryhiner "had heard improbable but nevertheless intriguing rumors. It was said in the bazaars of Bangkok that Gillmore lived at the end of the pipeline on the Siak River, in a remote station on the edge of the impenetrable forest and that there, among Indonesians who thought him a god, he kept a hairy dwarf rhino for a pet" (Lapham, 1964). This pet, of course, was Dimples.

Hearing that there were rhinos to be had, Ryhiner quickly talked the Basel Zoo into a contract and received $40,000 in advance. After some silence, Gillmore did contact Ryhiner, who made his way to Sumatra. Finally, "on the boat landing at Buatan, Harry Gillmore stood under a banyan tree, a tall and sorrowful man wearing faded khaki pants. He was then superintendent for the terminal of the pipeline that ran 100 miles inland to the Standard Vacuum oil fields at Liric. The natives called him

'*Tuan Besar*' or 'The Big Man,' " recounted Ryhiner to the reporter Lewis Lapham. "We shook hands. For me," Rhyiner said, "it was like Stanley meeting Doctor Livingstone" (Lapham, 1964).

Taken right away to the rhino, Ryhiner described it as the most fantastic thrill of his life. There was Dimples, a full-grown *sumatrensis*, affectionately named by Gillmore for a girl he had once known in Murphysboro, Illinois. Ryhiner said he sat gazing at Dimples for two or three hours. After being shown around Gillmore's place and assured the other male rhino was in an enclosure some meters away, Ryhiner rushed off to try to obtain the correct papers of transport.

Ryhiner finally did receive the right permits, but his troubles had just begun. First he had to build an enclosure for the Indonesian government at Bogor for 100,000 rupiah (about $2250 at the time). They wished to capture other rhinos for themselves and wanted a proper cage for them. And then once back at Buatan, Ryhiner discovered that Gillmore had been falsely accused of smuggling animals on and off oil tankers and that his contract with Standard had expired. He had been forced to release the two rhinos.

Luckily, within a week, Dimples did what so many wild animals that have become pets do: she walked back into Gillmore's stockade. Ryhiner quickly renamed her Betina to try to avoid any association with Gillmore and quickly, according to his retelling of the story in the *Saturday Evening Post*, arranged her passage out of the country on a Standard Vacuum Oil motor launch. Ryhiner recalled very romantically that he sat beside Betina's cage all the way across the Strait of Malacca, sipping warm beer and listening to American jazz on the radio (Lapham, 1964).

But was the story as Ryhiner told it? Irrgang remembers it this way:

> The affair with Peter Ryhiner was a tragic one for Harry. We met P. R. at Buatan with another man, and later he visited us in Rumbai. We all knew that Dimples was a very valuable piece of merchandise, especially after Harry had tamed her to be a docile pet. Peter promised to split the profits from the sale of Dimples with Harry, and the latter believed him and spent some of his last money to pay for her shipment and handling. Harry paid more than $10,000 of his own money for the transport of Dimples from Indonesia to Switzerland, and Peter Ryhiner never reimbursed him for a penny of that expense, nor did he pay Harry anything from the sale of the animal.
>
> Harry visited us one last time in August, 1959 before leaving for Singapore to await his payment of at least part of the profits from Peter. After some weeks in Singapore and some unanswered cables to P. R. it was evident that P. R. never intended to pay Harry a penny. Harry was without sufficient funds to pay his airfare home to the States, and he asked us to help. We sent him a check for $200, and he was able to get home (Irrgang, 1988).

Meanwhile, Dimples/Betina did reach Europe. Taken from Sumatra on March 17, 1959, she lived only until September 8, 1961, at the Basel Zoo in Switzerland where she died of a severe worm infestation probably as a result of transport stress (Basel Zoo, 1988).

BACK FOR MORE

After Betina's delivery, Ryhiner went back to Sumatra with hopes of obtaining a male rhino. Instead, what he found upon arriving was a second expedition. This one was led by two Danes—Arne Dyhrberg (who during 1970 to 1978 was the director of the Copenhagen Zoo) and Hakon Skafte (who was a writer for the Danish weekly magazine sponsoring the expedition). Dyhrberg, then a consultant to Indonesian nature park services, was to capture a rhino for the enclosure built by Ryhiner at the Bogor Zoo, and Skafte was to get one for the Copenhagen Zoo. Knowing that they had the political connections and he did not, Ryhiner semi-signed on with their efforts. They used his men and his traps.

The story turns cutthroat. Ryhiner's visa expired, and he was away trying to renew it when word reached him that a male rhino had been caught. His chief animal trapper, Sabran, was left alone for three days and nights on top of the trap. Ryhiner said that Dyhrberg was wining and dining the Danish trade commissioner who had come to Sumatra, and that Skafte was off for a weekend in Pakanbaru. Ryhiner remarked to Lapham years later, "They were in it for the money and the glory and not for the sake of the rhino" (Lapham, 1964).

The male rhino escaped and Sabran got malaria. Some 600,000 rupiah later, Ryhiner returned, visa in hand, but the rhino was back in the bush. As Ryhiner gloomily commented: "That's the end of my story. I had the only male *sumatrensis* captured in the century and I lost it" (Lapham, 1964). That does seem to be the end of the line for Ryhiner's Sumatra rhino involvement. Peter Ryhiner died a few years ago, apparently of the long-term effects of alcoholism, never having realized his dream to capture a male *sumatrensis*.

The Danish/Indonesian expedition of Dyhrberg and Skafte did meet with some success, however. Besides the one Ryhiner-involved male, they captured nine females. Skafte, in an article published in two different natural history journals, notes that of three females caught with the male, one died and two went to Copenhagen and Bogor (Skafte, 1961, 1962). The other female captives were all released due to political pressures from the local government (Anderson, 1961). What is confusing is that the official records of these 1958–1959 "field operations" in the State of Riau, Sumatra, tend not to separate the Gillmore/Ryhiner rhino (Dimples/Betina) from the others.

Anyway, the female that went to Bogor died in 1962, and the most famous Sumatran rhino of all time, Subur, lived at the Copenhagen Zoo until her death in February 1972. She is now part of a naturalistic diorama at the Copenhagen Zoological Museum.

A Special Link?

When alive, Subur was an oft-photographed example of what was called in the 1950s a living fossil—an animal seemingly left over from a prehistoric time. And here we get very close to understanding the Sumatran rhino's special link to Tom Slick and orang pendek. Slick was after something he believed was left over from bygone days, and he felt the best way to find the orang pendek was to ask the advice of someone looking for other prehistoric animals. That the Sumatran rhino has been and is considered in this light is rather apparent from an overview of the literature. For example, in *Zoos of the World*: "A living form closely related to Merck's rhinoceros [an iceage animal] is the Sumatran rhino, now in danger of extinction. The specimen [shown in the book] is in the zoo at Copenhagen, Denmark" (Fisher, Simon, and Vincent, 1969). And again *Wildlife in Danger* comments that this genus of hairy forest rhinoceros, not the plains and tundra wooly rhino, is the one represented in the Lascaux cave paintings. The Sumatran rhinoceros, "the sole living survivor is indeed but a relic of a successful Pleistocene genus" (Fisher, 1967).

Slick decided that the best way to get more information on the orang pendek was through Peter Ryhiner. It is not clear how much financial support Slick supplied for the hunt. We do know that Rhyiner would have received some funds from the Basel Zoo for the rhino quest and would have been going into the right areas for Slick's purposes. We also are certain that Ryhiner's contacts via Harry Gillmore proved the most fruitful for the rhino portion of the operation and probably for the orang pendek segment too. The linkage of the sponsor (Slick), his naturalist consultants (Heuvelmans and Sanderson), and their animal collector contacts (Ryhiner and Gillmore) is reflected in the connection between the two Sumatran expeditions. And it is from Sanderson that we learn of at least one concrete find of the so-called Slick-Johnson Orang Pendek Expedition.

Footprints in the Mud

Sanderson, in *Abominable Snowmen: Legend Come to Life*, touches on Gillmore's involvement with orang pendek. In a passage discussing the creature's footprints, Sanderson writes: "In 1958 some plaster casts of prints were obtained about halfway between the Siak and Kampar Rivers by Harry Gilmore [sic]. These, however, are most undoubtedly those of the Malayan Sun-Bear" (Sanderson, 1961a). Unfortunately, I suspect that something is wrong with this conclusion.

Irrgang was there with Gillmore when the footprints were discovered, and I questioned him extensively about their find. Irrgang tells me that no plaster casts were made. After he described the tracks and commented on their humanlike appearance, I asked him if they were bear tracks. Irrgang gave me a negative answer during our telephone interview, but in a follow-up letter he emphatically set the record straight:

> I can assure you that making the distinct tracks of a four-footed animal (rather than that of a two-footed person), all bear tracks I saw in Sumatra show the marks of the long claws, especially the front feet, which are the outstanding characteristic of this animal's feet since one of them is capable of tearing a tree asunder to get at honey or grubs. It is pointless for me to try to sketch the footprints Harry and I saw of a strange human or humanoid near our tree house. I could coat the sole of one of my feet with ink and then make a print while lifting my heel and standing on the ball of the foot. However, you could do the same and then reduce it to one-half size and you would have a picture of the prints we saw. We followed these two-footed tracks for some yards in the jungle, but when the ground became covered with thick grass and weeds, we could no longer follow them. Believe me, Malayan bears have *very* long claws. No trouble recognizing their tracks (Irrgang, 1988).

Peter Ryhiner may have obtained casts of probable bear prints said to be from an orang pendek. Osman Hill, the London primatologist Slick had contacted during the yeti expeditions, got involved in the orang pendek business as well. In a letter dated February 9, 1959, to Peter Byrne, Hill wrote: "You will be interested to hear that Peter Ryhiner, who is in Sumatra, has just sent me casts of foot prints of what are supposed to be impressions left by an orang pendek. They are not Primate. He is apparently in touch with Tom Slick" (Hill, 1959e). In a February 26 confidential report to Slick, Hill summarized his sense of this foot cast: "Matches in every detail the impression of the Malay Bear. Unusual features: 1. large size. 2. abnormality in digital formula" (Hill, 1959d).

And that is all we know of the Slick search for the orang pendek, a cryptozoological side trip to Sumatra.

New Interest in Sumatra

The Sumatran rhino story has not been told since Slick's time. And now, after being endangered and ignored for years, a massive effort to capture five pairs of Sumatran rhinos for the North American captive breeding program is under way. Two females of this species arrived in the United States while I was writing this book. One, Mahatu, arrived at the Los Angles Zoo in November 1988 and moved to the Cincinnati Zoo in May 1989. The other female, Kumu, is doing well at the San Diego Zoo. I saw her there in the spring of 1989, and the attractive red-furred little rhino is certainly a treasure to behold. She is probably one of the rarest, yet most neglected, zoological garden specimens now in any zoo. Crowds stand in line to see a giant panda, but the Sumatran rhinos are perhaps ten times as scarce. According to the Survival Service Commission Red Data Book report on endangered species, only one hundred Sumatran rhinos may be left in the wild.

We can only hope that as these new animal collectors gather their breeding groups of Sumatran rhinos, they pay close attention to tales and traces of the orang pendek and other cryptozoological wonders. Indeed, more animals may remain to be discovered on Sumatra. When I interviewed Irrgang, he told me that he and his wife, on two occasions during their time there, saw a small bird like a hummingbird. Zoogeographically, he knows it could not be a hummingbird, but he does not know how else to describe it. The one-and-a-half-inch long bird flew twelve inches away from the Irrgangs' faces. The winged unknowns were yellowish, with dark brown bellies and little stripes. Well grounded in zoology and geology for his oil company work in Sumatra, Irrgang does not have any idea what they were but knows he saw something unidentified in zoological texts.

Stories such as Irrgang's, Gillmore's, and Ryhiner's give one a sense of the unexplored world in which Slick found himself, whether it was Sumatra, Nepal, or northern California of the late 1950s and early 1960s.

CHAPTER II

OTHER CRYPTOZOOLOGICAL
SIDE TRIPS

Tom Slick did not do things halfway. After
he began actively sponsoring inquiries into cryptozoological topics, he did
so with much vigor. In this chapter, we shall examine some of his other
treks in search of other unknown animals.

Giant Salamanders of the Trinity Alps

One segment of the Pacific Northwest Expedition's agenda dealt with the
pursuit of giant salamanders in the same mountains in which Bigfoot was
supposed to roam. Slick had specifically asked the men exploring the Trinity
Alps area for signs of Bigfoot to look for the salamanders, since he was
aware of the long history of sightings in that section of the wilderness.

It all started back in the 1920s. An attorney for the Keystone Mine on
the North Fork of the Trinity River, Frank L. Griffith of Weaverville,
California, was one of the first modern witnesses. He was hunting deer
near the head of the New River in the Trinity Alps. In a small lake in
the middle of a meadow there, Griffith said he spotted five salamanders
from five to nine feet long at the bottom of the lake. Although he caught
one on a hook, he could not pull it out (Rodgers, 1962).

Hearing the story of Griffith's giant salamanders in 1948 from Keystone's
mining engineer, John Hubbard, biologist Thomas L. Rodgers made two
trips on foot and two by air to try to locate the animals. He had speculated
out loud with Hubbard that they might be an isolated group of Pacific giant
salamanders, *Dicamptodon*, which never get to be much bigger than a foot
long. Or maybe they were a relic population of *Megalobatrachus*, the Asiatic
giant salamander, an animal measuring in the five-to-six-foot range (Myers,
1951). These inhabit swift moving mountain streams in Japan and China
similar to those found in the Trinity Alps.

Perhaps the giant salamanders of the Trinities *are* American examples of *Megalobatrachus*. The amphibian family that the Japanese and Chinese *Megalobatrachus* belong to is Cryptobrachidae. It has only one known North American member, *Cryptobranchus*, the Hellbender. The Hellbender is often described in words such as those used by Hobart M. Smith in his *A Guide to Field Identification: Amphibians of North America.* "Ugly—frighteningly large—but harmless—nocturnal salamanders found in streams and rivers, often under rocks" (Smith, 1978). It is the largest known American salamander, at some twenty-nine inches, but hardly the five and a half feet for the Asiatic giant salamanders. Like its cousins in China and Japan, the Hellbender is found in the mountains, namely the Appalachians and the Ozarks in the United States.

Still, nothing like *Megalobatrachus* is zoologically known in the Pacific Northwest. From a prehistoric distributive frame of reference, however, giant salamanders in the Trinity Alps make sense. California and China share a number of unique species, such as redwoods, so maybe giant salamanders can exist in both places, as well.

Such an idea clearly occurred to herpetologist George S. Myers. Writing in a scientific journal during 1951, Myers recalled his encounter with a giant salamander captured in about 1939 in the Sacramento River. A commercial fisherman who had found the animal in one of his catfish nets gave Myers the opportunity to examine the specimen carefully for over thirty minutes.

"The animal was a fine *Megalobatrachus* (unquestionably identified generically by its closed gill openings), in perfect condition," commented Myers.

It was between 25 and 30 inches in length. . . . The creature exhibited coloration quite at variance not only with that of the several live Japanese examples I have seen, but also with the published accounts of the color of Chinese specimens. The dorsum was a uniform dark brown, with an irregular sparse sprinkling over all the back of rather well defined dull yellow spots, these being of irregular outline and about one centimeter in diameter. There were no small spots, darker than the ground-color, which is the common color pattern of all the examples of *Megalobatrachus* I have seen, and the ground-color was definitely brownish, not slaty gray. Also, it must be emphasized that there was nothing to indicate that the coloration was due to disease. The animal appeared to be in the very best of condition.

The source of the specimen is, of course, unknown. Its strange coloration even suggested the possibility of a native Californian *Megalobatrachus*, which would not be zoogeographically surprising, but no other captures have been reported (Myers, 1951).

Biologist Rodgers, trying to clear the air in 1962, theorized the Sacramento River *Megalobatrachus* was only an escaped pet because a fish fancier quickly stepped forward to claim this giant salamander as his own once the story hit the local papers. The notion that such finds are escapees from zoos, wrecked circus trains, or some exotic pet lover is more than familiar. The press and local "experts" often jump on such explanations to quiet uncomfortable questions as to the origins of a weird beast. Some captive animals do escape, but just as common is the greedy or shrewd pet trader or circus owner who is able to add a unique specimen to his collection by being on top of such media reports, showing up to claim the thing, and departing before background checks can be made. We do not know whether this happened in California in 1939, but it is as likely a scenario as Rodgers's. Whatever the case for or against the Sacramento River *Megalobatrachus*, the beast fits nicely within a larger context.

Reports of strange creatures in the waterways of the area go back many years. Warren Thompson passed on some of these to me. Of particular interest is an 1891 report of the sighting of the "head of a gigantic lizard." The thing caused quite a disturbance in the Sacramento River near Woodland, California, and was shot at when it tried to climb onto dry land. It was last seen swimming away in hasty retreat (*Semi-Weekly Independent*, 1891). Native Americans, including the Hoopa, have reported "giant serpents" in the Trinity River for years. A reporter commenting on a new report noted that "all three Indian tribes along the Trinity River have a name for it in their language" (Steen, 1959).

With such a history late in the 1950s, the giant salamander phenomenon began to gain steam. John Hubbard had been collecting stories from old-timers for years and was pretty well convinced that there was something in the mountains. More importantly, perhaps, he was able to persuade his brother, Reverend Bernard Hubbard of Santa Clara University, to look into the matter.

Father Hubbard (1888–1962) was a forminable character. A Jesuit scholar known throughout the world as the "Glacier Priest" because of his early affinity for climbing the Alps of Europe, Hubbard was an explorer, naturalist, photographer, and popular lecturer. His best known expeditions took place during the 1930s in Alaska: a 1600-mile dogsledding mush down the Yukon River to visit missions; a trek into the crater of the erupting Aniakchak volcano; and a trip to the Valley of Ten Thousand Smokes. When Father Hubbard decided to take an interest in the Trinity Alps giant salamanders, people noticed.

During 1958 and 1959, both Hubbards appear to have been associated with a couple of expeditions in search of the salamanders. Father Hubbard was quoted in 1960 as saying that these inquiries had definitely established that the salamanders were in the Trinity region (*Humboldt Times*, 1960c). Besides the Hubbards, no other expedition members were ever mentioned, except for Coast Guard Lieutenant Larry Desmond, who was said to be a member of the second expedition.

In 1960, the whole giant salamander affair bloomed. Slick, Hubbard, Rodgers, and many others became involved in multiple expeditions in pursuit of the prize. News stories hit some of the California papers during mid-January of that year. Animal handler Vern Harden of Pioneer claimed he had hooked one of a dozen salamanders he said he had seen in a remote Trinity Alps lake. Harden had named the body of water Lake Hubbard after Father Bernard Hubbard. Because of a threatening snowstorm, Harden had taken a quick measurement of the salamander's length—eight feet four inches—and released it. With no evidence for his story, he still decided to tell Stanford University biologist Victor Twitty about it. Twitty's comment: "Spectacular, if true" (Boquist, 1960). Father Hubbard's reaction: "Yes, I know Harden. He's a nice fellow and I think he ought to write fiction" (*Humboldt Times*, 1960c).

Despite Father Hubbard's public reaction to Harden, he did send him to see his brother, Captain John D. Hubbard of Paradise. Father Hubbard noted that although the whole thing sounded fantastic he was rather certain there were giant salamanders. "And next fall we expect to prove it," the seventy-two-year-old Hubbard said at the time, "if I have to lead an expedition from the university myself" (Boquist, 1960). "This next time," Father Hubbard was quoted by another paper, "we'll try to fly in and really go to town. The plans still are in the remote stage. The only time of the year is around November when the Pony Butte region is in a condition of drought. Then, beneath the dry mud there is a well in the bedrock and an underground river. That is where the salamanders are. They grow five and six feet long in Japan and there's no reason why they wouldn't reach the same proportions here. . . . We expect to be well prepared for this next trek. I can assure you that the Pony Butte terrain is tougher than anything I encountered in Alaska. We'll be prepared for it" (*Humboldt Times*, 1960c).

If they made it, no record of the fall 1960 Hubbard expedition now exists. Nor is there any knowledge of what happened to Father or John Hubbard's files of eighty-year-old clippings and collected interviews from oldtimers on giant salamander sightings. Ms. Julia O'Keefe, Santa Clara University Archivist, searched the "Bernard R. Hubbard, S. J. Collection" and contacted the widow of Hubbard's nephew, Bernard Stanley, on my behalf, and found none of the material we know the Hubbards once had on the salamanders.

Enter zoologist and herpetologist Robert C. Stebbins of the University of California–Berkeley. One of Stebbins's students overheard the Harden story from Twitty and took the word back to Stebbins. Although skeptical, Stebbins did want to follow up. He called biologist Rodgers of Chico State College and proposed an expedition. In the press accounts of January 1960, Stebbins declared that if Hubbard and Santa Clara University did not mount an expedition, he would (*Humboldt Times*, 1960d).

On September 1, 1960, three zoology professors—Stebbins, Rodgers, and Nathan Cohen of Modesto Junior College—left Willow Creek on their giant salamander expedition. A couple years later Rodgers noted in a scientific journal that they were accompanied by "ten laymen." We know from local accounts of the expedition that the "laymen" were seven Explorer Scouts, their leader, Rodgers's brother Don of El Sobrante, and someone unidentified. Stebbins was excited and hopeful as the group departed. He noted that if a big salamander existed, it might be exactly in the area near Mount Shasta, Pony Mountain, and Limestone Ridge (*Humboldt Times*, 1960d). We do not know what Stebbins felt about the expedition, but Rodgers wrote harshly of the giant salamanders after his involvement with this venture. Rodgers said that some of the boys mistook logs for salamanders and that the group collected only about a dozen *Dicamptodon*, the largest of which was eleven and a half inches long. Rodgers ended his article: "It is hoped that this evidence will kill rumors about any giant salamanders (much less *Megalobatrachus*) in the Trinity Mountains of California" (Rodgers, 1962). Rodgers is the Edmund Hillary of the giant salamander, for his official debunking seems to have ended most zoological interest in the giant salamanders of the Trinities.

Rodgers's comments, of course, came after Tom Slick's 1960 involvement with the giant salamanders. In his usual low-key way, Slick let it be known that he wanted to join the leagues of giant salamander seekers and told the members of the Pacific Northwest Expedition to try to find one. I confirmed this goal in talks with members of that group and by way of one haphazard mention in a weekly newspaper in the Trinity Alps area. I have also been permitted to view slides of Tom Slick and his children hunting for giant salamanders at Fish Lake in the Trinity Alps.

That Slick was after the salamanders as well as Bigfoot was not generally known. For example, Father Hubbard, in a story about the giant salamanders, was asked to comment on Slick's search for Bigfoot (which supposedly was then taking second billing to the *Megalobatrachus* pursuits). "Slick's money comes right out of the ground in oil," Hubbard was recorded to have observed wryly, "and this is a good way to spend it" (*Humboldt Times*, 1960c).

We know, of course, that Tom Slick was no more successful than the others looking for the giant salamanders. Furthermore, some of his hired Bigfooters became angry with him for what they saw as a silly side trip. But for Slick the salamander episode seems to be more evidence that he was adventurous in his cryptozoological thinking and not afraid to look for new animals that might be found just around the next peak or lake.

Others are continuing Slick's inquiries regarding gigantic amphibians. In Mark A. Hall's just published book, *Natural Mysteries*, an entire chapter is devoted to the so-called "monster lizards" of some specific sites in Kentucky and Ohio. Having collected and analyzed reports of the three- to six-foot-long creatures, Hall states: "These giant animals appear to be amphibians and not reptiles. . . . They sound like a giant version of a living amphibian known as the axolotl" (Hall, 1989a). Probably if he were alive today, Slick would take an active interest in Hall's writings and thoughts on those giant amphibians, just as he had with the giant salamanders of the Trinity Alps.

THE LAKE MONSTER OF ILLIAMNA

Slick was a hunter and enjoyed going off into the wilds of Alaska frequently after moose or other game animals. My talks with his sons confirmed that he took them along for these hunts and also on a monster chase in Lake Illiamna.

Illiamna, located on Alaska's southern coast, is the seventh largest freshwater lake in the world. It is about eighty miles long, twenty-five miles wide in spots, and covers an area of 1000 square miles. The depth average is 660 feet; in Pile Bay at the eastern end, on one sounding, the lead dropped to 1350 feet and then the line ran out. Once part of the ocean, the lake is now less than a hundred feet above sea level.

The January 1959 issue of *Sports Afield* carried the kind of article that would have caught Slick's attention. Entitled "Alaska's Monster Mystery Fish," the story by Gil Paust chronicled over thirty years of reports of huge fish in Lake Illiamna. In a breathless fashion, the author details his adventures in trying to catch this mysterious monster fish. Paust, along with Illiamna lake monster hunters Slim Beck, John Walatka, and Bill Hammersley, used a Bushmaster seaplane as a dock and some homemade monster-fishing gear. They attempted to catch the big one with a hook made from a foot-long, quarter-inch-thick iron rod baited with a chuck of moose flank. Their line was several hundred feet of sixteenth-inch stainless-steel aircraft cable. A fifty-five-gallon oil drum was the bobber. The thing snapped the line (Paust, 1959).

For some thirty years before this report appeared in a national sports magazine, sightings of the monster fish had been circulating around the shores of Lake Illiamna. Formerly the stories had been placed in the netherworld of Eskimo folklore, and local whites refused to acknowledge any truth in the reports, wanting to doubt that something so unexplained lived so close. But then certain respected local folks and visiting sportsmen saw it, and the word spread.

Perhaps local guide Babe Aylesworth and fisherman Bill Hammersley made the best sighting in September 1942. Crossing at Big Mountain, they were on a direct flight over the twenty-five miles of the lake to get to the village of Illiamna. Bush pilot Aylesworth was taking his Stinson ferry plane across at a steady pace over the deep, blue-black water when he noticed some unusual specks in the water near the unnamed island in the middle of the lake. All of a sudden, the normally calm Aylesworth shouted "Oh my God, what big fish!" and swirled the plane around for a closer look. Both Hammersley and Aylesworth got a good look. They described the things as dull aluminum in color with heads that were broad and blunt. The width of the long tapered bodies was the same as that of their heads, and vertical tails slowly waved side to side. (Whale tails go up and down; fish and reptile tails go side to side.) They saw several dozen of them (Paust, 1959).

Spiraling the plane from 1000 feet down to 300 feet, they soon saw that Aylesworth's estimate of their length at ten feet was low. The fish were easily longer than the plane's pontoon; they looked like mini-submarines. They circled for several minutes, then suddenly surged in the water and disappeared in a distinct wave disturbance. As they continued on their journey, the two men discussed and debated. No, it couldn't have been a whale, walrus, or seal, because they never blew or surfaced. Sharks would have been much smaller (Paust, 1959).

Local folks, such as high profile skeptic Arthur Lee, thought they might be cod. No way, said the two witnesses. Once word got around Illiamna, authorities told Hammersley that he had only seen some belugas. This was ridiculous to Hammersley, as he had seen thousands of belugas during his years of fishing Bristol Bay, and their white backs, tapering heads, and horizonal tails were very different from what he and Aylesworth had seen (Paust, 1959).

The mere fact that the lake is so close to the ocean leads many to quickly speculate that the monster fish are landlocked sturgeon or some unknown prehistoric fish. Nevertheless, no dead sturgeon or even landlocked belugas have ever washed up on the shores of Lake Illiamna. And we are still waiting on the prehistoric fish, too.

In 1947, after leaving his defense job, Hammersley published a short piece on the mystery fish to try to get others to look into the matter or to come forth with reports. One who did was Larry Rost, a U.S. Coast and Geodetic Survey pilot. Flying across Lake Illiamna in the fall of 1945, he was so startled by what he saw in the water that he turned around and flew over at a height of one hundred feet to get a good look at this giant fish, over twenty feet long, the color of dull aluminum (Paust, 1959).

I tracked down Aylesworth, now retired in Hawaii, and he reaffirmed the details of his 1942 sighting. He added that he thought the majority of the things were well over ten feet long, swimming in water that was only forty feet deep. Aylesworth recalled that Tom Slick hired him several times to fly Slick and his boys to moose hunting sites, and in the fall of 1959 to attempt specifically to find the monsters of Lake Illiamna. (These facts were confirmed by Slick's sons and Slick-Heuvelmans correspondence.) Slick had offered a reward of a $1000 to anyone who could catch one of the mystery creatures, and Slick himself was in charge of getting lines set with barrels for buoys. He even hired a helicopter to hover over the exact spot where Aylesworth had had his encounter. The bush pilot remembers Slick as a hard driver who was interested deeply in whatever he was after, whether shooting a big bull moose or catching a lake monster. Aylesworth and Slick never saw the big unknown animals on these flights and, indeed, the pilot said he went over that place in the lake more than one hundred times without seeing them again.

In 1967, Sanderson wrote in his book *"THINGS"* of Tom Slick's teaming up with a Commander Stanley Lee (who we have not been able to track down) looking for the "Things," as Sanderson termed them, in Lake Illiamna (Sanderson, 1967). Elwood Baumann noted in *Monsters of North America* that "Texan Tom R. [sic] Slick spent thousands of dollars in search of strange creatures in Lake Illiamna, Alaska" (Baumann, 1978). As Michael Newton observed in his *Monsters, Mysteries and Man*, Slick and Lee "organized an expedition to search for the elusive creatures. Slick was unsuccessful, and after his tragic death, Commander Lee teamed up with others to continue the hunt. Still the monsters remain unidentified" (Newton, 1979).

Newton appears to have picked up Sanderson's lead here: "Captain Lee of Kodiak, Alaska, together with the well known nature photographer, Leonard Rue of New Jersey, made still another stab at the monsters of Lake Illiamna in 1966" (Sanderson, 1967). Indeed, both Newton and Baumann, who write primarily children's books, may have taken all they knew about Slick's Lake Illiamna adventures from Sanderson. That Slick spent "several thousand dollars" in search of the mystery fish of Illiamna is only speculation.

Excursion into New Guinea

In some press accounts of Tom Slick's various expeditions, mention is made of an investigative trip into the wilds of New Guinea. For a long time I thought this was merely an incorrectly placed reference to Slick's attempt to learn more about the orang pendek in Sumatra. After all, the two countries are on the same side of the globe, and journalists are frequently less than accurate about their geography.

But what if this was not the case? I looked for an explanation. Bernard Heuvelmans's *On the Track of Unknown Animals*, which Slick read late in the 1950s, gives little attention to New Guinea's cryptozoological offerings. One tale from Charles "Cannibal" Miller discusses the *row*, a "dinosaur" he says he saw in New Guinea, but clearly Heuvelmans meant this tale to be a cautionary one. The Belgian wrote about Miller's animal: "The *row* looks damnably like an ill-digested memory of a bad Science Fiction film made by a producer ignorant of zoogeography" (Heuvelmans, 1958). Heuvelmans did not and does not believe this man was doing any more than telling a traveler's yarn. Today, cryptozoologists rather universally put Cannibal Miller's report in the hoax category.

Writing in the 1986 issue of the annual journal *Cryptozoology*, Heuvelmans mentions several hidden but as yet zoologically uncatalogued animals in Papua, New Guinea.

1. gigantic amphibious monitor lizards, a little under thirty feet in length, called *au angi-angi* by the Papuans
2. large tapirlike marsupials known as *gazekas*, reported from the mountains of the Owen Stanley Range
3. large, doglike animals on Mount Giluwe (perhaps a relic population representing living examples of the local fossil finds of thylacine) (Heuvelmans, 1986).

Were any of these unknown animals what Slick was after in New Guinea? The records are too scant to tell.

CHAPTER 12

THE DEATH OF TOM SLICK

EARLY IN OCTOBER 1962, TOM SLICK WENT TO A
Canadian meeting of the Board of Directors of Bailey-Selburn Oil and Gas.
Then he took a hunting trip for pheasant and quail, also in Canada. Some
speculate that he also checked up on his Sasquatch operations north of
the border. Press reports said he was scheduled to fly to Salt Lake City
on October 6 (Light, 1962), but his family has told me that he was on his
way to Phoenix to have dinner with his children in nearby Scottsdale, at
the home of his former wife, Patty.* They will never forget waiting for
that meal (Slick, C., 1988 and 1989; Slick, T., 1988). Slick's old Exeter
and Yale buddy, S. S. Wilson will never forget that night either. He and
his wife were waiting in their isolated upstate New York hunting cabin
for Slick's still later arrival. It was a couple days before the terrible news
reached the Wilsons (Wilson, 1989).

Saturday night at about 6 P.M., October 6, 1962, Slick and pilot Shelly
Sudderth of Dallas were killed in the crash of their Beechcraft Bonanza
35. This is the same kind of plane that the 1950s rock and roll innovators
Buddy Holly, Richie Valens, and J. P. "the Big Bopper" Richardson were
in when they died in a wreck on February 3, 1959. Don McLean's 1971
hit, *American Pie*, immortalized the date of the Holly tragedy as "the day
the music died," and I note October 6, 1962 as a similarly sad date in the
decline of the pursuit of yeti and in other creative cryptozoological quests
Slick had sponsored. The era of adventure and Slick's passion was over
for the young science and study of yet-to-be caught "hidden animals."

---

*Slick inherited his fatherly traits from his own dad. Tom Slick, Sr., only once gave an
interview to a newspaperman, in 1929, and the reporter described how the elder Slick "often
disappears for a whole day, in summer, and takes his boys out in a boat somewhere and
spends the day, digging worms for them, baiting their hooks, cooking their meals, building
a camp on shore." When the newsman asked about a recent illness of Earl's and whether
the boy was in danger, old Tom replied: "No none at all. Say, if there was any danger with
that boy I wouldn't be here. Money! I'd give the last cent of it rather than have anything
happen to either of those boys of mine" (Macdonald, 1929). His son Tom felt similarly, and
spent a good deal of time with his children.

Slick's death, combined with the after-effects of Hillary's 1960 yeti-debunking expedition and his 1962 book, changed attitudes toward crypto-zoology field studies forever.

No one knows exactly how or why Slick's plane went down. The plane's wreckage was found forty miles south of Dillion in extreme southwestern Montana, near the town of Dell. Residents near Dell reported hearing a "noise like a crash" (*The Light*, 1962a). Harold Briggs, search and rescue coordinator for the Federal Aviation Administration (FAA) and the local sheriff's department, said the plane apparently disintegrated in flight. One wing was found intact and one engine was found a considerable distance from all other wreckage. Slick's bag of game birds was strewn over the area. Searchers reported that Slick's and Sudderth's bodies apparently fell free from the plane because they were not close to the wreckage. Briggs reported that the backs of both seats were found together about three-quarters of a mile from the bodies. The bodies, both badly burned, were found alongside a rural country road about three-quarters of a mile from the center of the crash site.

THE WEATHER THEORY

Briggs reported a day after the accident that there had been storms along mountain peaks in the Dell, Montana, area on the night of October 6, 1962. One of several of his theories was that the plane had been struck by lightning.

Did the weather conditions support Briggs's lightning theory? At the National Climatic Data Center, which keeps thorough records of surface weather observations for the United States, I was able to locate material for the dates in question. The only "storm data and unusual weather phenomena" that was recorded in Montana for the entire month was that of a rain/sleet/wet snow storm on October 15 in the extreme northeastern corner. Dell and Dillion are in the southwestern part of Montana, near Idaho, so I searched that state's records. "None reported" is what I found (NOAA, 1962). On-site observations for Dillion, Montana, for October 6 show winds of ten to twelve miles per hour through the night. No evidence of a storm is in the record.

The weather theory for the Slick plane crash takes on a folkloric tone in one author's discussion of a Native American curse on whites. Nat Freedland writes in *The Occult Explosion* that he heard from an informant: "It was Indians singing something not quite as powerful as their 'Last

Song'* because of the arrest of Indian fisherman in the Trinity River area of northern California which brought on the Great Killer Thunderstorm of Columbus Day, 1962, that caused fifty deaths in the Pacific Northwest. The first storm victim was millionaire Houston [sic] oilman Tom Slick" (Freedland, 1972).

The weather had been relatively harsh during that first week in October 1962, at least on the East Coast. Hurricane Daisy had lashed the East Coast, and on October 6, the one-two punch of a northeaster followed by Daisy socked Boston. But how could anyone link Slick with the storms that hit the West Coast six days after he died? Friday, October 12, saw the worst storms in the history of the Pacific Northwest, according to the *New York Times*. From British Columbia to central California, a massive windstorm hit the coast, killing forty-seven and causing millions of dollars worth of property damage. On October 16, 1962, President John Kennedy declared most of Oregon's coast a disaster area because of the tremendous storms of the previous week. But this "Great Killer Windstorm of Columbus Day," as Freedland (1972) termed it, had little if any effect in Montana, and certainly none days before it struck. Freedland's informant is stretching the facts greatly to include Slick in this version of the "Last Song" curse.

The Beechcraft Theory

Questions have arisen as to whether Slick was pulled into the whirlwind of small plane accidents that were rapidly zeroing in on the design of the Beechcrafts themselves. I already mentioned that Buddy Holly and his fellow musicians went down in one of these planes. And, as the FAA's Briggs theorized, maybe the plane simply fell apart because it was flying too fast.

Based on investigations done in the late 1960s, James T. Bruce and John B. Draper, engineering graduates of Princeton University and Ralph Nader associates, compiled a report in January of 1970 highly critical of the general aviation industry. Citing 1400 fatalities involving small planes in 1968, their studies found that seventy percent of the small planes then in production would eventually be involved in an accident. They specifically pointed a finger at Beech Aircraft Corporation for not having followed through on providing shoulder harnesses in the 1950s because of the negative results of a marketing acceptance survey (Draper and Bruce, 1970).

Perhaps Slick was merely in the wrong plane at the wrong time.

*The "Last Song" deals with the final days of the Earth and the new tomorrow for Native Americans who have been exploited in the U.S.

THE BOMB THEORY

Tom Slick, a murder victim? His plane did not get hit by lightning, but disintegrated due to a bomb? Farfetched, outlandish? Yes, but among some people who were close to Slick, the bomb theory ranks very high on the list of possible causes of death. One of Briggs's observations that was not picked up by most press accounts was the possibility that the plane could have experienced, in his words, "an internal explosion" (Light, 1962a). Two sources that wish to remain unnamed quote the local sheriff's office in Montana as saying that Slick's death was murder.

Some of the thinking runs to the notion that Slick was an embarrassment to his research associates, to rivals, to disillusioned relatives, because he was wasting his money on his Snowmen/Bigfoot pursuits, and murder was the only way to stop him. Around some stove fires in the Pacific Northwest, even today, such discussions are seriously held. Folks see how suddenly the Johnsons died, Sr. within a year of Slick's death and Jr. within six, and they speculate.

Others wonder if Slick's peace work was rubbing certain folks the wrong way. After all, President John F. Kennedy was killed in Texas, Slick's home state, only fourteen months after Slick died. Maybe the conservative forces in America were trying to send someone a message with a special Texas flair. Some people mention the power struggles at the Southwest Research Institute and point to the changes that occurred in the leadership after Slick's guiding hand was removed from the picture.

We do not know what caused Slick's plane to crash, and we may never discover the official verdict. I attempted to learn exactly what the final FAA report had concluded by filing a Freedom of Information Act request; badgering the FAA and the National Transportation Safety Board; asking the Slick family to search their files; and getting the able assistance of Ralph Nader's Aviation Consumer Project, General Aviation Aircraft Owners data center, and countless librarians throughout the country, but to no avail. Finally the FAA told me that such general aviation accident investigations are the "responsibility of the National Transportation Safety Board (NTBS)" (Stewart, 1988).

The NTBS sent me a form letter with the date of Slick's "accident" handwritten in blue pen in the appropriate blank spot, but noting they were "unable to fill my request." The report on Slick's crash investigation was required to be kept for only seven years. "The report(s) requested by you fall under the statute of limitations category and have been destroyed" (Stevenson, 1988). I then searched the Library of Congress for a copy but had no luck.

THE WORD SPREADS

Most newspapers did not carry a notice of Tom Slick's death until their Monday edition. "Oilman Tom Slick Dies in Air Crash," "Tom Slick Crash Probe On," and simply, "Tom Slick" are examples of typical headlines about his sudden death. The *New York Times* carried an obituary in their October 8 issue headlined, "Thomas Slick, 46, Dies in Air Crash: Oilman and Philanthropist Is Killed in Montana" (*New York Times*, 1962a). Like his father before him, he died at the very young age of forty-six. All the media treatments went over the usual stuff about his oil, the Southwest Research Institute, and, of course, his yeti expeditions. Tom Slick was an important individual of the late 1950s, although few know it today.

The President of the Southwest Foundation for Research and Education (SFRE) and the Southwest Research Institute (SwRI), Harold Vagtborg, was far afield when he heard the news, and wrote: "Early in October 1962, I had left San Antonio for my trip to Nairobi, Kenya, to consult with government officials regarding our baboon project. As I registered at the New Stanley Hotel, I was handed the following telegram:

418 AM

HAROLD VAGTBORG NEW STANLEY HOTEL NAIROBI TOM SLICK KILLED IN PLANE CRASH STOP WILL BE IMPOSSIBLE FOR YOU TO RETURN FOR FUNERAL TOM SLICK TO BE BURIED TUESDAY OCTOBER 9TH STATEMENTS BEING HANDLED BY HARMON FEITH AND HARTMAN EVERYONE RECOGNIZES YOU WILL BE UNABLE TO ATTEND FUNERAL WIRE INSTRUCTIONS IF YOU WISH ME TO DO ANYTHING SPECIAL

FEITH SOUTHWEST FOUNDATION

COL 9TH

I cannot describe my reactions! Was the telegram a hoax? Surely not, I concluded after some thought; Tom was often flying into dangerous areas in small planes. I recalled a narrow escape he had had in the Brazilian [sic] jungle a few years before when Bill Mather of SwRI was with him on a geological exploration. Also, I knew he had taken many risks on his trips to Tibet [sic] and elsewhere in search of the Abominable Snowman. Having brought myself to the reality of what had happened, I at once set about to finish my work in Kenya so that I could hurry home. . . . Our research center was never the same again (Vagtborg, 1973).

Vagtborg was behind an effort to name a wing of the main Urschel Memorial Research Laboratory at SFRE the Tom Slick Memorial Laboratory. Vagtborg later noted that much of the $578,000 for this lab was underwritten by friends of Tom. Indeed, Slick's "reward to all of us," wrote SFRE's president, "was a legacy of over $9,000,000 (approximately $6,000,000 to SFRE and $3,000,000 to SwRI); moreover, his persistent encouragement prompted his mother to bequeath the Foundation an additional amount in excess of $2,500,000" (Vagtborg, 1973).

Because Slick had founded the Southwest Research Center of which SFRE and SwRI were parts, Vagtborg's book on its history begins with the transcript of the Memorial Service held for Slick in 1962. Speakers at the service noted irony in the fact that Slick's death had occurred within only a few days of the anniversary marking the Institute's fifteenth year. All those that spoke of Slick did so with warmth and personal friendliness. As Vagtborg said in his dedication: "Tom was one of the most gracious, thoughtful, and considerate human beings we have ever known—an outstanding example of a man truly dedicated to the well-being of his fellow-man" (Vagtborg, 1973).

Perhaps most fitting to the way a good many cryptozoologists feel about Slick is this passage from Dr. James W. Laurie's closing prayer at the memorial service: "Truly we would thank Thee for Thy servant, Tom, who being dead yet speaks to us" (Vagtborg, 1973).

Whatever the truth behind Slick's death, one thing is certain: almost everything cryptozoological he represented came to a grinding halt thereafter. Men were left in the field in Canada and California still under Slick's orders to find a Sasquatch/Bigfoot. Files on old expeditions were quietly put away. Ideas about publishing results were shelved for lack of support.

Nineteen sixty-two was the last year that anyone of Tom Slick's stature supported spiritually and financially the innovative and in-the-field cryptozoological research so important to the ultimate quest. What Slick did back in the late 1950s and 1960s was to assist in propelling the search for hidden animals out of the shadows of legends and into the light of legitimate scientific inquiry. If Slick were alive today, establishment zoologists would view the new science of cryptozoology more supportively. There is no doubt about that. Over and over again, people have told me Tom Slick left the world of cryptozoology too soon.

YETI AND THE CINEMA
Mark Chorvinsky

INTRODUCTION

I WAS HONORED WHEN LOREN COLEMAN ASKED me to do an essay on yeti cinema. He explained that he was interested in getting my opinion as to the effect that films can have on the public and suggested that I survey and analyze the Slick-era yeti films. Studying the influence of dramatic narrative feature films on the public has not been a regular part of cryptozoological/fortean research and investigation. Yeti feature films are not mentioned in any of the major abominable snowman (ABSM)/yeti, Bigfoot, and/or Sasquatch books that we know. The attitude that fictional films are not an important part of the picture is old-fashioned. Today more of us find that the serious study of strange phenomena involves such fields as sociology and cultural anthropology. Researchers who have firsthand knowledge of the strong influence exerted by the visual media realize that the effects of the release of dramatic films should not be ignored.

THE EFFECTS OF FILM

As a filmmaker and theorist, I have spent many hours considering the question of what effect films can have on individuals and society. I have reached the conclusion that films have had and continue to have a great impact on the public, although sometimes in subtle ways. Kenneth Macgowan, in his history of the motion picture, *Behind the Screen*, quotes disparate sources in support of these notion. Macgowan quotes Khrushchev as saying that "There is nothing to compare with the cinema in its power of impact on human minds and hearts and in the breadth of audience it reaches among the people." There is rare agreement about this fact among leaders with very differing worldviews, as demonstrated by Pope Pius XI's statement: "There exists today no means of influencing the masses more potent than the cinema."[1]

Cinema realizes the fantastic, and in that sense it is intrinsically a fortean medium. Something that does not exist is made to exist, and legends may be given life, as may anomalous phenomena. Films have had a much greater effect in the field of cryptozoology than in many others due to the fact that the creatures being studied are rarely seen and largely remain in the imagination of those who study them. That is, the cinema can mold the image and attributes of the creatures since the film version of the creature presents an image that becomes a part of one's mental "yeti-amalgamation." It is a fact that both laymen and cryptozoologists have seen more yetis in movies than they have seen in "real life." Unlike films such as the Patterson-Gimlin film purporting to show a Bigfoot, there are no such equivalents with regards to the yeti, which has a "looser," more malleable image.

Films also influence cryptozoology by creating a favorable climate for the discussion of monster sightings in the media. When monsters are in the public eye, there tends to be an increase in monster sightings, something that rationalist debunkers would make too much of and that forteans might tend to discount. In his article "Monsters of Maryland: Bigfoot (Part 1)" in *Strange Magazine* Number 3, Bigfoot investigator Mark Opsasnick notes that during the Sykesville wave of monster sightings in 1973, reporters pointed out that public consciousness may have been affected by the popular movie *The Legend of Boggy Creek*, which was playing in area theaters at that time.[2] "*The Legend of Boggy Creek* may also have had an effect on some Anne Arundel County reports, specifically those mentioned in the July 21, 1973, edition of the [Annapolis] *Evening Capital* where it states that a Glen Burnie woman reported seeing the beast in a tree and that the very next night a county police officer claims a similar creature ran in front of his car on Sudley Road near Lothian. These alleged eye-witnesses remained anonymous and the paper's reporter conveniently pointed out the presence of *The Legend of Boggy Creek* in local theatres," Opsasnick writes.[3] The influence of such films may or may not provide a viable explanation for some alleged Bigfoot sightings. While *Boggy Creek* may (or may not) have affected monster sightings it certainly raised public aware-ness of the Bigfoot phenomenon in the United States.[4,5]

In what other ways do films involving strange phenomena have an effect on the public? An interesting example of a delayed effect may be found in the field of ufology. *Close Encounters of the Third Kind* (1977) did not incite the rash of UFO sightings predicted by the rationalist ufologists. This fact was much-discussed in the UFO press at the time. However, while *Close Encounters* did not affect the number of UFO sightings as much as had been predicted, it did increase the public awareness of the phenomenon and I have received correspondence from individuals who became ufologists after seeing the film. (If there is doubt that the relationship between film and strange phenomena is worth studying, it is valuable to keep in mind that more people undoubtedly saw *Close Encounters* than have read every UFO book ever published, excluding perhaps the Bible.)

In the manner that *Close Encounters* inspired some viewers to study UFOs, the 1972 Bigfoot film *The Legend of Boggy Creek* encouraged some of its viewers to study hairy hominids. I have interviewed several Bigfoot researchers who credit *The Legend of Boggy Creek* with inspiring their interest in the subject. Aforementioned Bigfoot expert Opsasnick is one: "I was 11 years old when I saw *The Legend of Boggy Creek* and got interested in it after I saw the film. The idea that some unknown creature like this existed outside the Pacific Northwest was a new concept to me. I realized for the first time that there was nothing supernatural to it—that it was just an animal that hadn't been classified. It made a lasting impression that something so strange was roaming so close to home." Opsasnick envisioned himself traveling to Arkansas to investigate the Fouke monster case portrayed in *Boggy Creek*, and in later years when he found that there were Bigfoot sightings much closer to home, he became a Bigfoot investigator, thus realizing his youthful fantasy.[6]

Other Bigfoot researchers, such as Danny Perez, have written of *Boggy Creek*'s influence on them. In the preface to *Big Footnotes*, Perez writes: "My personal interest in monsters was first ignited at about the tender age of 10, by the movie *The Legend of Boggy Creek*. . . . This was the trigger which led to casual to casually serious to serious full-fledged involvement in this subject matter."[7]

In a 1979 newspaper interview author Loren Coleman attributed his interest in the field of strange phenomena to his viewing of a yeti movie. I asked him about this, wondering if he could expand on his brief film reference. His response is further evidence of the influence of hairy hominid films:

I fully credit the movie *Half-Human*, Inoshiro Honda and John Carradine, for my life long passion in pursuing yeti, abominable snowcreatures, hairy hominids, cryptozoological species, unexplained phenomena and forteana in general.

On one cold winter/early spring night in 1960 (probably March), I sat up late watching this incredible story about a giant hairy abominable snow-family in Japan—with words of scientific wisdom from Carradine—and was totally intrigued. As fate would have it, my local Decatur, Illinois, television station rebroadcast the previous evenings' movies again the next morning (at about 10 A.M. I recall). Therefore, I watched *Half-Human* all over again. I just could not shake its impact!

What was this 'abominable snowman'? Why hadn't I heard about it? Where could I read more about it? I started my research then, and soon ran across Heuvelmans, Sanderson, and Fort. One thing led to another, but forever I have directly pointed to *Half-Human* for opening my eyes to the notion that not everything is known or has been discovered.[8]

It may be interesting to note that in all three of these examples of researcher/investigators who were inspired by hairy hominid movies (as well as in several other cases that I know of), the influential film was viewed when the researchers were youths of ten to twelve years of age. Perhaps at this age one's worldview is not yet firmly set and these films may leave big impressions on curious minds. Adults may not take some of these films as seriously—some of the yeti movies were extremely bad— but youths may be more accepting of them. Films like the *The Legend of Boggy Creek* and *Half-Human* are aesthetically horrible, but include ideas that may be extremely exciting to someone who is young, inquisitive, and still open to new ideas.

THE SLICK-ERA YETI FEATURE FILMS

According to yeti expert Ivan T. Sanderson "the 'birth' of the Abominable Snowman per se may be precisely dated as of 1921." [9] This was the year that the yeti first came to the attention of the English-speaking public, as a result of a widely publicized telegram from Colonel C. K. Howard-Bury, who was on an expedition to Everest. The telegram described large tracks, the sighting of unknown dark moving forms, and Sherpa tales of a creature they called metoh-kangmi. Henry Newman, columnist for the *Calcutta Statesman*, mistranslated this term as "Abominable Snowman," and the British press had a field day.

Unfortunately, as far as we know, no films were inspired by the 1921 ABSM press attention. There may be several reasons for this. The film industry was still young in 1921. Feature films had been around for only ten years and had been a force in the industry for only about six. Sound had not yet come to the cinema. England would have been a good bet to release an early ABSM film since the British press had made such a brouhaha about it, but the film industry was largely dormant between

World War I and 1925. For whatever reason, it would take thirty-three years from the birth of the ABSM before yeti would be the subject of a feature film.

The press, in the form of a 1954 expedition sponsored by the (London) *Daily Mail*, was the first group to launch an expedition to the Himalayas with the yeti as its *raison d'être*. Reporter Ralph Izzard led the expedition and "publicized the whole matter and served notice on everybody that the press was no longer overawed by what they had termed 'scientific opinion,' but from then on took the affair for granted as having graduated from the category of the 'silly season filler.' "[10]

Less than a year later the first yeti film, *The Snow Creature*, was released. The relationship between media exposure and the first yeti feature film production mirrors that of Nessie, the Loch Ness Monster. In 1933 Nessie was publicized in the press for the first time, and the following year the first feature film about the famous lake monster, *The Secret of the Loch*, was produced and released.

We will now take a brief look at the early yeti feature films, paying particular attention to their approach to and portrayal of the yeti.

● *The Snow Creature* (1954). A Planet Filmways, Inc. production. Released through United Artists. Producer/director: W. Lee Wilder. Story and screenplay: Myles Wilder.

The Snow Creature is the first yeti feature film that we are aware of. It is certainly the first feature film in which the yeti is undeniably the title creature of the film and in which the term *yeti* is used.[11] The title *The Snow Creature* is interesting because the aforementioned Howard-Bury telegram used the term "kang-mi," which Ivan Sanderson translated as "snow creature."[12]

According to its narrator, *The Snow Creature* is the story "of how a small group of people found themselves in pursuit of a crude and primitive civilization, which once only existed as a figment of the imagination." The plot revolves around an expedition led by Dr. Frank Parrish to find and study previously inaccessible unknown plant life in the Himalayas. While in the mountains, the wife of Subra, the Nepalese guide, is abducted by a yeti. "Yeti always want to steal women!" explains Subra. Dr. Parrish is skeptical: How come no one ever sees them? The guide explains that they smell humans and then hide. After some plot complications the yeti is captured. A special cage is ordered from the United States and when it arrives, the creature is shipped to Los Angeles.

The immigration authorities need to clarify the immigration status of the yeti—is it a man or an animal? (And all this time I thought man was an animal.) Dr. Parrish, who is a botanist, is convinced it is an animal. The expedition photographer, however, has lost no time in selling photos of the yeti to the newspapers and the headlines reads "Snow Man," thus confusing the immigration and customs people. While they argue over what it is and wait for expert opinion, the creature escapes into the sewer system and terrorizes the city. After several murders by the yeti, it is captured and killed by the police.

The critics disliked the film. "Bush league science fiction, a routine low-budget shocker," pronounced "Herm" in the November 10, 1954, issue of *Daily Variety*. Many critics found fault with the portrayal of yeti. The script and direction are actually more problematic than the yeti, which is fairly eerie-looking because it is shot in very little light. However, several shots of the yeti are repeated over and over again. The creature is seen so briefly in such little light that a description of it is almost impossible.

● *Man Beast* (1955), copyright 1956. A Jerry Warren Productions, Inc. production. Producer/director: Jerry Warren. Screenplay: B. Arthur Cassidy.

Professor Erikson is directing an expedition in the Himalayas, and guide Steve Cameron explains the plan: "His purpose is to capture one of the Abominable Snowmen. That's what the natives call the yeti. A kind of people covered with hair, supposedly living above the 21,000-foot level . . . nobody seems to know whether they are man or beast. Everyone thought they were a fable until some famous explorers found traces of them just before World War I. Since then, many people have claimed to have seen them."

The ludicrous expedition sets out and everyone wears funny hats. They find a white, very nonhuman and monstrous-looking yeti (which doesn't look as bad as it should considering the overall quality of the film). Professor Erikson places the yeti "somewhere between the Rhodesian Man and the Danish Stone Age Man." The yeti seems to be under the control of Varga, the leader of the climb. Everyone else is very cold, but Varga is warm. He was brought up in Calcutta, which was too warm for him, so he moved to Sweden. His mother, a "mountain woman with Mongol [read 'yeti'] blood" died in childbirth. In addition, he has very bizarre hairy eyebrows. Thus, it comes as no great surprise that Varga is part yeti. Varga kills off most of the team one by one, explaining to the professor that he will kill any expedition that finds out about his people, the yetis. Varga wants to breed yetis with human women and hopes to do so with the female lead. He has kidnapped five human women so far just that year. He wants to raise the intelligence (and, evidently, lower the acting ability) of yetis, who are nice but kind of slow. He wants to "breed out the yeti strain," which makes no sense considering his yeti pride. (The notion that Varga is a fifth-generation yeti is reminiscent of Stanislav Szukalski's strange ultra-fringe theories concerning the yetisyn, the offspring of human women raped by yetis). Varga kills the professor and then falls to an anticlimactic death in a climbing accident.

This film falls into the "so bad that it's good" category. The script, acting, and directing are so ludicrous that they are entertaining, and the film has become known as a classic example of bad fifties cinema. Horror–science fiction film expert Bill Warren suggests that parts of the film, such as the yetis and the mountain climbing scenes, could have been cannibalized from other films, since Jerry Warren's later films were pieced together from parts of other movies, often Mexican productions. Bill Warren humorously typifies the critical reaction to *Man Beast* when he writes: "I am proud and even anxious to say that I am not related to Jerry Warren, the auteur of *Man Beast* and other even worse films. His credo seems to promise that no matter how terrible his previous film was, his next will be worse."[13]

● *Half-Human* (1957). Released in Japan in 1955 as *Jujin Vukiotoko* or "*Monster Snowman.*" Subtitled *The Story of the Abominable Snowman.* Made by Toho Co., Ltd., Tokyo. Released in the United States by Distributors Corp. of America. Producer: Tonoyuki Tanaka. Japanese sequences directed by Inoshiro Honda. U.S. sequences directed by Kenneth G. Crane. Original story: Shigeru Kayama.

Japanese students mountain climbing in northern Japan discover a yeti living on a high peak. A group of Japanese anthropologists organizes an expedition to find and investigate the yeti. A carnival director also searches for the creature and finds its cave. Living inside is the yeti's shaggy son. During an attempt to capture the father, the snowkid is killed and his angry dad throws the carnival men and their truck over a cliff. He also kills all of the residents of a mountain village except one girl, who runs away. The yeti abducts a student from the anthropologists' camp. He drops her, though, when he sees the mountain girl that fled from him earlier. (The "yeti needs women" motif is present again, as it was in *Snow Creature* and *Man Beast.*) Pursued into a cave by the scientists and their entourage, the yeti and his captive fall to their deaths into a steaming volcanic pit.

This story is told in flashback with voice-over narration by John Carradine playing anthropologist Dr. John Rayburn. The film is a stylistic curiosity since there is no dialogue throughout the Japanese sequences that make up the bulk of the film. Instead, Carradine tells the audience what the Japanese characters are saying. This Japanese horror film was intercut with American scenes so that a U.S. release would be possible, and this is exactly how the film comes across. While the adding of American scenes is a clumsy device, it nevertheless provides some interesting dialogue for the yeti enthusiast (the "words of scientific wisdom from Carradine" that intrigued and inspired Loren Coleman as a youth). How could anyone interested in yeti not be fascinated by scenes of "scientists" speculating about the origin and the behavior of the yeti, even if they are often nonsensical. Indeed, the yeti theories proposed in each of these films are some of the most entertaining parts. *Half-Human* includes something not found in the other yeti films: a yeti autopsy. Near the end of the film Carradine reveals that he has acquired the body of the dead child yeti and has asked a surgeon to perform an autopsy on it. The surgeon proclaims, with a tone of finality: "It is my belief that this species is one-half animal and *half-human*." (A few minutes later, in response to a speculative question about the creature's behavior, the doctor guesses that "he is probably more human than animal.") The surgeon explains that "the respiratory system is almost identical to ours, as are the lungs." (I thought the lungs were a part of the respiratory system.) The nervous system is "smaller" than the human nervous system, but the creature can feel emotions in a half-human way.

The yeti looks fairly good compared to those in some other yeti films, but visually comes across as more ape than human.

● *The Abominable Snowman* (aka *The Abominable Snowman of the Himalayas*) (1957). Made in England by Exclusive Films, an arm of Hammer Studios. Released in the United States by Twentieth Century–Fox. Producer: Aubrey Baring. Director: Val Guest. Story and screenplay: Nigel Kneale.

In this British feature, an English botanist* studying plants in the Himalayas, Dr. Rollason (played with great intelligence and thoughtfulness by Peter Cushing), agrees to join an American expedition searching for the yeti led by Dr. Friend (Forrest Tucker). The yeti is spotted and shot by one of the men, who, it turns out, plans to exploit the creature. They try to bring the yeti down the mountain, but on the way one of the men falls off a cliff due to a leg wound that had been caused by his stepping into one of the yeti spring traps. Another man dies of a heart attack when

---

*One of the interesting details in these movies is the fact that they often involve a botanist on a yeti expedition. Indeed, at the same time the *New York Times* story about Slick's 1956 yeti expedition with helicopters and dogs broke, there was in fact a British Museum botanical expedition lead by A. E. Stainton in the Arun Valley, Nepal, from April to October 1956, according to the *Times of India.*—LC

he sees the yeti and learns that the gun that he has been given by the contemptuous Dr. Friend contains blanks. The porters desert the expedition and only Rollason and Friend are left. They are cornered in a cave by a yeti, and Friend goes outside and tries to start an avalanche to trap the yeti and Rollason in the cave, but let him escape. Instead, he is killed in the avalanche. Rollason comes face to face with a living yeti for the first time and blacks out, coming to later when he is found by a search party further down. When asked about the existence of the yeti, Rollason replies that there are no such creatures. His memory of the yeti has either been obliterated by the yeti's implied advanced mental powers or Rollason has chosen to help protect the yeti by denying their existence.

The story and screenplay for *The Abominable Snowman* were written by Nigel Kneale, who had written several very fortean scripts for the first two renowned Hammer "Quatermass" films. The film was based on "The Creature," a BBC teleplay written by Kneale. It is certainly the finest crafted yeti film and possibly the most problematic as well. Unlike the previous yeti features, *The Abominable Snowman* had a director who (if unsubtle) knew how to craft a film, as well as the support of Hammer Studios, a small independent British production company whose forte was the creation of evocative films of horror and science fiction that were sometimes well scripted, acted, and directed.

Here was an opportunity to make the classic yeti film. Instead, the film's anti-American message in yeti clothing is blatantly obvious as the plot is constantly held hostage by the theme, and to make matters worse, Kneale uses one of the least subtle techniques available to the screenwriter by having the main character announce the theme of the film near its conclusion. The theme, by the way, is that humans, not yetis, are the monsters.

Forrest Tucker's Dr. Friend is a grotesque exaggeration of all the negative traits often attributed to the Ugly American—he is loud, brash, and rude for starters, and things go down from there. He turns out to be an unscrupulous and self-centered carnival con man. He is indirectly responsible for four deaths, including his own and that of a yeti. By way of contrast, the British scientist Rollason, played by Peter Cushing, is quiet, sincere, and thoughtful. He cares deeply for his fellow man (and beast) and ultimately puts the good of the yeti ahead of his own. He is clearly the voice of the author.

An intriguing question has been raised by Loren Coleman: Is the character portrayed by Forrest Tucker based on or inspired by Tom Slick? Coleman's research has shown that between October 1956 and February 1957 Tom Slick received major press coverage including pieces in the *New*

York Times, *Newsweek*, and Reuters news service concerning his proposed first yeti expedition planned for 1957. There is usually a year or more between an actual event and the movie based on it. The fact that there was only a little lag time between this media storm and the production of *The Abominable Snowman* does not rule out the possibility that the film may have been inspired by Nigel Kneale's knowledge of the Slick expedition. Indeed, the fact that the movie was developed from a teleplay (which may be written one or two months after the event inspiring it), may have shortened the time between the media event and the film based on it.

While there is no certain relationship between Kneale's work and Slick's efforts, tantalizing hints of some correlation do exist in *The Abominable Snowman*. The American antagonist is named Tom Friend, sharing with Slick the same first name and a single-syllable last name. This is a common screenwriter's gambit when a thinly disguised character based on a real individual is desired. If the Tom Friend character is based on Tom Slick, then this portrayal is pretty far off the mark, because Slick was quite unlike the demonized caricature of the film. It may be worth noting, though, that partway into their climb, Dr. Rollason is repulsed to learn that the Americans had stashed guns and large traps at higher altitudes during a previous climb. This is an interesting detail in light of Loren Coleman's research discovering that the guns and equipment carried by the Slick expedition meant that they were prepared to kill and/or trap a yeti to bring back to the U.S. Articles in British and Indian newspapers during the early spring of 1957 talked of Slick rather coldly as an "American millionaire" out to capture a yeti alive and holding special permits to shoot one in self-defense (see the "Slick Yeti Reconnaissance" chapter). It does not take much reading between the lines to notice that the English press was wondering aloud about Slick's definition of "personal safety." The weaving of the British perception of Tom Slick into the character of "Tom Friend" is not entirely outside the realm of possibilities.

Dr. Rollason's theory (based on looking at the dead creature's face for a few moments) is that yeti are older and wiser than Homo sapiens and that we are the savages. Rollason supports the theory of parallel development versus that of the notion that the yeti may be an evolutionary "missing link."

Critics have pointed out that the yeti are basically background figures in *The Abominable Snowman*. The yeti is not seen until the end of the film, when it is shown to have an owlish face with very human eyes and expression. A telepathic ability on the part of the yeti is strongly implied. The addition of this motif adds to the thematic concept of the yeti being an advanced race, contrasting with the part-human but essentially "subhuman" yetis of the earlier yeti films.

● *Gergasi* (1958). Made in Singapore by the Shaw Brothers Studios. Produced in Malayan. The Malayan title supposedly means "*Abominable Snowman*" in English.

Little is known about this, the last Slick-era yeti film, and I don't believe that it is available outside of Malaysia. It is very possible that prints of it may not exist. The only reference to the feature that I can find is in *Far East Film News*, October 10, 1958, p. 17. Perhaps future research will turn up more information or perhaps even a print of this extremely obscure yeti feature that was, to the best of my knowledge, never seen outside of the Far East.

Loren Coleman has pointed out that "During the period that is relevant, through early 1960, the Himalayan yeti appears to have been the lead character, with the Bigfoot and Boggy Creek types taking over during the 1970s and 1980s. The gap during the 1960s is incredible."[14] The gap is striking and calls out for analysis. Coleman has suggested that the debunking of the yeti by Sir Edmund Hillary in December 1960 may explain what was essentially the demise of the Himalayan yeti film, and I agree with this cogent conclusion.[15]

The official Soviet news agency Tass covered the Hillary expedition results, and on January 11, 1961, an article ran in *Izvestia* titled "End of A Myth. No Snow Man Had [sic] Ever Existed." Ivan T. Sanderson watched the Hillary press circus make its rounds and wrote in early 1961 that the Hillary expedition and the press aftermath had "done nothing to prove the nonexistence of ABSMs. But it has led a great body of the public to believe that the whole concept of such creatures existing has finally been debunked."[16]

Conclusions and Speculations

Motion pictures simultaneously act as a reflection of the consciousness of the public and as fuel and fodder to feed that consciousness. Films can have an appreciable effect on the viewer, as evidenced by the cryptozoologists we have interviewed who set off on their lifelong searches after seeing a film concerning a hairy hominid. It is easy to underestimate the effect of cinema on society. Hairy hominid films in general and yeti films in particular have provided an interesting mini-genre that has allowed us to consider possible effects of cinema on a small scale. The early yeti films had a great impact, and some of this impact is only now being felt (in the form of the book that you are now reading, which may not have been written if the author hadn't viewed one of the yeti films). Before embarking on this essay, I was uncertain as to whether films could really have an effect—a positive effect—on an individual or a subculture. As a result of my analysis of hairy hominid films, I can conclude that films can affect an entire field of study in a positive way.

We have surveyed the Slick-era yeti films and considered their historical context. None of these films was particularly successful or influential on a large scale, but each served to introduce and/or reinforce the notion of yeti existence in the public imagination. This creation/reinforcement may have had latent effects. Bigfoot investigator Mark Opsasnick finds it significant that the so-called "birth" of Bigfoot in 1958 was preceded by the Slick-era yeti films.

"The American public had access to these films a few years before Bigfoot per se made his appearance. There were a good deal of Bigfoot-type creatures reported in America before 1958, but the term 'Bigfoot' did not originate until 1958."[17] In 1961, Ivan T. Sanderson wrote: "In 1958 I received a number of reports of an ABSM in California. At first, this sounded quite balmy even to us—and we are used to the most outrageous things. . . ."[18] Those of us who grew up while Bigfoot was becoming a part of American popular culture may not realize that just thirty-one years ago Bigfoot was hominid non grata. Bigfoot has become such a fixture on the cryptozoological scene, with thousands of alleged sightings throughout the U.S., that Sanderson's statement is surprising.

The yeti films of 1954 to 1957 brought the idea of hairy hominid existence to a much larger public than ever before, and in so doing, helped create fertile conditions for the growth and flourishing of societal consciousness of Bigfoot, a creature that would ironically usurp the yeti's throne as the hairy hominid media darling.

APPENDIX NOTES

1. Macgowan, Kenneth, *Behind the Screen: The History and Techniques of the Motion Picture*, Delacorte Press, New York, 1965.
2. Opsasnick, Mark, "Monsters of Maryland: Bigfoot (Part 1)," *Strange Magazine*, No. 3, p. 21.
3. Opsasnick, Mark, unpublished manuscript, on file with *Strange Magazine*.
4. The early 1970s Bigfoot/monster films (unlike the yeti films that preceded them) did extremely well at the box office. *The Legend of Boggy Creek* made it onto *Variety*'s list of "All-Time Film Rental Champs" (*Variety*, Vol. 315, Num. 2, May 9, 1984, p. 168) with

film rentals received by distributors in the U.S. and Canada totalling $4,800,000. The 1975 Sunn/Taft production of *Mysterious Monsters* was even more successful with $10,960,000 in film rentals received by the distributors of the film. The actual box office gross (total ticket sales) of these films would be two to three times these figures.

5. Unlike the later Bigfoot films, the yeti films most likely had no effect on actual yeti sightings in the Himalayas. In 1985 when touring Washington, D.C., the Royal Cultural Minister of Nepal visited my film studio and we had occasion to discuss the film scene in her region. In the early 1980s film exhibition in Nepal and Tibet consisted largely of traveling motion picture shows in tents. Thirty years earlier, during the heyday of the yeti film, there was no film exhibition to speak of. Marshall McLuhan's notion of a media-connected global village had not extended to the Himalayas in the 1950s. Thus, yeti films most likely did not influence the locals, and the effect of yeti films on the local population does not become a consideration as it has with later hairy hominid films such as *The Legend of Boggy Creek*

6. Interview with Mark Opsasnick, March 19, 1989.

7. Perez, Danny, *Big Footnotes: A Comprehensive Bibliography Concerning Bigfoot, the Abominable Snowmen and Related Beings*, D. Perez Publishing, Inc., Norwalk, California, 1988, p. 7.

8. Correspondence between Loren Coleman and Mark Chorvinsky, July 17, 1988.

9. Sanderson, Ivan T., *Abominable Snowmen: Legend Come to Life*, Chilton Book Company, Philadelphia, 1961, p. 10.

10. Ibid., p. 16.

11. Loren Coleman has suggested that the 1935 Universal horror film *Werewolf of London* may warrant inclusion in a listing of yeti features as the first yeti film. It shares with two of the Slick-era yeti films (*The Snow Creature* and *The Abominable Snowman*) the motif of a botanical expedition in the Himalayas. In this film two scientists search for a flower that blooms during the full moon and is a cure for lycanthropy. A hairy creature (one of the doctors is a werewolf) attacks the other doctor, who becomes the werewolf of the title. Coleman feels that the Himalayan setting and the nature of the beast suggest the yeti. I can't quite call it a yeti film as much as I can a film that shares certain elements with yeti films. Despite the setting and the fact that a hairy man-beast is involved, the creatures in the film are clearly werewolves in appearance and behavior. (*Werewolf of London* was the second werewolf feature film, the first

was made by Universal in 1913 and was based on the American Indian legend of the werewolf.) For the record, I believe that the first short film involving a hairy hominid was Willis O'Brien's 1917 stop-motion film *The Dinosaur and the Missing Link*, which stars an apelike creature that walks upright. The first feature film involving a hairy hominid was First National's 1925 production of *The Lost World*, in which ex-wrestler Bull Montana donned an excellent ape suit (by makeup pioneer Cecil Holland) and played a missing link.

12. Sanderson, op. cit., p. 11.
13. Warren, Bill, *Keep Watching the Skies!*, Vol. 1, McFarland, Jefferson, NC, 1982, p 294.
14. Correspondence between Loren Coleman and Mark Chorvinsky, June 6, 1988.
15. The only yeti (as opposed to Bigfoot) films after 1958 were the 1964 George Pal production of *The Seven Faces of Dr. Lao* (in which an "abominable snowman" is one of the seven characters); the curious Italian yeti/UFO film *Snow Demons* (aka *Snow Devils*) released in 1965; *Yeti*, a fanciful 1972 Italian production filmed in Canada; the 1972 Spanish/English *Horror Express*, in which a hairy monster is being shipped from China, circa 1906, on the Trans-Siberian Railroad; and the film *Night of the Howling Beast*, a 1976 Spanish production also released as *The Werewolf and the Yeti*, that was set in Tibet. A long list of pre-Slick era "missing link" creature films do exist, mostly set in Africa, and, of course, there are numerous Bigfoot, Skunk ape, and related non-Himalayan hairy beast movies that have been produced since the Slick-era cinema.
16. Sanderson, op. cit., p 488. I recall reading the *World Book Encyclopedia*'s debunking of the yeti when I was a child and (like most of the rest of the largely uninformed public) accepting it as fact. (The *World Book Encyclopedia* had been one of the sponsors of the Hillary expedition and had a vested interest in making a big deal of the whole thing, indeed a much bigger deal than it was with respect to the release of new information about the yeti.)
17. Telephone conversation between Mark Opsasnick and Mark Chorvinsky, March 19, 1989.
18. Sanderson, op. cit., p. 20.

Mark Chorvinsky has degrees in film from the University of Maryland and Temple University. He has been making films since 1972 and has written many articles on cinema. He has lectured on film history and technique internationally, most recently at Pinewood Studios in England. Chorvinsky is a researcher and investigator of fortean phenomena and is editor/publisher of *Strange Magazine*.

For yeti enthusiasts who wish to view these films, they occasionally appear on television and may be viewed by special arrangement at the Library of Congress film archives. *The Snow Creature, Man Beast,* and *Half-Human* are available on VHS videocassette from Strange Bookshop, P. O. Box 2246, Rockville, MD 20852.

WHAT CRYPTOZOOLOGY IS ALL ABOUT

Large Animals Discovered by Western Science Since 1900

In 1812, the "Father of Paleontology," Baron Georges Cuvier, rashly pronounced that "there is little hope of discovering new species" of large animals and that naturalists should concentrate on extinct fauna. In 1819 the American tapir was discovered, and since then a long list of "new" animals have disproved Cuvier's dictum. Even within the present century rather astounding zoological finds have been announced, and the fact remains that other animals are out there waiting to be "found" by modern scientists. Tom Slick wanted to add the yeti to this list!

1. Okapi

By saving a group of Congolese Pygmies from a German showman who wanted to take them to the 1900 Paris Exhibition, Sir Harry Johnston immediately gained their trust. He then began hearing stories about the okapi, a mule-sized animal with zebra stripes. In 1901, Sir Harry sent a whole skin, two skulls, and a detailed description of the okapi to London, and it was found that the okapi had a close relationship to the giraffe. In 1919 the first live okapi were brought out of the Congo River basin, and in 1941, the Stanleyville Zoo witnessed the first birth of an okapi in captivity. The okapi, striking in appearance, are now rare but popular attractions at the larger, more progressive zoological parks of the world.

2. Mountain Nyala

First discovered in the high mountains of southern Ethiopia in 1910, the mountain nyala remains a relatively unknown species. The male has gently twisting horns almost 4 feet long and can weigh up to 450 pounds. The coat is a majestically grayish brown with white vertical stripes on the back. After it was first described by Richard Lydekker, the eminent British naturalist, it was ruthlessly hunted by field biologists and trophy seekers through some of the most inhospitable terrain in existence. The mountain nyala lives at heights above 9,000 feet, where the sun burns hotly in the day and the night temperatures fall to freezing. Its existence is now threatened by illegal hunting.

3. Pygmy Hippopotamus

Karl Hagenbeck, a famous German animal dealer, established a zoological garden near Hamburg that was the prototype of the modern open-air zoo. In 1909, Hagenbeck sent German explorer Hans Schomburgk to Liberia to check on rumors about a "giant black pig." After two years of jungle pursuit Schomburgk finally spotted the animal thirty feet in front of him. It was big, shiny, and black, but the animal clearly was related to the hippopotamus, not the pig. Unable to catch it, he went home to Hamburg empty-handed. In 1912, Hans Schomburgk returned to Liberia, and to the dismay of his critics, came back with five live pygmy hippos. A full-grown pygmy hippopotamus weighs only about 400 pounds, one tenth the weight of the average adult hippopotamus.

4. Komodo Dragon

These giant monitor lizards are named for the rugged volcanic island of Komodo, part of the Lesser Sunda Islands of Indonesia. Unknown to science until 1912, the Komodo dragon can be up to twelve feet long and weight over 350 pounds. The discovery of the giant lizard was made by an airman who landed on Komodo island and brought back incredible stories of monstrous dragons eating goats, pigs, and even attacking horses. At first no one believed him, but then the stories were confirmed by Major P. A.

Ouwens, director of the Buitenzorg Botanical Gardens in Java, who offered skins and photographs as proof. Soon live specimens were caught by William H. Harkness and exhibited. The world's largest living lizard is now a popular zoo exhibit.

5. Andean Wolf

The Andean wolf was identified from only one skin obtained by Karl Hagenbeck's son Lorenz, who had inherited his father's zoological business. The Hagenbeck find was made in 1926 when Lorenz bought one of four such skins shown him in Buenos Aires. It was from a large canine, said to be from the Andes. Finally in 1947, Dr. Ingo Krumbiegel of the Munich Museum reconstructed the animal from the skin and announced that it was a large blackish-brown-maned wolf more adapted for a cold climate than the pampas. Thus far, no living specimen of the Andean wolf has been caught.

6. Congo Peacock

Some animal discoveries are made in museums. In 1913, the New York Zoological Society sent an unsuccessful expedition to the Congo in an attempt to bring back a live okapi. Instead one of the team's members, Dr. James P. Chapin, brought back some native headdresses with curious long reddish-brown feathers striped with black. None of the experts could identify them. In 1934, Chapin, on another of his frequent visits to the Congo, noticed similar feathers on two stuffed birds at the Tervueren Museum. They were labeled "Young Indian Peacocks," but Chapin immediately knew that was not what they were. As it turned out, a mining company in the Congo had donated them to the museum and labeled them "Indian peacocks," but Chapin soon discovered that they were a new species. The following year he flew down to the Congo and brought back seven birds. Chapin confirmed them as the first new bird genus discovered in forty years. They were not peacocks after all, but pheasants. The Congo peacock is now commonly found in European and North American zoos.

7. Kouprey

The most recent large animal to be discovered in Asia is found along the Mekong River in Cambodia and Laos and has been the source of much controversy. In 1937, the director of the Paris Vincennes Zoo, Professor Achille Urbain, went to North Cambodia and reported that a large wild ox, unlike the gaur and the banteng, was to be seen in Cambodia. Other naturalists felt he was wrong and suggested that the kouprey might be just a hybrid of the gaur and the banteng. Finally in 1961, a detailed anatomical study of the kouprey proved it to be so different from the area's other wild oxen that it might belong in a new genus. Urbain's 1937 discovery was upheld. The Vietnam War was responsible for killing many koupreys, and not more than 200 now exist in the wild. A 1975 New York Zoological Society expedition was unable to capture any, although they did see a herd of fifty.

8. Coelacanth

This five-foot-long, 127-pound, large-scaled, steel-blue fish was brought up in a net off South Africa in December 1938. The huge fish crawled around on deck for three hours before it died. The only problem was that the coelacanth was supposed extinct for sixty million years. Ms. M. Courtenay-Latimer and ichthyologist James Smith of Rhodes University, South Africa, identified the coelacanth after it already was dead and had begun to decay. Professor Smith then began years of searching for a second living coelacanth and finally was rewarded in December 1952, when a fishing trawler off the Cormores island of Anjouan, near Africa's east coast, brought up an excellent specimen. Dr. Smith was soon shocked to learn the local inhabitants of the Cormores had been catching and eating the "living fossils" for generations. Not until January 17, 1987, was the first live coelacanth found and filmed in its natural habitat by Hans Fricke.

9. Long-Nosed or Chacoan Peccary

This "rangy big pig," as biology professor Dr. Ralph M. Wetzel of the University of Connecticut termed his 1975 discovery, was a big surprise, since it was a Pleistocene Epoch survivor—a species thought to have died out about two million years ago. The long-nosed peccary, a relative of pigs, boars, and warthogs, weighed in at over 100 pounds. Wetzel found it in the wilds of Paraguay and stated that it differed from other known peccaries by its larger size; longer ears, snout, and legs; and proportionately shorter tail.

TOM SLICK'S CONFIDENTIAL LIST OF YETI CONSULTANTS

BEGINNING IN 1957, TOM SLICK ASSEMBLED A worldwide group of consultants to examine and analyze the evidence gathered by his Nepalese expeditions during the search for the yeti. The following is the never-before-published list of those individuals and their affiliations noted by Slick, as of September 1959.

Dr. George A. Agogino—University of Wyoming

Dr. Paul Baker—Physical Anthropologist, Pennsylvania State University

Dr. Carleton Coon—University Museum, Pennsylvania State University

Dr. Floyd Falz—Biochemist, South Dakota Medical School

Dr. Stanley M. Garn—Chairman, Physical Growth Department, Fels Research Institute and Associate Professor of Anthropology, Antioch University

Dr. Leon Augustus Hausman—Professor Emeritus of Zoology, Rutgers University

Dr. Heberer—Primatologist, Germany

Dr. Bernard Heuvelmans—Belgian Royal Institute of Natural Sciences

Dr. Osman W. C. Hill—The Zoological Society of London

Ralph Izzard—England

Dr. Carl Kootman—Vertebrate Zoologist, Academy of Natural Sciences, Philadelphia

Dr. Charles A. Leone—Professor of Zoology, University of Kansas

Dr. G. A. Matson—Technical Director, Minneapolis War Memorial Blood Bank

Dr. Boris Porshnev—Moscow State University Anthropological Institute

Dr. Anne Porter—Associated with Dr. Osman Hill

Dr. Adolph H. Schultz—Anthropologist, Zurich University

Dr. Selby—Pediatrician, Fels Research Institute, Ohio

Dr. Shaw—X-Ray Diffraction Expert, associated with Dr. Agogino

Fred Stark—San Antonio Zoological Society

Frederick A. Ulmer, Jr.—Curator of Mammals, Zoological Society of Philadelphia

Dr. F. G. Wallace—Associate Professor, College of Science, Literature and the Arts, University of Minnesota

SOURCES

THIS BIBLIOGRAPHY CONTAINS ALL THE REFER-
ences cited in the text of *Tom Slick and the Search for the Yeti*. Additionally,
some other supportive materials which were consulted but not cited have
been listed to assist interested researchers and readers. For descriptive
convenience, the following abbreviations have been used throughout the
referencing, except when the author's name is listed wholly: "pc"—"Personal Communication"; "TS"—"Thomas Baker Slick, Jr."; "PB"—"Peter
Byrne." When a reference to personal communication is not followed by
an individual's name, you may assume this is an interview, a letter, and/
or some form of communication given to the author of this book. The style
of this "Sources" section generally follows the form established by the
journal *Cryptozoology*, the official publication of the International Society
of Cryptozoology, P.O. Box 43070, Tucson, AZ 85733, U.S.A. Please note
that when more than one date in a year refers to an author or citation
heading, the year is sequenced by "a," "b," "c," etc., in the order in which
that reference first appears in the book, not alphabetically or by oldest date
first.

Agogino, George
    1958   pc to TS (December 31).
    1959a   pc to TS (May 7).
    1959b   pc to TS (July 13).
    1959c   pc to TS (November 4).
    1959d   pc to TS (January 8).
    1959e   pc to TS (June 30).
    1959f   pc to M. Stamps (July 20).
    1959g   pc to Jeri Walsh (September 8).
    1971   pc to J. Schoneberg Setzer (January 28).
Alix, Ernest Kahlar
    1974   *Ransom Kidnapping in America, 1874–1974* Carbondale, Illinois: South-
            ern Illinois University Press.
    1988   pc.
Allen, Donald A.
    1958   pc (North American Newspaper Alliance) to TS (April 10).
Anon.
    1988   pc.

Anderson, John Gottsberg, editor
1987 *Nepal*. Singapore: APA Productions.
Anderson, Svend
1961 Sumatran Rhinoceros in Copenhagen Zoo. *International Zoo Year Book*, Vol. II.
Anderson, Teresa H.
1981 San Antonio has World's Biggest Baboon Breeding Colony. *Houston Chronicle*, Houston, Texas (November 26).
Aylesworth, Leon (Babe)
1988 pc.
Basel Zoo (Basel, Switzerland)
1988 pc.
Baumann, Elwood D.
1978 *Monsters of North America*. New York: Franklin Watts.
Berkeley Gazette (Berkeley, California).
1958 Two Abominable Snowman Types, Says Photographer. (July 12).
Beynon, Thomas Roger
1983 The House That Slick Built. *Southwest Airlines Magazine* (March).
Bezruchka, Stephen
1985 *A Guide to Trekking in Nepal*. Seattle: The Mountaineers.
Bishop, Barry C.
1962 Wintering on the Roof of the World. *National Geographic* (October).
Boquist, William
1960 Sea Monster in Trinity Alps Lake? *San Francisco Examiner*, San Francisco, California (January 18).
Bowman, Natalie
1984 Zen and the Art of Mind Science Maintenance. *San Antonio Monthly* (June).
Braud, William
1981 Mind Science Foundation. *PSI News: Bulletin of the Parapsychological Association*, Vol. 4, No. 3 (July).
Bruce, James and John Draper
1970 *Crash Safety in General Aviation Aircraft*. Washington, DC: Nader Group (privately published).
Bruckner, D. J. R.
1960 Hillary is Skeptical: 'Snowman' Scalp Arrives for Study. *Chicago* (Illinois) *Sun-Times* (December 12).
Business Week
1951 The Slicks: What Rich Men's Sons Can Do. (November 17).
Byrne, Peter
1956a pc to TS (May 26).
1956b pc to Cathy Maclean (November 27).
1956c Search for Snowman. *The Australian Women's Weekly* (October 10).
1957a pc to TS (January 18).
1957b unpublished documents.

1958a The Search for the Abominable Snowman. *New York Journal-American*, New York, New York (April 27, May 4, May 11, May 18, May 25, June 15).

1958b pc to Jeri Walsh (January 6).

1958c pc to TS (March 12).

1959a pc to TS (February 3).

1959b pc to TS (September 20).

1959c pc to George Agogino (September 18).

1975 *The Search for Bigfoot: Monster, Myth or Man?* Washington, DC: Acropolis Books.

1987 pc.

1988 pc and archival material.

1989 pc.

Caen, Herb

1961 Column (re: Nancy Cooke de Herrera in Trinity Alps). *San Francisco Chronicle/Examiner*, San Francisco, California (August).

Chicago Daily News (Chicago, Illinois)

1961 The Abominable Snowman Only Legend: Hillary. (January 11). Chicago Daily News Service.

1960 Hillary Expedition Extended Following Discovery of Pelt. *Toledo Blade*, Toledo, Ohio (November 2).

Chicago Sun-Times (Chicago, Illinois)

1960a Hillary Describes His Plans for Adventure in Himalayas (June 1).

1960b Hillary, Crew Test Freeze-Dried Menu. (June 2).

Collins, George B.

1976 *Wildcats and Shamrocks*. North Newton, Kansas: Mennonite Press.

Contemporary Authors

1981 Bernard Heuvelmans. Vol. 97–100. Detroit: Gale Research Co.

Cooke, Catherine Nixon

1987 Sir Edmund Hillary to Address Research Partners. *Mind Science Foundation News*, San Antonio, Texas, No. 13 (Fall).

1989 pc.

Coon, Carleton S.

1959 pc to TS (March 7).

1962 *The Story of Man*. New York: Alfred A. Knopf.

1978 pc.

1984 Why There has to be a Sasquatch. In *Markotic*, 1984.

Costello, Peter

1979 *The Magic Zoo*. New York: St. Martin's Press.

Cowals, Dennis

1971 The Thing in Lake Iliamna. *Anchorage Times*, Anchorage, Alaska (December 28).

Cronin, Edward W., Jr.

1979 *The Arun: A Natural History of the World's Deepest Valley*. Boston: Houghton Mifflin.

Current Biography
1941   James Maitland Stewart. New York: H. W. Wilson Co.
1948   Cyrus Stephen Eaton. New York: H. W. Wilson Co.
1960   James Maitland Stewart. New York: H. W. Wilson Co.
1965   Norman Gunther Dyhrenfurth. New York: H. W. Wilson Co.
Daily Express (London, England)
1960   Hillary Will Try to "Shoot" the Abominable Snowman. (June 26).
Daily Mail (London, England)
1960   Knock-out Drug Rifles Go to Catch a Yeti. (June 29).
Daily Telegraph (London, England)
1958   U.S. Party Seeks Snowman. (February 17).
1960a Snowman to be "Shot" by Drug. (June 7).
1960b Hunt is on for "Snowman." (September 14).
1960c Hillary Trek Begins. (September 15).
1960d Scalp of Yeti for Overseas. (November 22).
1960e Rebuke for Sir Edmund Hillary. (November 9).
1960f Sir E. Hillary Sees King. (December 8).
1960g "Yeti" Scalp on Way Home. (December 29).
Davies, R. E. G.
1972   *Airlines of the United States Since 1914*. Washington, DC: Smithsonian Institution Press.
Dee, Michael
1988   pc (Los Angeles Zoo) (February 25).
Doig, Desmond
1958   Is This The Yeti?: A Rare Find in Remote Bhutan. *Statesman*, Calcutta, India (n. d.).
1960a Chinese Jam Camp Radio. *Sunday Times*, London, England (November 13).
1960b Hillary's Men Buy a "Yeti" Skin. *Sunday Times*, London, England (October 23).
1964   Clues to Yeti Get "Scalped." *Chicago Daily News*, Chicago, Illinois (April 4).
Dyhrenfurth, Norman
1958   pc to PB (May 9).
1959   Slick-Johnson Nepal Snowman Expedition. *The American Alpine Journal*, Vol. 11.
1988   pc.
Earle, Howard
1960   The Abominable Snowman—Man, Myth or Monster? *Chicago Tribune Magazine* (n. d.).
Eberhart, George M.
1983   *Monsters: A Guide to Information on Unaccounted For Creatures, Including Bigfoot, Many Water Monsters, and Other Irregular Animals*. New York: Garland Publishing.

Ellis, John
   1975   *The Social History of the Machine Gun.* New York: Pantheon Books/
           Random House.
Ellis, Leon
   1958   Mr. Slick of Texas Will Hunt the Snowmen. *Sunday Dispatch*, London,
           England (January 5).
Encyclopedia of Biography
   1932   Thomas Baker Slick. New York.
Exeter Academy
   1934   Thomas Baker Slick. (Academy Yearbook) Exeter, NH: Exeter Acad-
           emy.
Farrell, Adrienne
   1956   Lean Year For Himalayan Expeditions. Reuters dispatch (May 28).
Federal Bureau of Investigation
   1988   Archival material on Charles Urschel, Sr., and George "Machine Gun"
           Kelly. Washington, DC.
Fisher, James
   1967   *Zoos of the World.* Garden City, New York: Natural History Press.
Fisher, James; Noel Simon and Jack Vincent
   1969   *Wildlife in Danger.* New York: Viking/Studio.
Forth Worth Star-Telegram (Fort Worth, Texas)
   1963   Oil Man Dies on Trip in California *and* Oil, Ranching, Zoo Among
           Interests of F. Kirk Johnson. (June 12).
Fowler, Guy
   1960   All in A Day. Column on TS, *Humboldt Times*, Eureka, California
           (January 12).
Frates, Joseph Anthony
   N. D.   Biography of Joseph Anthony Frates, Sr., unpublished autobiographical
           document.
Freeland, Nat
   1972   *The Occult Explosion.* New York: G. P. Putnam.
Friedrick, R. H.
   1957a   San Antonio Zoological Society sponsorship letter (February 11).
   1957b   San Antonio Zoological Society "duty free" letter (n. d.).
Fuller, Curtis
   1958a   The Lair of the Snowman. *FATE*, Vol. 11, No. 10 (October).
   1958b   The Year of the Yeti? *FATE*, Vol. 11, No. 9 (September).
Garn, Stanley
   1959   pc to TS (January 14).
Geckler, Ralph
   1989   pc.
Genzoli, Andrew
   1961   RFD. *Humboldt Times*, Eureka, California (October 1).
Green, John
   1973   *The Sasquatch File.* Agassiz, British Columbia: Cheam Publishing.

1978   *Sasquatch: The Apes Among Us.* Seattle: Hancock House.

1980   *On the Track of the Sasquatch: Book One.* Victoria, British Columbia: Cheam Publishing.

Gregory, Robert

1984   *Tom Slick: Oil in Oklahoma.* Tulsa, Oklahoma: KTUL-TV.

1986   King of the Wildcatters. *Oklahoma Today* (September–October).

Grubb, R. B.

1939   pc to Robert Ripley (January 12).

1988   pc (April 4).

Gunderson, Edna

1989   Rock Hero Was Robbed of His Future. *USA Today,* Arlington, Virgina (February 3).

Haas, Joseph

1960   Believes the Yeti Is "Missing Link": Oilman Hands Snowman Data to Zoo Chief Here. *Chicago Daily News,* Chicago, Illinois (May 21).

Hall, Mark A.

1987   pc.

1988   pc.

1989a   *Natural Mysteries.* Bloomington, Minnesota: Hall Publications.

1989b   pc.

Hansen, Harry, editor

1970   *Colorado: A Guide to the Highest State* (FWP), New York: Hastings House.

Harkness, Ruth

1938   *The Lady and the Panda.* New York: Carrick & Evans.

Head, Deborah Johnson

1988   pc.

Herald (Plymouth, England)

1960   Yeti Search Near China Border: Hillary's Project. (July 28).

Heuvelmans, Bernard

1955   *Sur la Piste des Bêtes Ignorées.* Paris: Plon.

1958   *On the Track of Unknown Animals.* London: Rupert Hart-Davis.

1959a   *On the Track of Unknown Animals.* New York: Hill and Wang.

1959b   pc to PB (February 1).

1959c   pc to PB (April 26).

1960   pc to Ivan T. Sanderson.

1961   Caption notes added to French edition of Ivan T. Sanderson's *Abominable Snowman: Legend Come to Life.*

1972   *On the Track of Unknown Animals.* Cambridge, Massachusetts: MIT Press. (updated and abridged)

1986   Annotated Checklist of Apparently Unknown Animals With Which Cryptozoology is Concerned. *Cryptozoology,* Volume 15.

1987   pc (December 17).

Heuvelmans, Bernard and Boris F. Porchnev

1974   *L'Homme De Neanderthal Est Toujours Vivant.* Paris: Plon.

Hill, Osman W. C.
    1958a pc to TS (October 14).
    1958b pc to PB (December 17).
    1959a pc to PB (April 17).
    1959b pc to TS (February 2).
    1959c pc to TS (July 5).
    1959d pc to TS (February 26).
    1959e pc to PB (February 9).
Hillary, Sir Edmund P.
    1961   Epitaph to the Elusive Abominable Snowman. *Life* (January 13).
    1962   Hillary Expedition. *The World Book Encyclopedia 1961: Annual Supplement.* Chicago: Field Enterprises Educational Corporation.
    1975   *Nothing Venture, Nothing Win.* New York: Coward, McCann and Geoghegan.
    1988   pc (January 4).
Hillary, Sir Edmund P. and Desmond Doig
    1962   *High in the Thin Cold Air.* Garden City, New York: Doubleday and Co.
Holton, Lo
    1988   pc (April).
Hopkins, Harry
    1938   *New Hampshire.* (FWP/WPA) Boston: Houghton Mifflin.
Hopper, Dick
    1988   pc (Caltex Pacific Oil Co.) (April).
Humboldt Times (Eureka, California)
    1959a Big Game Hunter and Safari Trail Bigfoot. (December 10).
    1959b "Bigfoot" Escapes Worry as Tycoon Fires Hunters. (December 16).
    1960a Slick Thinks Bigfoot Kin of Abominable Snowman. (January 19).
    1960b Bigfoot Sleuth in County Jail. (March 25).
    1960c Father Hubbard Spotlights Salamanders. (January 24).
    1960d Professors Trying to Unravel Old Legend of Lizard. (September 1).
    1960e Texas News Man Checks on Bigfoot. (January 10).
Hunter, Don and Rene Dahinden
    1973   *Sasquatch.* Toronto: McClelland and Stewart Ltd.
Irrgang, Otto R.
    1988   pc, Caltex Pacific Oil Co. (April–May).
Izzard, Ralph
    1955   *The Abominable Snowman Adventure.* London: Hodder and Stoughton.
    1958   The Snowman May Be In For A Shock. *London Daily Mail* (September 29).
    1959a pc to George Agogino (May 4).
    1959b pc to PB (November 23).
    1959c pc to PB (May 4).
    1988   pc (June 4).
Jackson, Peter
    1959   Pelt Stirs Hopes of Finding "Snowman." *Toledo Blade*, Toledo, Ohio (September 13).

Johnson, Bess
    1961   *Safari Diary/Africa, 1961.* Fort Worth, Texas: Self-published.
Johnson, David
    1989   pc.
Johnson, F. Kirk Jr.
    1958   Diary. Unpublished document.
Johnson, F. Kirk III
    1987   pc (December 18).
Jorgensen, Bent
    1988   pc, Copenhagen Zoo (January 18).
Kenyon, Kay
    1988   pc, National Zoo Library.
Kirkpatrick, Ernest E.
    1947   *Voices from Alcatraz: The Authentic Inside Story of the Urschel Kidnapping.*
            San Antonio: Naylor.
La Pe, John and George Gatto
    1959   Two Eureka Hunters Follow Huge Prints in Wilderness. *Humboldt
            Times*, Eureka, California (November 29).
Lapham, Lewis H.
    1964   A Passion for Rhinoceros. *Saturday Evening Post* (February 1).
Lee, Dale
    1988   pc (January 12).
Lee, Gail
    1958a   pc to N. Dyhrenfurth (January 21).
    1958b   pc to TS (April 9).
Leone, Charles
    1959   pc to George Agonino and TS (July 16).
Lewis, Howard T. and James W. Culliton
    1956   *The Role of Air Freight in Physical Distribution.* Boston: Harvard Uni-
            versity Press.
The Light (San Antonio, Texas)
    1962a   Tom Slick Crash Probe On, *and* Tom Slick Brought Nobility to Wealth.
            (October 8).
    1962b   Tom Slick (editorial). (October 9).
Los Angeles Times (Los Angeles, California)
    1958a   Fabled Snowman Hunt Continues. (February 23).
    1958b   Nepal Reports Death of Strange Creature (Mustang animal). (June 15).
    1958c   The Snowman Hunt. (July 10).
    1958d   Snowman Skin Reported Found. (December 28).
Lubar, Robert
    1960   Tom Slick. *Fortune* (July).
Lucas, George, Executive Producer
    1981   *Indiana Jones: Raiders of the Lost Ark.* Story by George Lucas and Philip
            Kaufman; screenplay by Lawrence Kasdan; directed by Steven Spielberg.
            A Lucasfilm.

Macaluso, Betty Jo
  1962   pc, "In Search of the Abominable Snowman" lecture information through the Lincoln Park Conservation Association (October 10).

Maclean, Cathy
  1958   pc to TS (January 7).

Macdonald, A. B.
  1929   Why Tom Slick, Who "Sold Out" for 35 Million Dollars in Cash, Cannot Retire From Business. *Kansas City Star*, Kansas City, Missouri (May 5).

Markotic, Vladimir, ed.
  1984   *The Sasquatch and Other Unknown Hominoids.* Calgary: Western Publishers.

Marshall, Robert E.
  1961   *The Onza.* New York: Exposition Press.

Matson, G.
  1959   pc to George Agogino (July 9).

McCarty, Diane
  1988   *Lhasa Apsos.* Neptune City, NJ: TFH Publications.

McClarin, Jim
  1975   pc and notebooks.

Meier, Don
  1987   pc.

Miles, Ray
  1987   King of the Wildcatters: Tom Slick and the Cushing Oil Field. *The Chronicles of Oklahoma*, Vol. 65 (Summer).
  1988   pc.
  1989   pc.

Miller, Marc E. and William Cacciolfi
  1986   Results of the New World Explorers Society Himalayan Yeti Expedition. *Cryptozoology*, Vol. 5.

Morris, Ramona and Desmond
  1966   *Men and Pandas.* New York: McGraw-Hill.

Morton, D. E.
  1987   pc (November 25).

Mother Land (Kathmandu, Nepal)
  1959   Yeti Still Remains A Mystery. (July 16).

MS Arms and Ammunition
  1958   Deposit receipt for two guns received from T. B. Slick through B. D. Byrne, New Delhi, India (July 5).

Muskogee Democrat (Muskogee, Oklahoma)
  1939   "Goat Hog" photograph and caption (January 11).

Myers, George S.
  1951   Asiatic Giant Salamander Caught in the Sacramento River. *Copeia*, No. 2 (June).

National Observer
  1969   Minor Oversight Won't Wipe Clean on Texas Tower. (June 2).

New York Times (New York, New York)

1930   T. B. Slick Dead; Wealthy Oil Man. (August 17).

1933   Oil Men Kidnapped in Oklahoma City. (July 23, continues for several months).

1956   Texan Balked in Nepal Hunting. (October 7).

1957a   Texan Will Lead "Snowman" Hunt. (February 5).

1957b   Soviet Sees Espionage in U.S. Snowman Hunt. (April 27).

1958   U.S. Team Seeks Snowman. (December 7).

1962a   Thomas Slick, 46, Dies in Air Crash. (October 8).

1962b   46 Dead on Coast in Wake of Storm. (October 14).

The News (San Antonio, Texas)

1962   Oilman Tom Slick Dies in Air Crash, *and* Slick: Realist, Idealist. (October 8).

Newsweek

1957   Looking for a Legend. (February 18).

1958   Man, Monster—Or Both? (February 24).

1960   Chase for the Snowman. (July 11).

Newton, Michael

1979   *Monsters, Mysteries and Man.* Reading, Massachusetts: Addison-Wesley.

NOAA

1962   *Storm Data.* Vol. 4, No. 10 (October), *and* Surface Weather Observations for Dillon and Monida, Montana and Salmon, Idaho. Washington, DC: Department of Commerce.

Norgay, Tenzing and James Ramsey Ullman

1955   *Tiger in the Snows.* New York: G.P. Putnam.

North American Newspaper Alliance

1958   Hunt Extended for Snowman of Himalayas. *New York Journal-American,* New York, New York, (June 22).

Ogawa, Teizo

1959   pc to PB (December 1).

O'Keefe, Julia

1988   pc (Santa Clara University—Bernard R. Hubbard Collection).

Paust, Gil

1959   Alaska's Monster Mystery Fish. *Sports Afield,* Vol. 141, No. 1 (January).

Perkins, Marlin

1982   *My Wild Kingdom.* New York: E. P. Dutton.

Perry, Richard

1969   *The World of the Giant Panda.* New York: Taplinger.

Peterson, Janet T.

1988   pc (World Book, Inc.) (January 14).

Poppy, John (photography by Phillip Harrington)

1968   You Dive for Gold and Find Pieces of the Past. *Look* (March 5).

Porter, Annie

1959   pc to TS (April 9).

Renick, Nancy
  1984   The Mind Science Foundation Takes a Look at the Brain and Beyond. *The Tinitonian*, Trinity University, San Antonio, Texas (November 30).
Rhyiner, Peter and Daniel P. Mannix
  1958   *The Wildest Game*. Philadelphia: J. B. Lippincott.
Ripley's Believe It or Not!
  1939   "Goat Hog" cartoon (February 10).
Rodgers, Thomas L.
  1962   Report of Giant Salamander in California. *Copeia*, No. 3 (September).
Roosevelt, Kermit
  1930   The Search for the Giant Panda. *Natural History*, Vol. 30.
Russell, W. M. (Gerald)
  1958a Report on the 1958 Slick-Johnson Nepal Snowman Expedition. Unpublished document (June 27).
  1958b pc to PB (May 2).
Sacramento Bee (Sacramento, California)
  1959   Texas Millionaire Enters Bigfoot Hunt. (October 14).
Sage, Dean
  1935   In Quest of the Giant Panda. *Natural History*, Vol. 35.
San Francisco Chronicle (San Francisco, California)
  1958   Abominable One is a Frog-Eater. (June 17).
  1959   Explorers Back—But No Snowman. (December 25).
San Antonio Express (San Antonio, Texas)
  1962a Slick's "Snowman" Hunt was Famous. (October 8).
  1962b Rancher-Scientist Tom Slick Lived Many-Faceted Life. (October 8).
Sanders, Garth
  1960   Taxidermist Wants Information on Bigfoot. *Redding Record Searchlight*, Redding, California (February 27).
Sanderson, Ivan T.
  1961a *Abominable Snowmen: Legend Come to Life*. Philadelphia: Chilton Book Company.
  1961b *The Continent We Live On*. New York: Random House.
  1967   *Things*. New York: Pyramid Book.
Seeligson, Ramona Frates
  N. D. Joseph Anthony Frates. Unpublished document.
Semi-Weekly Independent (Red Bluff, California)
  1861   Sea Serpent in Sacramento River. (June 11).
Shackley, Myra
  1983   *Still Living? Yeti, Sasquatch and the Neanderthal Enigma*. New York: Thames and Hudson.
Shaw, Edwin H., Jr.
  1959   pc to George Agogino (January 6).
Shoemaker, Alan
  1988   pc.

Singh, N. M.
    1956   pc (Ministry of Foreign Affairs, Nepal) to PB (January 20).
Skafte, Hakon
    1961   A Contribution to the Preservation of the Sumatran Rhinoceros. *Acta Tropica*, Vol. 18.
    1962   A Contribution to the Preservation of the Sumatran Rhinoceros. *Natural History Bulletin of the Siam Society*, Vol. 20, No. 2.
Slick, Charles
    1988   pc and notes on Slick-Frates geneology.
    1989   pc.
Slick, Tom
    N. D.   Introduction. Unpublished manuscript.
    1951a   *The Last Great Hope.* San Antonio, Texas: Naylor.
    1951b   Tom Slick, Jr., Interview. Benedum and Oil Industry Collection, Oral History Collection, Interviewers Alan Nevin and Frank E. Hill, Columbia University (July 30).
    1952   Some Comments on the Life of Tom Slick, Sr. Presented on the occasion of a testimonial award at the Cushing Petroleum Festival, Cushing, Oklahoma (September 9).
    1956a   pc to PB (December 5).
    1956b   Proposal/Nepal Himalaya Zoological Expedition. Unpublished document.
    1957a   Findings of the 1957 Reconnaissance. Unpublished document.
    1957b   pc to PB (June 12).
    1957c   pc to Mary E. Barber/*Life* (September 20).
    1958a   *Permanent Peace: A Check and Balance Plan.* Englewood Cliffs, NJ: Prentice Hall.
    1958b   The Search for the Abominable Snowman. *New York Journal-American*, New York, New York (April 20).
    1958c   Yeti Expedition. *Explorers Journal*, Vol. 36, No. 4 (December).
    1958d   pc to expedition members (March 3).
    1958e   Addenda (to the Gerald Russell Report) by Tom Slick as the Result of His Conferences. Unpublished document (October 9).
    1958f   Elusive Snowman Still in the Hills. *New York Journal-American*, New York, New York (June 22).
    1958g   Cable to Bryan Byrne (October 7).
    1958h   pc to PB (March 17).
    1959   Information on Physical Evidence. Confidential unpublished report (September).
Slick, Tom (III)
    1988   pc.
Smith, Hobart M.
    1978   *A Guide to Field Identification/Amphibians of North America.* New York: Golden.

Snyder, Richard G.
1978   *General Aviation Crash Survivability*. Warrendale, Pennsylvania: Society
of Automotive Engineers.
Soule, Gardner
1966   *Trail of the Abominable Snoman*. New York: G. P. Putnam's Sons.
Southwest Research Institute
1988   A Guide to Southwest Research Institute. San Antonio, Texas.
Stacy, Dennis
1981   Tom Slick: The Forgotten Millionaire. *Sunday Magazine, San Antonio
Express-News*, San Antonio, Texas (October 25).
1988   pc.
1989   pc.
Statesman (Calcutta, India)
1957a   Slick to Confer With Tenzing. (March 4).
1957b   Helicopters May Be Used. (March 6).
1957c   Slick's Team Not to Shoot Yeti. (March 20).
1957d   Snowman Not Found: Slick Expedition is Returning. (April 18).
Steen, Maye
1958   Bigfoot, Giant Serpent Again Reported at Hoopa. *Humboldt Times*, Eureka, California (n. d.)
Stejneger, Leonhard
1907   *Herpetology of Japan and Adjacent Territory*. Washington, DC: United
States National Museum (Bulletin 58).
Stevenson, Susan
1988   pc (National Transportation Safety Board) (April 28).
Stewart, Gladys
1988   pc (Federal Aviation Administration form reply with notes) (April 12).
Stewart, James
1989   pc (June 19).
Stoner, Charles
1955   *The Sherpa and the Snowman*. London: Hollis & Carter.
Sunday Express (London, England)
1958   Snowman Hunter Keeps Secret. (October 5).
Swedrup, Ivan
1974   *The Pocket Encyclopedia of Dogs*. New York: Macmillan.
Sydney Sun Herald (Sydney, Australia)
1955   Aust. Expedition to Hunt the Yeti. (August 14).
Tait, Samuel W., Jr.
1946   *The Wildcatters: An Informal History of Oil Hunting in America*. Princeton: Princeton University Press.
Tcherine, Odette
1961   *The Snowman and Company*. London: Robert Hale Limited.
Thomas, Tony
1988   A *Wonderful Life: The Films and Career of James Stewart*. New York:
Citadel Press.

Thomas, Warren D.
  1988   pc (Los Angeles Zoo) (February 25).
Thompson, Warren
  1987   pc.
  1988   pc.
Tiemann, Robert L. and Mark Rucker
  1989   *Nineteenth Century Stars*. Kansas City, Missouri: The Society for American Baseball Research.
Time
  1958   The Ape Trade. (December 1).
Times of India (New Delhi, India)
  1957   Tom Slick Convinced of Snowman's Existence—Move to Capture Yeti Alive on Next Expedition. (April 25).
Toronto Sun (Toronto, Canada)
  1971   Zoologist Talks on Abominable Snowman Quests. (Perkins on 1960 expedition) (December 2).
Turner, Norman I.
  1988   pc (SWRI Architect).
Ulmer, Frederick
  1958   pc to TS (December 31).
  1959a pc to TS (March 6).
  1959b pc to TS (May 13).
Ungar, Sanford J.
  1975   *FBI*. Boston: Atlantic Monthly Press.
United Press
  1957   Nepal Order Protects Its Snowman. Unknown newspaper (March 19).
Vagtborg, Harold
  1973   *The Story of the Southwest Research Center: A Private, Nonprofit, Scientific Research Adventure*. San Antonio, TX: Southwest Research Institute.
Vogel, Shawna
  1988   The Domino Building. *Discover* (January).
Wallace, Amy; David Wallechinsky and Irving Wallace
  1983   *The Book of Lists #3*. New York: Wm. Morrow.
Wallace, F. G.
  1959   pc to G. Albin Mattson (May 27).
  1959   pc to TS (May 27).
Walsh, Jeri
  1958a pc to Gerald Russell and PB (February 5).
  1958b pc to PB (December 18).
  1959a pc to PB (February 5).
  1959b pc to PB (August 27).
  1959c pc to PB (December 7).
Wendt, Herbert
  1956   *Out of Noah's Ark*. London: Weidenfeld and Nicolson.

Western Morning News (Plymouth, England)

1960   Drug Guns for Yeti Hunt. (June 29).

Whitehead, Don

1956   *The FBI Story*. New York: Random House.

Whyte, Constance

1957   *More Than a Legend*. London: Hamish Hamilton.

Williams, Don

1960   Yeti, Yeti Up in That Tree, Are You Real or Imaginary? *Fort Worth Star-Telegram*, Fort Worth, Texas (n. d.).

Willis, Paul, ed.

1970   A Monster from the Trinity Alps. *INFO Journal*, Vol II, No. 2.

Wilson, Stewart Strong

1989   pc.

Wood, C. V.

1988   pc.

Woodland Daily Democrat (Woodland, California)

1891   Did He See the Sea Serpent? (August 8).

Yale University

1989   Thomas Baker Slick. Archival material—pc.

Zhujian, Huang

1982   The Chinese Salamander. *Oryx*, Vol. XVI, No. 3 (February).

NAMES INDEX

(PLEASE NOTE THAT THE NAMES OF SHERPAS ARE ORganized as whole words without surnames, whereas Indian and Nepalese names do reflect their use of surnames. This follows the usage demonstrated in indices in many works, from Heuvelmans [1958] to Hillary [1975].)

ABOUT THE AUTHOR

LOREN COLEMAN HAS BEEN INTERESTED IN TOM Slick and the search for the yeti since 1960. Majoring in anthropology and zoology at Southern Illinois University in Carbondale helped him to fine-tune his desire to be a cryptozoologist; obtaining a master's degree in psychiatric social work has helped him to understand *Homo sapiens* a little better.

This is the book that Loren Coleman has wanted to write for twenty years. In the meantime he has authored other Faber and Faber, Inc., books, namely, *Mysterious America* (1983), *Curious Encounters* (1985), and *Suicide Clusters* (1987). Coleman is a research associate at a human services institute at the University of Southern Maine. Someday he would like to found the Tom Slick Center for the Study of Cryptozoology. Until then, Coleman spends his free days driving between mysterious incidents, base-ball games, zoos, and family outings in a car with the only plates in Maine proclaiming proudly to the world: "YETIS."